FLIGHT AND REBELLION

Flight
and Rebellion

Slave Resistance in Eighteenth-Century Virginia

GERALD W. MULLIN

OXFORD UNIVERSITY PRESS

London   Oxford   New York

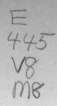

OXFORD UNIVERSITY PRESS

London   Oxford   New York
Glasgow   Toronto   Melbourne   Wellington
Cape Town   Ibadan   Nairobi   Dar es Salaam   Lusaka   Addis Ababa
Delhi   Bombay   Calcutta   Madras   Karachi   Lahore   Dacca
Kuala Lumpur   Singapore   Hong Kong   Tokyo

To Martha

Acknowledgments

A graduate research grant from Colonial Williamsburg Incorporated, and a faculty grant from Smith College made possible my work in southern archives. Among their staffs, my special thanks to John Selby and Harold Gill, Assistant Director and Archeologist, respectively, of the Colonial Williamsburg Research Center; Mrs. Matte Russell, Director, and Virginia Grey, Chief Archivist of the Duke Library Manuscript Division, and Harold Eads, Assistant in Manuscripts at the Alderman Library, University of Virginia.

Martha McCart helped with the maps and also with the editing and proofreading, as did Stella Thalinger, Bill Spurlin, and Alan Lewis. My colleagues, Ed Jordan and Mike Cahn, at the City College of San Francisco, Michele Aldrich and Alan Lawson at Smith College, made useful criticisms of portions of the manuscript. I am especially grateful to Robert Middlekauff and Winthrop Jordan who offered important suggestions and encouragement while reading this as both a dissertation and a manuscript. They are in no way responsible for any errors or stylistic infelicities. I cannot adequately express my appreciation to Martha, my wife, who has worked with me from beginning to end, but I would like to acknowledge it by dedicating this book to her.

Introduction

In 1726 William Byrd II, a wealthy planter and writer, described to an English earl the most cherished ambitions of his class:

> Besides the advantage of a pure Air, we abound in all kinds of Provisions without expence (I mean we who have Plantations). I have a large Family of my own, and my Doors are open to Every Body, yet I have no Bills to pay, and half-a-Crown will rest undisturbed in my Pocket for many Moons together. Like one of the Patriarchs, I have my Flocks and my Herds, my Bond-men and Bond-women, and every Soart of Trade amongst my own Servants, so that I live in a kind of Independence on everyone but Providence. However this Soart of Life is without expence, yet it is attended with a great deal of trouble. I must take care to keep all my people to their Duty, to set all the Springs in motion and make every one draw his equal Share to carry the Machine forward. But then 'tis an amusement in this silent Country and a continual exercise of our Patience and Economy.[1]

In this pastoral setting the patriarch's "Bond-men" were slaves, most of whom were born in Africa and enslaved as young adults. For Africans the plantation was virtually a total experience: cut off from the larger society, they learned slowly and incompletely about whites and their ways. This process, and the plantation setting itself, channelled and controlled their rebellious reactions to enslavement. Robert "King" Carter, for example, wrote his overseer in 1727: "Now that my new negro woman has tasted the hardships of the woods she'll stay nearer to home where she can have her belly full." [2]

While most slaves were comparatively unacculturated, the colony conformed to Byrd's bucolic portrait and was a secure "slave society." The era of the American Revolution changed much of this: the slave trade was sharply curtailed, while economic developments accelerated the growth of towns, commerce, and the influence of "enlightened" slaves. According to St. George Tucker, poet, lawyer, and aristocrat, the very nature of the slave community and slavery had in fact changed perceptibly by 1800.

> There is often a progress in human affairs which may indeed be retarded, but which nothing can arrest. . . .Of such sort is the advancement of knowledge among the negroes of this country. . . . Every year adds to the number of those who can read and write. . . .This increase of knowledge is the principal agent in evolving the spirit we have to fear. The love of freedom. . . .In our infant country, where population and wealth increase with unexampled rapidity, the progress of liberal knowledge is proportionally great. . . .The growth and multiplication of our towns tend a thousand ways to enlighten and inform them. . . .Fanaticism is spreading fast among the Negroes of this country, and may form in time the connecting link between the black religionists and the white. . . .It certainly would not be a novelty, in the history of the world, if Religion were made to sanctify plots and conspiracies.[3]

Tucker's letter to the state legislature was an analysis of Gabriel Prosser's Rebellion, Richmond 1800. This insurrection was organized by a small group of relatively assimilated slave-artisans who used religious gatherings and the whites' outmoded permissiveness and sense of security, to promote the first large-scale and widespread insurrection in our country's history. Their preacher, Gabriel's brother Martin Prosser, addressed a meeting of conspirators in the following manner: "Their cause was similar to [the] Israelites' I have read in my Bible where God Says, if we worship him, we should have peace in all our land and five of you shall conquer an hundred & a hundred a hundred thousand of our enemies." [4]

Seventy-five years after "King" Carter's letter to his overseer, native African slaves had largely been replaced by their American-born children. But the most essential arrangements among whites and blacks were still based on assumptions about slave behavior established when most slaves were "outlandish" Africans. This book, which offers a new perspective on slave behavior, is about these men, their American-born descendants, and the relationship between the acculturative process and resistance to slavery before the ante-bellum era.

* * *

Historians of American Negro slavery have overlooked the colonial
era when the process of cultural change in native Africans and their
American-born descendants was an important element in the development of slavery before the end of the slave trade in the early nineteenth
century.[5] By examining slavery topically, concentrating on the last few
years of its long existence, and using models based on modern industrial
society, they have limited our understanding of the changes in slavery
over a period of time and obscured our view of the slaves themselves.
Scholars have characterized slavery variously: as a business enterprise,[6]
a school,[7] and one type of "total" institution or another (a prisoner-of-
war or concentration camp,[8] or maximum security prison[9]). These
static models, which have sustained the ahistorical treatment of ante-
bellum slavery, indicate that slaves were unable to influence the total
society in any important non-economic manner, and they are anachronistic when used to explain slavery in the agrarian, aristocratic,
and God-fearing societies of colonial North America. But in the
absence of a synoptic study of the institution in the colonial era, this
approach has dominated our view of slavery since its inception, it is
illustrated by the following comments on three critical features of
American Negro slavery—chronology, structural characteristics, and
the African background:

> The rigid and static nature of ante-bellum slavery, 1830–1860,
> makes it possible to examine it institutionally with only slight regard
> for chronology.[10]
> In the slave system of the United States—so finely circumscribed
> and so cleanly self-contained—virtually all avenues of recourse for
> the slave, all lines of communication to society at large, originated
> and ended with the master.
> Something very profound, therefore . . . intervene[d] . . . to
> obliterate all this [the "resourcefulness and vitality" of African
> tribal life] and to produce, on the American plantation, a society
> of helpless dependents.[11]

Structural factors predominate in studies such as these; roles and
status are emphasized at the expense of individuals, interpersonal relations, or even events. The system was implacable: slaves were
merely the creatures of slavery; only a few whites, whose functions
were typically custodial, shared slavery with them; and like our own
corporate capitalist system, the slave society, it would seem, could
absorb all types of resistance.
Thus when historians have tried to deal with slaves themselves,

their views are what one might expect were a slave a prison inmate or in a labor-management relationship with his master. Historians' insights have emphasized the lack of cooperation, fellowship, and cultural cohesion among slaves: freedmen looked down on all slaves; house slaves felt superior to field laborers, and slaves ridiculed those recently imported from Africa.[12] These are important generalizations—and perhaps may have been the case in the ante-bellum period, although they do not apply to the colonial era—but, they cry out for more precise examination. Something more than an example or two is needed, some routine kind of quantification perhaps, so we could be sure that slaves were really like that. At this point, Jesse Lemisch's views on history from the bottom up are most appropriate.

> No generalization has much meaning until we have actually examined the constituent parts of the entity about which we are generalizing. No contention about the people on the bottom of society—neither that they are rebellious nor docile, neither that they defer to an authority whose legitimacy they accept nor that they curse an authority which they deem illegitimate, neither that they are noble nor that they are base—no such contention even approaches being proved until we have in fact attempted a history of the inarticulate.[13]

The sources that have been used to study slavery have also encouraged us only to see the institution from the top down. Travelers' narratives, letters, essays in agricultural magazines on slave management, and polemical pro-slavery tracts are prominent sources in studies of slavery. These are what Professor Daniel McCall (in *Africa in Time-Perspective: A Discussion of Historical Reconstruction from Unwritten Sources*) calls "narrative sources," written by authors who consciously intended to inform (or misinform) their readers. Documents of another kind are what the great French medievalist Marc Bloch called "witnesses in spite of themselves"—such bits and pieces of the historical record as census returns, ledgers, wills, court records, and newspaper advertisements for runaway slaves in our case—that were never intended to be examined by historians. This "unconscious evidence" is more appropriate than narrative sources for the study of a people who could not or were not inclined to write things down.[14]

In past investigations of slavery in North America historians have not "attempted a history of the inarticulate": to see slavery also from the bottom up, and to discover the importance of slave culture for whites

and blacks alike. Locked into a view of slavery on the eve of its ex-
tinction, employing models and sources that do not encourage us to
discover how slavery developed and transformed the entire society,
historians have told us more about masters than slaves. But most important, they have sealed all of us off from slavery's meaning for this
country. To see slaves as a "society of helpless dependents" is to make
a judgment that ultimately rests on one's view of the relationship of
slavery to the rest of society. And the impression from these studies
which remains is that slavery was simply an "institution," the "peculiar institution," one of several (like the churches, cities, Whig and
Democratic parties) which gave the ante-bellum South its identity,
and that slavery was essentially for those who occupied the lowest
caste.

There is, however, a fundamentally different way of looking at the
problem; one that insists on focusing on the slaves themselves and on
their impact upon the total society. In 1946 Frank Tannenbaum, a man
who saw slavery in this hemisphere from the vantage point of Latin
America, argued that there were basically two ways of viewing a slave
labor system: as merely an "institution," or as a system so pervasive
that we may call the whole a "slave society." Arguing that slavery in
any society was the latter—a way of life—Tannenbaum came to realize
that as slavery encompassed the whole society, it changed profoundly all
of its most important institutions: the family, law, religion, politics, and
even diet and architecture. Indeed, he wrote, "nothing escaped, nothing
and no one." [15]

The direction of American Negro slavery historiography is even
more unusual in light of recent interpretations of slavery in Latin
America. Taking for granted the existence of a viable slave culture
with African antecedents, historians of Latin American slavery usually
deal both with the colonial dimension of slavery as well as its change
in time. This approach, which is still largely unexplored, will yield
rich returns in comparative studies: while different legal and religious
traditions may have eventually produced sharply contrasting slave
systems in the Americas (*vide* the Tannenbaum-Elkins thesis),[16] the
preponderant number of Africans among all colonial slave populations,
more than we have previously recognized, made them more alike than
not and therefore highly comparable. Two recent and excellent studies
are especially noteworthy: Elsa V. Goveia, *Slave Society in the British
Leeward Islands at the End of the Eighteenth Century* (New Haven,

1965) and Orlando H. Paterson, *The Sociology of Slavery* [Jamaica] (London, 1967). They argue that the African heritage was a variable in adjustments to slavery, in slave revolts, and in relations among slaves and their masters.[17] These interpretations, which provide a richer view of slave life than their North American counterparts, picture the African as much more than "Sambo," a creature of the white man. So they stand in sharp contrast to much of the work on slavery in this country, which seems so inappropriate when applied to the colonial period and to a non-Western, traditional folk, the African tribesmen, who came into the colonies by the thousands before the end of the slave trade. Slaves in eighteenth-century Virginia, for example, did have a life of their own, which for a time was partially based on African values. And an understanding of the gradual transformation of these traditional ways, which led to important changes among all slaves and in the slave society itself, allows one to build-in a new series of perspectives on slave behavior and slavery before the ante-bellum period.

Contents

Maps

Map design by David Lindroth

Tables

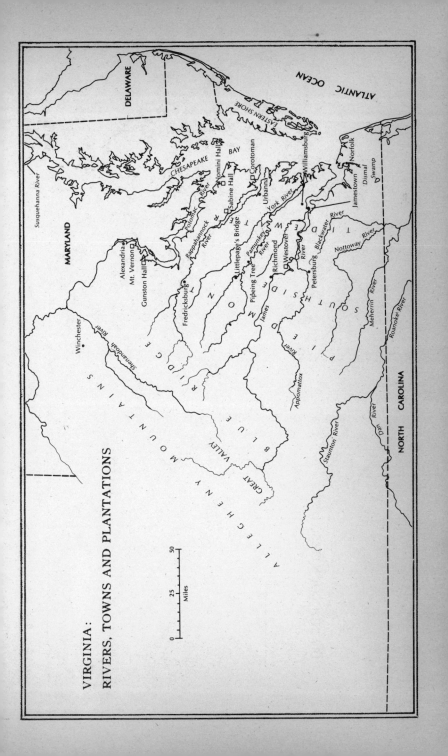

VIRGINIA:
RIVERS, TOWNS AND PLANTATIONS

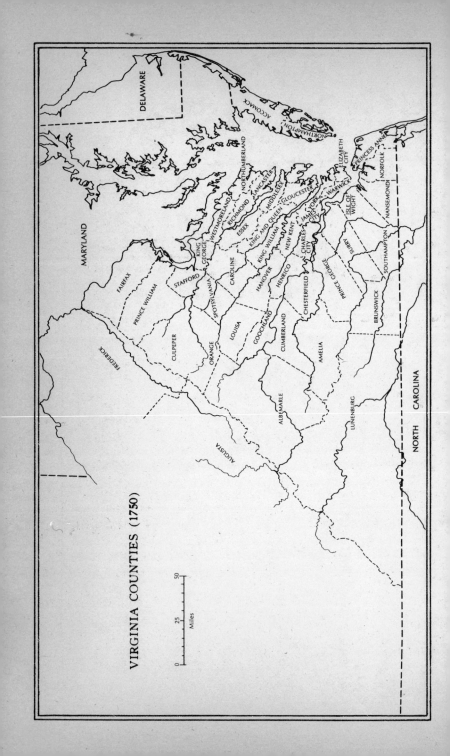

VIRGINIA COUNTIES (1750)

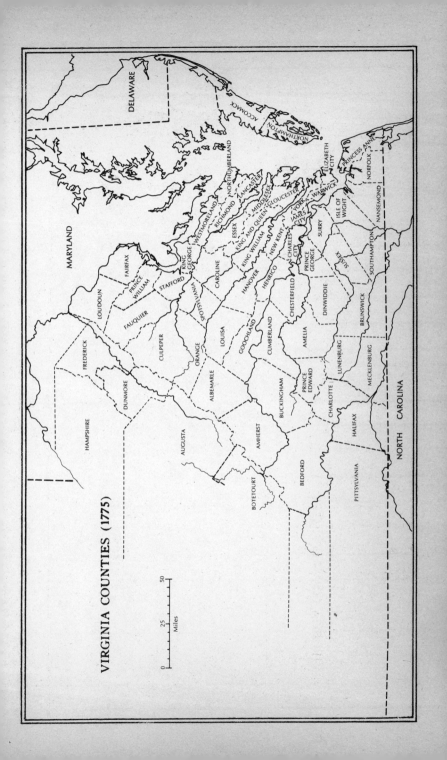

VIRGINIA COUNTIES (1775)

FLIGHT AND REBELLION

1

The Plantation World of William Byrd II

Great planters like William Byrd II would "live in a kind of Independence on Every one but Providence" even though they were destined to be colonial staple producers and slaveowners in a mercantilist empire.[1] This was the central paradox of their careers. As colonists, Byrd and his countrymen understood that authority for the most important political and economic decisions for Virginia originated outside its boundaries, in England. As staple producers, they were subject to the mother-country's mercantile community and its manufactured goods, credit, and prices. As slaveowners, they exploited Africa as a cheap and consistent source of labor, only to gradually realize how thoroughly dependent they were on slaves.[2]

To achieve a measure of control over their circumstances, wealthy slaveowners sought to make themselves patriarchs of plantations which were far more self-contained than their nineteenth-century counterparts. These economically diversified plantations, which the gentry worked so hard to create and maintain, were absolutely dependent on acculturated, skilled slaves. They were also the vehicle by which the great planters would realize their dream of self-sufficiency—and ultimately of mastery—over a society in which this was largely impossible. Not only were they colonial agriculturalists but most important, their leading objective, the autarkic plantation community and its corollary, acculturated artisans, created a cruel dilemma: cultural change made Negroes less suitable for plantation slavery.

"THIS SILENT COUNTRY"

Africans in slavers entered Virginia on majestic tidal rivers that carried them from the Chesapeake Bay to the great planters' wharves in a land which, even a century after its settlement, remained a densely forested, sparsely populated wilderness. Waterways and forests, the tidewater region's most distinctive features, provoked the images whites used to convey their awed impressions of primeval splendor and vast distances. "The land, an immense forest extend[s] on a flat plain, almost without bounds," wrote an Englishman in 1787, "Nature here being on such a scale that what are called great rivers in Europe, are here considered only as inconsiderable creeks or rivulets. . . . The Rivers," he continued, "large expanses of water of enormous extent spread . . . under the eye as far as it can comprise." Another late eighteenth-century traveler, the Marquis de Chastellux, saw "the great part of Virginia [as] very low and flat and so divided by creeks and great rivers, that it appears in fact redeemed from the sea and entirely of very recent creation." [3]

Carved in the last glacial age, the Chesapeake Bay and its great tributaries, the Potomac, Rappahannock, York, and James rivers, comprise over 1,100 miles of waterways.[4] The Bay (the ancient bed of the Susquehanna River) is 200 miles long and, at one point 40 miles wide. The four rivers rise as fresh-water streams high in the gently rolling hills of the piedmont, the transitional zone between the Blue Ridge mountains and the tidewater. At the head of navigation their character changes. They widen, deepen, and become brackish; shrimp, oysters, and clams appear off the docks of such fall-line towns as Alexandria, Fredericksburg, Richmond, and Petersburg. Fall-line towns on the Potomac and Rappahannock could accommodate the largest ships built in the colonial period. At their mouths the rivers lose their identity altogether, and roll into the Great Bay in estuaries, which divide the coastal area into necks of land, or peninsulas, where the large slave-owners built their homes.

Accessibility to distribution points largely determines the character of staple-producing regions. In New England the well-worn coastal ranges in some areas march nearly to the beaches; the terrain is rocky and difficult to farm extensively, and marked by few rivers navigable by ocean-going vessels. Here Englishmen settled in communities and turned to the sea for their livelihood. In contrast the rich alluvial soil and web of waterways in Virginia drew the people into the interior, where they built plantations, not towns. Jamestown too, unlike Massachusetts-Bay Colony, was founded as a commercial venture by a London corporation intent on making a swift, neat profit on its investment. Although the Company's settlers initially tried to establish such staples as precious metals, wine, silk, and glass, by the 1620's tobacco became the cash crop. Tobacco planters also grew Indian corn, grain, and fruit and raised horses, cattle, and swine. By the late seventeenth century the supply of African slaves increased rapidly and the more profitable large plantations—often at the expense of the yeoman's farm—came to dominate the arable land in the tidewater and to move inexorably west up the river basins. But as late as 1750 the fresh-water sources for the great rivers sprang from an interior that was still largely unknown. In a report to the Board of Trade, a wealthy planter described his country's western boundary by reference to the mysterious "South Sea": "Virginia is Bounded by the Great Atlantic Ocean to the East, by North Carolina to the South, by Maryland and Pennsylvania to the North, and by the South Sea to the West, including California." [5]

Political divisions, trade, and the plantations themselves were oriented to the river courses. Large slaveowners like Byrd, who once described Westover as "two miles above where the great ships ride," preferred to build on "roads," sections where the rivers broadened to two or three miles. A location on deep water had obvious economic advantages: the planter could control slave sales, and serve as a distributor for his inland neighbors' commodities. But a mansion situated on a tidal river had its own magical appeal. While explaining his countrymen's aversion to town life, one contemporary historian noted that Virginians preferred their "dispers'd way of living," because they would not be "coop'd up." Indeed, wrote Hugh Jones, another early eighteenth-century historian, "they love to build near water." [6]

Most of the great home plantations of the one hundred wealthiest eighteenth-century Virginians were clustered off the coastline, a few miles downstream from the head of navigation on the great rivers. Professor Jackson Turner Main's analysis of the wealthiest taxpayers in the 1780's indicates that the median value of their property was about £25,000 (based on a computation of their amounts of taxable property in land, slaves, cattle, horses, and carriage wheels. One pound sterling equaled roughly $50 in food, clothing, and shelter in 1965). Slaves made up slightly more than one-fifth of the total sum of the gentry's property. These men owned an average of 70 slaves at home and 60 elsewhere. Only about one in ten owned 300 or more slaves; the largest with 785 was a Carter. George Mason of Gunston Hall was a representative member of the "One Hundred." He paid taxes on 7,649 acres, 118 slaves, 63 horses, 116 cattle, and a four-wheeled carriage.

Slaves and land were widely dispersed along the river basins. Only 58 slaveowners kept more than 100 slaves in a single county; and the average wealthy planter owned about 3,000 acres, both in the county where he lived and in counties upriver from his estate. Nearly all manors were broken up into small, isolated tracts referred to as "quarters." Half of the men on Main's list, for example, held land in 4 or more counties; and only 4 (less than 1 in 20) owned all of their property in one county. These non-resident quarters were usually west of the home plantation. The river courses also largely determined where land was held: Potomac River planters speculated in Northern Neck properties, while aristocrats on the James River developed quarters along that waterway.[7]

Rivers, the main arteries of trade and travel for more than two hundred years, had tidal estuaries that opened up the interior, drew people into the land, and dispersed population.

Population density remained low even in the most populous counties throughout the colonial period. These were located in the oldest areas of settlement in the tidewater south of the Rappahannock River. These counties, which included the colony's few leading towns, were Gloucester (with 10,292 inhabitants), Elizabeth City (2,439), York (4,857), and James City (4,041). There were approximately 40 people per square mile in the first three; and James City County had about 30 people per square mile.[8]

In 1699 when large importations of Africans were under way, there were about 70,000 inhabitants in the colony; and nearly 138,000 a quarter-century later. In the first year of the American Revolution the population was about half a million, of whom 40 per cent were slaves. Town life did not influence many colonists. In 1790 after a perceptible growth of port and fall-line towns following the war, only 19,000 of nearly half a million whites lived in nine of the new state's largest towns. The ninth was a hamlet of 669 souls.

The important connection between the colony's severe shortage of towns and free artisans, on the one hand, and staple production with slaves, self-sufficient plantations, and the lack of capital accumulation, on the other, was understood as early as 1698. *The Present State of Virginia and the College,*[9] written by colonists for the Board of Trade, began, "[tobacco] swallows up all other Things"—towns, port facilities, educational institutions, and tradesmen. Artisans were especially "dear," because "for want of Towns, Markets, and Money," they had to be part-time farmers. Where else would they buy their meat, milk, corn, "and all other things"? Skilled laborers were perforce itinerants, "going and coming to and from their Work" in the "dispers'd Country." Instead of wages they were paid "straggling parcels of Tobacco," or worse, sides of beef, which had to be immediately salted and preserved. Planters refused to pay cash or even smaller quantities of payment in kind. The white artisan's loss, however, was the skilled slave's gain. Assimilated slaves, those who were sufficiently conversant in English to be taught work skills, were used in mines, salt- and ropeworks; and they trained as shipwrights, blacksmiths, and as various kinds of woodworkers, including carpenters, coopers, wheelwrights, and sawyers.

But the lack of town life and urban services was not an insurmountable problem for the large slaveowners, for the articles which they did not produce on their own plantations were shipped to their wharves directly from Europe. Hugh Blair Grigsby, a late eighteenth-century Virginia historian and an acute observer, used a comparison of habits of dress to call attention to the great planters' pre-eminence based on their slave-artisans, self-sufficiency, and strategic location. "You can tell the men who come from the bay counties and from the banks of the large rivers, and who, from the facility with which they could exchange their products for British goods are clothed in foreign fabrics," he wrote. "You can also tell those who live off the great arteries of trade, far in the interior, in the shadow of the Blue Ridge, in the Valley. . . . These are mostly clad in homespun, or in the most substantial buckskin."[10]

"A KIND OF INDEPENDENCE ON EVERY ONE BUT PROVIDENCE"

Conspicuous in a European finery symbolic of their dependence on metropolitan areas overseas, the great planters were also well known for their vaunted individualism which they displayed in all major aspects of their lives. "The public or political character of the Virginians," the Reverend Andrew Burnaby understood, "corresponds with their private one: they are haughty and jealous of their liberties, impatient of restraint and can scarcely bear the thought of being controuled by any superior power." Dependence on British culture, ministers, and merchants sharpened the Virginians' fears about becoming anyone else's "slaves"—a concept they often used in the Revolutionary era.

In order to master forces that were actually for the most part beyond their influence, the large planters became exemplary entrepreneurs in what C. Vann Woodward has aptly labeled "The Age of the Puritan Ethic." "I cannot allow myself," Robert "King" Carter wrote his London factor, "to come behind any of these gentlemen in the planter's trade." His son Landon understood that the quixotic quest for autonomy in a slave society began at home: Sabine Hall, he remarked, was "an excellent little Fortress . . . built on a Rock . . . of *Independency*." Indeed, the planters' economically diversified plantations, as well as their subsidiary business roles as slave dealers, home manufacturers, and retailers of European goods to their less fortunate neighbors, were ultimately the source of their power, their life style, and the means by which they would resolve the dilemma inherent in their role as colonial agriculturalists in a mercantilist empire.[11]

But to underscore the uniqueness both of slavery and the wealthy slaveowners' way of life on the large, self-contained plantations it is necessary to digress momentarily to consider the great majority of planters on small, inland farms, who were wholly dependent on outside sources for even the most essential household goods, manufactures, and services.

One rare but fairly complete account of a small plantation described a 690-acre farm in St. Thomas' Parish, Orange County. John Mallory put his estate together slowly.[12] In 1742 he paid quitrents on 249 acres; in the mid-1750's he made payments of £1.15.11½ on 690 acres, and two slaves (all slaves over 16 years of age were taxed). How many slaves he owned at this time is impossible to discover; but in his estate (attested in 1772) there was a costly imbalance between men and women, productive and non-productive slaves. Eight of his 11 slaves were women and 2 were "girls"; Dick, who was rated at £70 and the only male laborer, went to Mallory's eldest son. Two women, who were evidently expected to produce additional slaves, were valued at £70 and £60. The remainder were children, assessed at about one-half of the adult's value. These 11 slaves were worth less than £500.

Planters like John Mallory often required services, usually of the most menial, but not necessarily inexpensive, variety, that were provided by either the large planters' slave-artisans or an occasional itinerant white craftsman. A fragment of an account for household expenses from June through May 1760–61, included charges from 2 pence to 8 shillings for pointing a plow, sharpening a hoe, and "laying" [making] three hoes, a plow, and 2 horseshoes.

The Pocket plantation's critical dependence on outside support was even greater. John Smith, Jr., purchased this Pittsylvania County plantation of 713 acres from Peter Jefferson in 1755.[13] Smith, who sold tobacco and hemp to Scottish factors in New London, Bedford County, was a larger and more politically active planter than Mallory. He served as a sub-surveyor and sub-sheriff for Albemarle County in the 1750's, and as sub-surveyor for Goochland County in the 1760's.

Smith's expenses, upkeep, and repairs were also more varied and extensive than Mallory's. In 1772 he paid £25.5 alone for work performed by a carpenter and joiner. Earlier accounts with the county handyman recorded payments for a pair of "negro shoes"; the construction of a twelve-foot-square meat house; two 50-gallon "Cyder Cases," £3.10; for "your [the white jobber's] wife Laying [midwifing] two negro Wenches", £1; and, for "sundry sort of Work, 18/6." Evidently, Smith's slaves were only field laborers, because in 1757 he contracted for such simple tasks as the construction of a kitchen and a slave quarter, "mending an old Tobo [hogshead]." In June of that year he paid Thomas Allbrittain £2.5 for "getin & Nailing on 1500 bords." He also had to hire blacksmiths for such piddling jobs as pointing a plow, and mending a teakettle and padlock. Last, a James Faniken was paid for supplying the plantation with 309 pounds of beef, for 3 days' work in the "Cellar shelters," and for "riding 8 days in Search of horses." This odd-jobber's wife was also given a small recompense for weaving 15 yards of cloth.

These plantation accounts illustrate a problem of insufficient urbanization and home manufactures so severe one planter commented that "we have no merchants, tradesmen or artificers of any sort here but what become planters in a short time"—few of the larger slaveowners, he should have added, were not also merchants and tradesmen.[14]

Small planters like Mallory and Smith were the gentry's regular customers for retail goods and repairs as well as for slaves and home manufactures. They sold their crops to the large slaveowners who used them to increase their own credit purchases of European manufactured goods. As a type of resident factor, the great planter retailed these goods in "merchant stores," one of which is described in "King" Carter's estate inventory:

> Sundry goods in the Brick House Store, under the care of Captain thomas Carter: Gartrix, Kenting, blew linnen, Patterbons, Dowals, brown oz., ticking, fine chince, fine broad falls, fine Devon. Kersey, Shalloon, men's roll, knit hose, short hose, women's wash gloves, men's gloves, blankets, boots, shoes, men's & women's; men's new woodheeled shoes, round red heels do.; spectacles in case, men's felts, men's casters, pr. scales' weights, money scales, thread, cloves, drop shot, mould shot, brass kettles, bell metal skillets, double slint decanters, tape, gunpowder, mohair, tie buttons, other buttons, brads, broad hoes, brass chaffing dishes, brass & iron candlesticks, paddlocks, hasps & staples, pewter basin, lead inkstand, knives and forks, ivory combs, horse combs, sheep shead lines, drum hooks, perch hooks; sifters, lawn searches, 1 grammer, 2 testaments, chests, trunk, leather chair.[15]

Wealthy and powerful men like "King" Carter also supplied additional urban services based on their iron foundries, flour mills, textile weaving centers, and blacksmith shops. John Tayloe's Neabsco Ironworks in Prince William County, for example, did a thriving business in cutting new tools, repairing old ones, and in blacksmithing and locksmithing.[16]

Even the physical appearance and layout of the large plantations made abundantly clear why a few slaveowners excelled while so many others struggled. Robert "Councillor" Carter's Nomini Hall in Westmoreland County was surrounded by 33 outbuildings, including a mill, brewery, spinning center, wheat silo, and ironworks. Extensive outbuildings such as these prompted the German traveler, Dr. Johann Schoepf, to observe that "a plantation in Virginia has often more the appearance of a small village by reason of [its] many small buildings." [17]

Augustus John Foster, a British visitor to James Madison's Montpelier, remarked that the neighboring piedmont towns were so critically lacking in skills and services that it was necessary for Madison's slaves to be "able to do all kinds of handiwork." Accordingly, he discovered in his walks a forge, a turner's shop, a carpenter, and a wheelwright. While inspecting a very well-made wagon that "had just been completed," he noted that "all" of the farm implements were also "made on the spot." The Duc de La Rochefoucauld-Liancourt found the same thriving workshops close by at Monticello. Since Jefferson could not "expect any assistance from the two small neighboring towns, every article [was] made on his farm." His slaves were cabinetmakers, carpenters, masons, bricklayers, smiths, "&c." Although nearly all planters who recorded their views of slave children agreed that they were economic liabilities, Jefferson's young slaves manufactured nails. This small-scale household industry "yield[ed] a considerable profit"; his other unproductive slaves, the older women, spun clothing.[18]

In addition to archaeological remains and these narrative sources, accounts and inventories often illustrate the abundance of home manufactures on the great plantations. John Page's informal inventory for his beautiful estate, Rosewell, listed: [19]

> Emanual (Shoemaker), Oliver (Blacksmith) Sam (Carpenter), Jemmey (Cooper), Sharp (Waiter), Mary (Dairy Maid), Rachel (Cook), Kate (Laundress), and Edy, Jenny, Molly, and Kate (Maids).
>
> totals   10 in the Crop
> 12 Tradesmen & H[ouse] S[ervan]ts
> 8 Children
> 4 old
> ⎯⎯
> 35

On Philip Ludwell's plantation, Green Spring, the proportion of field to non-field workers was slightly higher. He owned 81 slaves, three-fourths of whom worked "in the crop." Twelve were house "servants" (a term preferred by slaveowners when they referred to house slaves); and there were 3 gardeners and hostlers, 4 carpenters, 2 shoemakers, and a wheelwright. Coachman Nat, a "governor," presided over this plantation "family." [20]

Great planters kept large and specialized staffs of "servants" and artisans on their home plantations; but their up-country, staple-growing quarters were comprised of tobacco fields, crop slaves, and little else. One of George Washington's periodic inventories listed 216 slaves: 67 of whom lived at Mount Vernon, and included 2 "val de Chambre," 2 waiters, 2 cooks, 3 drivers and stablers, 3 seamstresses,

2 house maids, 2 washers, 4 spinners, and (their numbers not indicated) knitters, blacksmiths and carpenters, a wagoner, a carter, and
a stock keeper. He also had 2 women "almost past service," lame
Peter, who had been taught to knit, and 26 children. At his mill
adjacent to the home quarter, he kept a slave miller and 3 coopers to
pack the meal. Thompson Mason had 50 slaves on his home plantation,
20 of whom were house "servants" alone, and many of the others were
artisans.[21]

The most complete description of a virtually self-dependent plantation is George Mason's. Describing his father's economic diversification at Gunston Hall, Mason wrote:

> My father had among his slaves carpenters, coopers, sawyers, black-
> smiths, tanners, curriers, shoemakers, spinners, weavers and knit-
> ters, and even a distiller. His woods furnish timber and plank for
> the carpenters and coopers, and charcoal for the blacksmith; his
> cattle killed for his own consumption and for sale supplied skins for
> the tanners, curriers, and shoemakers, and his sheep gave wool and
> his fields produced cotton and flax for the weavers and spinners, and
> his orchards fruit for the distiller. His carpenters and sawyers built
> and kept in repair all the dwelling-houses, barns, stables, ploughs,
> barrows, gates &c., on the plantations and the out-houses at the
> home house. His coopers made the hogsheads the tobacco was prised
> in and the tight casks to hold the cider and other liquors. The tan-
> ners and curriers with the proper vats &c., tanned and dressed the
> skins as well for upper as for lowere leather to the full amount of
> the consumption of the estate, and the shoemakers made them into
> shoes for the negroes. . . . The blacksmiths did all the iron work
> required by the establishment, as making and repairing ploughs,
> harrow, teeth chains, bolts &c., &c. The spinners, weavers and
> knitters made all the coarse cloths and stockings used by the negroes,
> and some of finer texture worn by the white family, nearly all worn
> by the children of it. The distiller made every fall a good deal of
> apple, peach and persimmon brandy. . . . All these operations were
> carried on at the home house, and their results distributed as occa-
> sion required to the different plantations. Moreover all the beeves
> and hogs for consumption or sale were driven up and slaughtered
> there at the proper seasons, and whatever was to be preserved was
> salted and packed away for after distribution.[22]

Although these accounts shed light on the most essential difference
between eighteenth- and nineteenth-century plantations—namely, the
considerable degree of occupational specialization of the former—they

do not tell us much about the slaves who were the basis for plantation self-sufficiency. Bernard Moore's advertisement for a lottery helps complete the portrait of the great slaveowner's plantation.

In 1768 Moore, a well-to-do planter and land speculator, faced economic ruin. To pay his debts he published a lottery scheme that laid bare the most essential economic and social arrangements in his extended "family." [23] Moore's first prize, valued at £5,000, was a gristmill and forge on 1,800 acres, astride a "plentiful and constant stream." Billy (£280), a Negro man about 22, and "a very trusty good forgeman, as well at the finery as under the hammer, and understands putting up his fire," was listed with "his wife Lucy, a young wench, who works exceeding well both in the house and field." Sam (£250) about 26, and "a fine chaffery man," was also listed with his wife, Daphne, "a very good hand at the hoe, or in the house." Abraham, like most of the other men, was in his late 20's; he was an "exceeding good forge carpenter, cooper and clapboard carpenter." Bob (£150) was a master collier. Peter was 18 and a wagoner; Dick was a blacksmith, and Sampson, 32, a skipper of Moore's flat. Rachel was listed with her "very fine" children, Daniel and Thompson. Hannah, 16, and Ben, 25, a good house "servant" and carter "&c." were also listed together. Pat, "with child," lame on one side, and a "fine breeding woman," was to be sold with her 3 children. Another family Moore recognized included Casear, 30, a very good blacksmith, his wife Nanny, and their 2 children, Tab and Jane (all valued at £280). Other families included Moses, a "planter," his wife Phebe, "a very fine wench," "her" child Nell; and Robin, a sawyer, and his wife Bella and their two little girls. Sukey, about 12, and Betty, about 7, completed this list of American-born slaves. Last, native African slaves as usual were carefully indicated as "outlandish" and without skills or training. Tom (£50), "an outlandish fellow," and Lucy (£20) also "outlandish," completed Moore's "family." [24]

"Outlandish" slaves like Tom and Lucy, strangers to the English language and seldom trained as artisans, were comparatively inexpensive. Thus they were usually purchased by smaller planters from the large slaveowners, who were slave traders as well as retailers and manufacturers. As middlemen in the trade, the great planters were indispensable to the ship captains and the companies they represented since they conducted all aspects of the sale in the colony. They evaluated the prospective buyer's credit, obtained a return cargo, provided

for the maintenance of unsalable slaves (those too old, young, or ill),
and sometimes they leased out Africans on a trial basis. Their com-
mission for these services, usually 10 per cent, was evidently not sufficient; many gentlemen sold only a cargo or two before they quit the
business.

"King" Carter, the wealthiest planter of his generation, has left one
of the more complete descriptions of a sale which he conducted in the
late 1720's. During the first half of the century, sales took place, not
on the great planters' docks or at the tobacco inspection stations, but
aboard the slaver. Thus, punctually at 1:00 p.m. each afternoon Carter
got up from a hearty meal and several glasses of port, and rowed out
from Corotoman to Captain Denton's slaver. He usually stayed until
dusk; but one rainy evening kept him aboard overnight. During the
three-week sale he was without customers on only two occasions.
Carter usually sold between 4 and 6 Africans (most often in pairs,
for between £25 to £40 per pair). The most critical part of this, or
any slave sale, from Carter's vantage point was his expertise in the
delicate job of appraising his neighbor's credit. Carter described his
financial arrangements with Denton in this way:

> I went abord Captain Denton, agreed to sell his negroes . . . I
> am to draw 10 per cent on the sale of commission to make good all
> debts in this manner, if any of exchange will not be paid, the protest
> to be mine. He is to run into Corotoman, there to lye for the sale,
> I am to be at no manner of charge, all to be charged to the owner.[25]

This transaction was unusually smooth, for in the early part of the
century, the trade was so unorganized that slave captains stopped at a
number of great houses along the rivers before they made the best
deal for themselves and the firms they represented. On one contract
examined by Carter, the captain's list of prospective slave dealers included his own name at the top of the list but crossed out, and "Tom
Nelson['s] interlined," then Carter's again, "Thomas Lee, Potomac,"
and one Mr. Bennet in Maryland.[26] On another occasion Captain
Haynes of the *Leopard* sailed into the York River in mid-September.
He first stopped off Yorktown at Nelson's, but "finding no Orders
for him there," he went north around the peninsula to Corotoman on
the Rappahannock. Carter took one look at the captain's orders, and
"upon Seeing [their] Strictness," said he would "not meddle with his
Slaves." The season was late, the terms "preemptory," so Carter "let

him go." The captain "immediately" went up the river to Carter's neighbor, John Tayloe of Mount Airy.[27]

The slave trading season was short, from late spring to the end of the summer. Convinced that cold, chilling climate was often lethal for Africans, the buyers watched the weather carefully, come mid-September, "when the mornings & Evenings are cool," they stopped buying slaves for the season.[28] When Governor Jenings explained to the Board of Trade why the separate traders were more successful than the Royal African Company, he wrote:

> when Negroes come in about the begin[n]ing of the Summer, the planters are abundantly more fond of them, and will give greater price for them, because they are sure of the advantage of their labour in that years Crop, whereas Negros bought at the Latter end of the year, are of little Service till the next Spring, and this is the true reason of that difference of price.[29]

"Outlandish" Africans were not systematically broken-in or "seasoned." But rather they were put immediately to work in the last harvest of the year. One prominent Norfolk merchant and slave trader, Charles Steuart, corroborated Jenings's report, when in March 1752 he wrote: "slaves will continue in great demand for at least two months, the planters having left room in their Crops for them." [30]

Most important, smaller slaveowners, according to one county study, provided the market for Africans. In Caroline, the county with the largest slave population, the wealthiest families (the Baylors, Corbins, and Beverleys) did not register a single African with the county court after 1732. (The age of young Africans had to be adjudged so they could be taxable at age 16.) The only wealthy families that purchased Africans were those who had numerous sons and many new homesteads. Thus, in addition to small planters, the chief registrants of young and taxable Africans were tavernkeepers, sailors, horse traders, small-time speculators, and such minor officeholders as constables and road supervisors.[31]

In 1671 there were only about 2,000 slaves in the colony; but twenty-nine years later—when the economy had achieved the critical mass necessary to give it a market capable of absorbing a cargo from Africa —the number had tripled. At this time only about 40 per cent of the whites owned any slaves, and the great majority who did, owned one or two. The white population in 1700 was about 70,000, and from

1698 to 1708 the number of slaves doubled to about 12,000, and then increased another two-thirds by 1730. After the 1730's blacks consistently made up between 40 and 50 per cent of the colony's population. By 1763 there were equal numbers of slaves and whites in a population of approximately 340,000, or about 170,000 of each according to Governor Francis Fauquier. In 1770 on the eve of the Revolution and the end of the slave trade, the blacks had increased another 18,000 to 188,000. In arriving at these figures, Governor Robert Dinwiddie said that he counted 3 Negro children per 2 blacks of taxable age.[32]

Population growth, dramatized by the slaves' ability to greatly increase in number by natural means, was the demographic reality behind the establishment of the great families' economically diversified plantations in the 1720's. Since 1710, Hugh Jones noted, "our Country may be said to be altered & improved in wealth . . . more than in all the scores of years before, that from its first discovery." Jones's contemporary, William Byrd II, viewed this growth more pessimistically: the colony "will some time or other be confirm'd by [the] Name of New Guinea." [33] Although the population figures are fragmentary, there were indications that the increase of the Africans' children was phenomenal. Elizabeth Donnan estimates that the slave trade brought about 55,000 slaves to Virginia between 1710 and 1769. Philip Curtin's estimate of a total importation to all British continental colonies to 1790, moreover, is approximately 250,000 to 300,000 Africans—a figure that could scarcely account for the size of the slave population in Virginia alone, which according to the Federal census in 1790 was 292,627. The Virginia slave population, unlike that of the British island colonies, experienced a rapid natural growth, a critical factor—so important to comparative studies of slavery in the Americas—which historians, Curtin reminds us, have neglected almost completely.[34]

"MY BOND-MEN AND BOND-WOMEN"

"Outlandish" Africans were absolutely essential to the aristocratic planters who would be "independent on Every one but Providence." Ironically, the Christian culture that supported that Faustian wish also sanctioned the view of newly arrived Africans as godless savages. This attitude and the whites' appraisal of a slave's comprehension of English and the colonial culture were the most important realities for slaves of all kinds. A slave's birthplace and the pace and level of his socialization were the basis for the most important decisions forced upon him: his sale, task assignment, and distribution in estates. At these times there were only two kinds of blacks: those who were "outlandish"—born in Africa—and those born in America.

Colonists and travelers alike clearly understood the critical importance of an African's background and his later adjustment to slavery. Hugh Jones, an early eighteenth-century historian, for example, made the usual references to the blacks' ugly bodies, slavish natures, and "delight" for his country's "violent Heat," before stating that among "New Negroes," the best slaves were those who had been servants in their own country. But "they that have been Kings and great Men are generally lazy, haughty, and obstinate." Visitors to the colony, who at first saw few differences among slaves, soon realized that the African's origin as well as his color was the basis for the colonists' hostile evaluation of his alien culture. "The more we observe the Negroes, the more must we be persuaded that the difference distinguishing them from us does not consist in color alone," the Marquis de Chastellux observed, and he soon came to understand his hosts' standards. When comparing Virginia and Jamaica slaves he reported: "most of the Negroes are born in this country [Virginia], and it is a known fact that they are generally less depraved than those imported directly from Africa." [35]

Virginians made similar distinctions between Africans and native American slaves when it came time to allot tasks—to decide which slaves remained in the fields and which ones came into the flourishing workshops on the home plantation to acquire the literate and technical skills that were the basis for the great plantation's self-sufficiency. This issue was viewed in a religious context, and since Christianity was at the heart of colonial culture, the African's apparent paganism was his greatest liability. Hugh Jones, for example, observed that most slaveowners believed that while baptism made slaves proud and unmanageable, this applied only to "Infidels," that is, to "wild Indians and New Negroes," who possessed neither the knowledge nor the inclination to "know and mind" our "Religion, Language, & Customs." Education and training (which he equated with conversion and baptism), on the other hand, were acceptable for American-born slaves, who were by

nature "sensible, good and underst[oo]d English." Drawing attention
to the fact that the source of the essential differences among slaves
was traceable to their origin, Jones wrote that "Africans would ob-
stinately persist in their own barbarous Ways." Thus he wondered
"whether Baptism of such (till they be a little weaned of their savage
Barbarity) be not Prostitution of a Thing so sacred." But, he concluded, the Africans' children, "those who are to live among Chris-
tians, undoubtedly they ought to be baptized." [36]

The Bishop of London concurred: it was the Church's duty to up-
lift and civilize the benighted Africans. In 1727, the same year that
Jones published his history, the Bishop sent an inquiry to his ministers
in Virginia. Their replies underscore the extent to which colonial
churches reflected the ethos of the aristocratic slaveowning families
they served. "Are there any Infidels, bond or free, within your Parish;
and what means are used for their conversion?" "My Lord," began a
typical reply, "our Negroe Slaves imported daily, are altogether ignorant of God & Religion, and in truth have so little Docility in them that
they scarce ever become capable of Instructtion; but my Lord, I have
examined and improved several Negroes, Natives of Virginia." [37] Almost invariably white ministers pointed to the relevance of the Africans' distinctive language patterns for religious instruction.

> The owners are generally careful to instruct those that are capable
> of instruction and to bring them to Baptism, but it is impossible to
> instruct those that are grown up before they are carried out of their
> own Country, they never being able either to speak or understand
> our Language perfectly.[38]

A few ministers did report that they had made significant gains in
the number of slaves converted and educated. One man taught cate-
chism classes for black youngsters every Saturday afternoon in the
chapter house; another, an Eastern Shore minister, said he had baptized about 200 slaves, whom from time to time he instructed on their
own plantations. But those educated were nearly always the Virginia-
born, so the planters' and ministers' efforts to ameliorate their slaves'
condition—to use their term—further widened the cultural gap between African and native American slaves.[39]

By 1750 these attitudes were sharply focused by important demographic and economic developments: the leveling off of the importations of Africans, the remarkable natural increase of American-born

slaves (nearly always referred to as "country-born"), and the wealthy planters' determination to offset the effects of both the severe depression of the tobacco market and their notorious debts to British merchants, by training slave-artisans and further diversifying their plantations. This required them to base their lives as well as their livelihoods on the rhythms of the plantation's intricate workings. Thus, in the final analysis, the great planter had to be the accomplished head of an extended plantation "family."

"LIKE ONE OF THE PATRIARCHS"

The large slaveowner served his plantation in essentially two ways: as an estate manager and as a patriarch. The first role was a function of his direction of the plantation's complex and demanding economic processes; it required a shrewd, calculating, and systematic regard for expenses, the delegation of authority, and the direction of slaves. The second role, defined by the master's relations to the members of a plantation "family"—composed of his kin as well as the overseer, servants white and black, field slaves, and artisans—required that the good patriarch maintain two positions, one in the neighborhood, by sumptuous living and feats of hospitality, and the other among his slaves on the plantation, by a benevolent, indulgent, and understanding view of their performance. Planters were usually more accomplished as patriarchs than estate managers, though this certainly was often not in their best interest. But their failure to achieve economic, political, and cultural self-determination in the Empire sharpened the view that the father was the source of authority on the plantation, and that this authority was indivisible. At this point particularly, the planter's two roles conflicted: it was absolutely essential to good estate management that the planter divide his authority in a rational way, so that those directly responsible for the slaves' work could supervise effectively.

To see the great slaveowner as a patriarch and estate manager is to begin to understand what it meant for him to be a product of a slave society, in which "nothing, nothing and no one escaped"; to understand, too, the nature of the "command experience"—that familiar notion historians have used to discuss the exceptional background of the famous Virginians who served the national government with such distinction during the Revolutionary and early National periods.

"A Continual Exercise of Our Patience & Economy"

Planters revealed themselves and the most intimate details of their plantation duties in accounts of their daily rounds. Poking into stores and shops, watching their slaves plant, hoe, and irrigate, persistently counting rows of corn, tobacco, and heads of cattle, they relentlessly pursued wealth and competence. "Made a Visit to my Plantations this day," Landon Carter, "King" Carter's son, noted, "that is, looked into every hole and corner of them." "I walk much about the family business," wrote a Huguenot minister and planter "and ride constantly every morning all over my plantation, giving my servants their several employments." [40] Landon Carter's account of the estate manager's "continual exercise" preserves the mood of this way of life:

> Rode out this day. Corn except where the land is very stiff is coming up, and with a broad blade.
> Mill dam in tolerable good order but a little wanting to make things there very strong, and troughs to let the ponds from the runs into the canals run off into the meadow which is to be.
> Making tobacco hills. Potatoes come up, want weeding.
> Fork Corn not quite done in the Peach orchard. Therefore Cotton can't be planted there before next Monday, the old May day.
> Wheat looks tolerable, only a trespass from the Cowpen last monday night.[41]

No item of production, no man, beast, or building was beyond the assiduous planter's purview, as this excerpt from "Councillor" Carter's papers will illustrate:

> To Richard Dozier, orders for the following summer crops: 64 acres Indian Corn; 2 acres peas, 2 acres Irish potatoes, 2 acres Turnips, 2 acres pumpkins, 1 in flax, 3 in cotton, 32 in tobacco.[42]

"Councillor" Carter's concreteness became obsession with detail for estate managers like George Washington and Landon Carter.

> Notwithstanding all Lawson's boast [one of Carter's overseers] I shall not do more than fill the Mangorike 60 foot double Shedded house with corn in the Shucks up to the Joice.[43]

Item counts of seedlings, stores, and crops took up much of each inspection tour because so many planters believed that their slaves and overseers took advantage of them at every opportunity. Landon Carter's way was to begin where even the most scrupulous planters left off. His counts involved each plant, literally tens of thousands of them:

> I find it wondered at how any hand can tend 28,000 corn hills planted at any distance. But surely it cannot be reasonable to do so, when it is considered that at 2 feet and 7 an acre holds 3,111 corn hills and at 6 and 5 it holds only 1,452; for it is in such a case evident, that at 7 and 2 the acre contains more than double to what it does when planted at 6 and 5 by 202 hills. Allow then that at 6 and 5 ten thouand hills only are tended; it will amount to near 7 acres that are worked each hand. Now at 7 and 2, 7 acres will contain 21,777 so that there only wants 6,223 to make up 28,000. Now that is Exactly 4 hill[s] short of 2 acres, So that the hand that tends 28,000 is only to tend 9 acres. And cannot a hand tend 9 acres of ground? [44]

The continuous assessment of the plantation's components, of course, also included the slaves. Even their peculiarities of appearance and grooming habits were scrutinized and became part of the planter's lore. One slaveowner advertised for a runaway whose lips were not thick, "but seem[ed] a little longer than common." Another described an African who had run off four years earlier: he had reddish eyes and a "remarkable loose jostling Way of walking." Sancho's master knew that his slave ran away in new shoes, "one tied with a leather thong, the other with an old black ribbon"; and another owner said that his slave's shoe heels "were pegged and nailed with 3d nails and 2d nails drove through the edges at the soles and clinched." [45]

During their long hours among crops, slaves, and shops, planters sought to make intelligible the larger world beyond the plantation. Richard Henry Lee, the Revolutionary War general and leader of the Virginia anti-Federalists, carried a memorandum book on his rides. It is small, hand-sized, and its leather cover is gently rounded, smoothed, and polished by the action of Lee's rear pocket, saddle, and the swaying of his horse. It is a distillation of his reminders, accounts, and reading notes over a few years, which included comments on the whereabouts of two slaves (his jobber Congo and a "yellow negro girl" named Grace); the disposition of iron bars sent from Stratford to various quarters; how much pork he cut from a hog sent in payment for the hire of Abraham; and plants in his window garden.[46] Lee, like so many Virginians then and now, lavished attention on his kitchen garden: it was the plantation in microcosm, but with boundaries sufficiently restricted that control, always a problem elsewhere, was readily achieved. "Sowed [s]quare next [to the] dining room with peas, the 6 rows next [to] the dining room window are Lawsons Hotspur & the 6 rows furthest off are the Greenspring May pea." [47] A few lines further he recorded having "counted the Sheep carefully & there were 32 head including the sic[k] one in the Cow house & the two in the fattening sheep pen. . . . Not one young Lamb yet." The planter's reading notes were scattered throughout in this manner: "Dissertations historical and political on the Ancient Republics of Italy" by Carol Denina, led to musings on standing armies in republics. Notes on the Reverend William Stith's *History of Virginia* (1747), included a reference to "Sir George Somers [who] paid [laid?] his ship's bottom seams with Lime and Turtle oil which made a fine cement for stopping the Seams of the Vesels." These observations were followed by a recipe for potato pone.[48]

Even while he was President, George Washington was also never too far from his plantation operations. In 1793, for example—a critical year for him—the cold war with the French and English navies and the bank bill were demanding realities. But in the midst of these crises, he pored over his steward's weekly reports from Mount Vernon and sent off revealing directives. His devotion to order carried his attention to a particular group of workers: the sewers "who made only Six Shirts a Week." [49] Then his concern was narrowed to one worker: "and the last week Caroline (without being sick) made only five"; and finally penetrated to the very items of production, and the intricacies of how they were made:

> Mrs. Washington says their usual task was to make nine with Shoulder straps & good sewing:—tell them therefore from me, that what *has* been done *shall* be done by fair or foul means; & they had better make a choice of the first, for their own reputation, & for the sake of peace and quietness.[50]

Then Washington, who after 1775 aptly called his diary "where, & how my time is Spent," concluded: "Their work ought to be well examined. The same attention ought to be given to Peter (& I supposed to Sarah likewise) or the Stockings will be knit too small." [51]

"I have a large Family of my own"

Washington's familiarity with his slaves and their routines stemmed from his patriarchal role as head of a large and varied plantation "family." The correspondence of several types of colonist indicates that the plantation slaves' status as family members was assumed. John Harrower, an indentured servant and tutor, wrote home to Scotland: "our Family consists of the Col[onel], his Lady & four Children, a housekeeper, an overseer and myself, all white. But how many blacks young and old, the Lord only knows." Robert Beverley, the historian, gently chided his father-in-law, Landon Carter, for his notoriety as a stern parent, while observing that Carter had not been "sufficiently indulgent" about allowing his 22-year-old daughter to visit a woman companion. He concluded: "My familey [sic] are all well now some few Negroes excepted." [52]

Accounts of the great planters as their peoples' doctors and judges clarify the patriarchal role and the familial, domestic character of eighteenth-century plantation slavery. In the first few days of the new year 1711, Byrd, for example, spent long hours during a fierce epidemic administering to his slaves:

> I spent most of my time in looking after my sick. . . . My sick people were some worse and some well enough to go home to the quarters. . . . In the afternoon I did nothing but mind them. . . . At night I look over all my people. . . . I tended them diligently and went to the quarters to see the negroes there and gave the necessary orders about them. . . . I visited my people again.[53]

The patriarchal role sometimes had an insidious influence on the master's behavior. Landon Carter's paternalistic care of his slave children changed his normally embittered outlook. Carter knew himself well enough to seek out situations that brought out his generous, humane qualities. He was especially gentle to those whom he perceived as weaker than himself, including "my negro children," whom he sometimes doctored. "How wonderfully has [God] blessed me both with skill and inclination to assist my poor fellow creatures." Or, "killed a fine mutton this day; ordered some broth for the sick, Nassau tells me they are all mending. I hope in God they are . . . they are human creatures and my soul I hope delighteth in relieving them." This from a man who said slaves were devils and should never be free. In momentarily drawing upon his own humanity, the old man discovered that of his slaves.[54]

But planters were more in character as their slaves' judges. Meting out punishment, they readily lost sight of the slave's individuality. At these times one important facet of the patriarchal role, his kindness and indulgence, gave way to another, his stern righteousness.

". . . I must take care to keep all my people to their Duty."

The tone and phrases masters used while punishing slaves indicate that they viewed slave rebelliousness in the context of the Fifth Commandment—Honour thy father and thy mother—assuming that both slaves and free had certain rights, duties, and responsibilities toward one another. "I must again desire you will keep Tommy strictly to his Duty & obedience." Or, "cruelty to the poor slaves is a thing I always Abhored. I would think myself happy could I keep them to there [sic] duty without being Obliged to correct them." "Began this morning," Landon Carter noted, "to enforce my resolution of correcting the drunkenes[s] in my family by an example on Nassau." Washington's order preserved the same tone: "As for Waggoner Jack, a misbehaving fellow, try further correction, accompanied by admonition and advice." When two runaways sent word to their master, John Tayloe, that they would not return unless he either hired them out or sold them, his response was typical of the elite of the era he represented: "I will do neither until they return to a sense of duty." [55]

Patriarchs also preferred to call slaves (house and field) on the home plantation "servants," and to view physical beatings as "correction" and "discipline." At the same time a few sensational and well-publicized whippings should not obscure our view of the masters' sharply equivocal feelings about beating their "people." In the era of the Revolution, which produced a mild effort to ameliorate slavery by prohibiting the trade, encouraging manumission, and discouraging sales that separated children from their mothers, some whites became openly defensive and apologetic about physically "correcting" slaves. Those who advertised runaways who had been whipped, occasionally felt compelled to explain away their slaves' wounds and scars. "His thefts were certainly the Cause of his Flight." Sam ran away "to avoid the Gallows; for he was never punished whilst with me," his master reported, "nor ever complained, neither had he any Cause to be dissatisfied at his Treatment." The manager of an ironworks said that his mulatto runaway had scars on his back, "which he got several Years before I had him"; and another advertiser simply noted: he has been "pretty much subject to the Lash by his former Master." [56]

As a substitute for physical beatings, planters used job placement to reward some and punish others because it simply was not feasible to attempt to contain the plantation slaves' clever "trifling about" in any other way. "Councillor" Carter's order for task assignments illustrates the extent of the master's control of this important method of expressing authority on the plantation.

> Negro Ralph Sawyer has committed so many offences lately that I propose to remove him from that Employment—Ralph to work as a Labourer in the crop at Colespoint.
> Frank lately of Taurus & now at Colespoint he to be delivered up to Oliver [an overseer] & to be a sawyer this Exchange to be made immediately.[57]

"To Set all the Springs in Motion"

Assigning tasks—deciding who remained on the distant quarters and who came into the plantation or household, and which young slaves were to be apprenticed—was one of the most important prerogatives of ownership, as well as a very effective way of controlling slaves. Masters seldom shared this responsibility, because "set[ting] all the Springs in Motion" allowed them to demonstrate their paternalistic concern for their "people's" welfare and best interests.

For some slaveowners, job assignment was also a way of establishing order in a more personal sense. "I would not live with too disorderly souls about me for no consideration in this life," wrote Battaile Muse, George Washington's rental agent and a distinguished Northern Neck steward. "If I cannot Keep order with Slaves I cannot do it with free men and where their is no regulations their must be much confusion—which will always be the Case unless Proper decorum is kept up." This conception of "order"—of inculcating in slaves "a sense of duty and responsibility" in order to make a confusing world more manageable—was apparently realized at Thompson Mason's plantation below Fredericksburg. The Colonel's New England tutor wrote that there were about 50 slaves on Mason's home quarter, among whom were "his weaver, his blacksmith, his carpenter, his shoemaker, as is the general practice with very independent planters." He concluded: "each one knows his place and business and every thing is conducted with the greatest order." [58]

The patriarch's knowledge of virtually every slave was, in the final analysis, a function of the colony's terrain, economic setting, land inheritance patterns, and a brief historical phenomenon. Usually at least once in their career wealthy slaveowners were forced to relocate much of their property. The use of reserve lands and partible inheritances to establish cadet lines, soil exhaustion, and population pressures in the tidewater prompted them to develop up-country quarters as new home plantations. Moving up-river and west was a perilous venture that required shrewd and rational planning, if the planter was to avoid a crippling setback from losses of slaves and livestock. Thus it was imperative that he attempt to extend family status even to slaves on the farthest perimeters of his holdings, that he know each slave as an individual, and that slave's idiosyncrasies and special skills.

Although for all these reasons patriarchs exercised almost exclusive control over task assignment, their stewards and overseers were charged with implementing as best they could the establishment of new quarters. The directives they received indicated that the patriarch often placed his people's well-being above economic considerations. James Mercer wrote Muse in 1777:

> I send 2 Negroe Wenches Amy & Sall, Daughters of Scipio. They are fine winches but I suspect [they are] too sick to thrive here. Amy has had a three months Spell & Sall has been sick two months. . . . [Sall] shou'd live on milk, butter milk is best, & use exercise every day on horse back . . . in particular she must not work 'till she is quite well.[59]

And Hugh Nelson, scion of the wealthy Yorktown merchant family, also wrote to Muse in 1789:

> The old Woman may serve to take Care of all the Children, and Grace may be employed any Way you please. Give Nanny 4 Pieces of Bacon . . . The little Girl, Dinah, you may keep in Fauquier as a Spinner. Nanny who has one of her Eyes very much hurt, which makes it necessary to keep her here till it is well. . . . I shall be up in May.[60]

When in 1779 John H. Norton, a member of another merchant family, established new quarters in the Valley, he carefully listed his resources, which included the abilities that enhanced the individuality of particular slaves.

> I have an old fellow called Charles & his Son Anthony who have been employed always at the Carpenters business & will be very useful, his Wife Betty, a favor'd house Servant assists in our Cooking.
> Mulatto Milly is the principal Spinner, she has several Children, one of which can spin & work at the Needle.[61]

He then indicated which men he wanted in the fields (which he called "working out"), and designated Jemmy "a plowboy." Also "there is a fellow named Jack who has had a bad Complaint in his Eyes but maybe useful in looking after Stock, or plowing occasionally." [62]

Families figured prominently in these moves, because patriarchs like James Mercer were often intent on keeping them intact:

> As Lot's Boy Harry (I believe that is his name) is now deprived of all his Friends & Connections & is of a size & sort to be usefull in a factory he must come down with them & so must Bet's Husband rather than part them unless they mutually agree to part.[63]

In many ways planters actively intervened in the slaves' fragmented family lives. Sometimes the desire to keep remnants of families together was a practical one: "as Dick is likely be troublesome I have wrote down to Mrs Burwell for his Wife even at the enormous price of £6. . . . Indeed the maintenance of her [the slave's wife] & Children is considerable more than the Hire of a Negro Fellow." At other times, masters seemed to be genuinely concerned about slave marriages, although one can never discount the strong probability that they wanted to encourage couples to produce as many children as possible. "May I beg the favour of you," one wrote his overseer, "to send Beck & her Child & purchase a likely young Virga. born Fellow between the Age of 18 & 22 or 23 Years." [64]

"Councillor" Carter who owned about 10 plantations in several counties, and more than 400 slaves (whose "correction" he personally directed), wrote a remarkable order which read in part:

> Sir, Child Negroe Molley—about two years old, [the] Daughter of Sukey of Cancer [Quarter] wants a Nurse. I understand that

Negroe Payne, 71 years old of the Forest Plantation, is the father
of said child—if it be agreeable to you . . . I now direct that Payne
be ordered to go to Cancer Plantation & live at Sukey's house he to
have the Care of both his grand Children.[65]

This same planter once exchanged men between two quarters because
he said "the Distance from Coles Point to Dicks Quarter is rather far
for a Walker"; so he asked that Dennis be moved nearer to his wife,
and that a slave be found to replace him.

Patriarchs also directly intervened in their slaves' domestic affairs.
Byrd wrote that he "threatened Anaka with a whipping if she did not
confess the intrigue between Daniel and Nurse." And when James
Gordon, a Northern Neck planter, was "alarmed" by news that
Cumberland was "abusing" his wife, he had him whipped the following morning. "Councillor" Carter, who was so well informed about
his slaves' liaisons and marriages, reported to an overseer: "Sir, Dennis
of Colespoint Quarter has Negro Frankey for a Wife, she living at Mr.
Fleet Cox's Quarter. . . . I hope that Dennis & Frankey Are Constant to each other." [66]

Wise, concerned but detached, and very understanding, the master
on some occasions could have it both ways: as owner and estate
manager, on the one hand, and as father for all members of the
plantation "family," on the other. Robert Wormeley Carter, 41 years
of age, dutifully reported to his father in Williamsburg about his
arbitration between an outraged overseer and a slave woman. Jackson,
the Sabine Hall overseer, recaptured a runaway on the road to
Williamsburg and "turned up her cloathes and whiped her Breach."
But, the son assured the old man, he "check[e]d" Jackson "for this
mode of correction," and "made the matter up between them." [67]

More often though, masters were caught in the inherent contra-
diction of their two roles. James Mercer in his role as patriarch wrote
to his steward in 1778: "I shall direct George to be well hunted after,
we must break the habit of runing away by severe example." But a
year later Mercer, the estate manager and entrepreneur, no longer the
kind patriarch, advised: "as to Negroes, Indulgence Spoils them, either
make them do their Duty or let them run away, when we save their
Corn & Cloathes & if idle at home they wont earn it." The master's
ambivalence about his roles, slaves, and slavery also directly contributed to the abusive, exploitative relations between plantation slaves
and their supervisors. Norton by his own admission worsened the

arrangements on one of his plantations. He mentioned to his steward: "I have told Payne [an overseer] & the People that I must have large Crops made & ordered that the people in any instance to do their Duty otherwise they should suffere for discharging him." [68]

Patriarchs, characteristically refusing to divide their authority, insisting on making the most trivial decisions, and demanding bumper crops while berating overseers for driving slaves, undermined their representatives' confidence in their own judgment. Thus absenteeism inevitably provoked widespread non-cooperation among the slaves. When the owner left the plantation in the hands of the demoralized overseer the situation rapidly deteriorated. "My spinners," wrote Landon Carter, "imagining I was gone yesterday instead of their usual day's work spun but 2 ounces a piece." While visiting another quarter he noted: "I must declare I saw no care on my whole plantation, but everybody did as they pleased, Came, Went, Slept or Worked as they would." [69]

The master's insensitivity to the overseer's position was even more remarkable in light of his own recognition that his slaves were tough, clever, and troublesome and that his representatives on the quarters must therefore be strong, talented men. Mercer directed his steward to hire an overseer who "must be what is called tight in order to learn my lazy Negroes how to work." Washington sized up one prospective overseer as "a tolerably good looking man and [he] has the appearance of an active one—but how far any man, unacquainted with Negroes is capable of managing them, is questionable." The President realized that slaves were quick to exploit weaknesses in an overseer's character. An old man who handled the "house People" and ditchers was honest, sober, well-meaning, and "something knowing," in Washington's estimation. Unfortunately, he was also "not accustomed to Negroes," who since they were in "no sort of awe of him—of course do as they please." Because they were not given the means to do their job, overseers were a convenient target for the persistently non-cooperative plantation and quarter slaves. Landon Carter understood the process of attrition that steadily wore them down. Overseers, he said, "tire as cornfields do." [70]

Overseers and their employers argued repeatedly about the question of payment in crop shares or salary; about problems of supplies for both slaves and overseer; about pasturage for the overseer's horse, milk cows, reports of untended fences and stray cattle and serving "wenches" for his wife and family. But the basic and most divisive issue was based upon the related problems of delegating authority in the master's absence and the use of slave informers.

Overseers who tried to imitate their employers' paternalism by using persuasion and incentives were moderately successful. They used what little authority they had at their disposal to manipulate and cajole slaves, occasionally overlooking a young pig cut out of season, discreetly keeping unlocked a corn or cider store, or simply allowing slaves to visit adjoining quarters or plantations during the evening and on Sundays. But when these privileges were cut off, the field workers balked. A familiar note of exasperation is heard in a report to John Hatley Norton from his York County overseer. The planter's quarter was about to be abandoned and the laborers, evidentally satisfied with the arrangements thereon, were in no mood to cooperate. Faced with this situation, the overseer reported that he had "to hurrey to get [his] Corn of hand as fast as posable tho the negroes Seem verey Dul and Sloath full Sense they have heared that the Plantation wase to be Broke up." He could, he noted apologetically, accomplish very little to date, and then "onley when [he was] Driveing and Storming at them and verey often [he was] a bliged to whipe." Charles Dabney, an estate steward, accounted for the problems on a Louisa County plantation in this way: his previous overseer "was so good natured to the Negroes under him [that] he suffered them to Impose on him very much." Dabney complained that under the present overseer "the Negroes are very unwilling to give up the privileges they were allowed." [71]

Overseers were seldom "good natured." Unlike masters, they were sometimes sadistic. "There are very few of the common Overseers that have the least feeling of humanity for Slaves," Hugh Washington, the President's relative, reported, "they treat them in general (when left to themselves) as if they were not of the same species." George Washington concurred: "I expect little of this from McKoy [an overseer]—or indeed from most of his class; for they seem to consider a Negro much in the same light as they do the brute beasts on the farms; and often times treat them as inhumanely." [72] In another letter to his steward, Hugh Washington wrote:

> I once wrote to You on the Subject of the Negroes ill treatment by the common Overseers; who in general have not the least

humanity in regard to the Slaves under them, & I know that they require much looking after to prevent their using them ill.

I know from experience, that Negroes are in general an ungrateful set of beings that there is no such thing as satisfying them in regard to their Overseers; but indeed Sir the common run of Overseers if left to themselves, woud be cruel to them.[73]

When Joseph Ball was notified of the loss of several of his slaves' children he replied: "You [his steward and nephew] let unmerciful overseers beat and abuse them Inhumanely and Break their hearts." [74]

The planter's source of information of this type was often a "trusted servant." This practice, which further weakened the overseer's position, was defended in a letter from James Mercer to his steward:

> I have allmost constantly found Nigroes tell Truth enough of distant overseers & I am now told that Moore has sold every grain of his own Corn yet Suds his own horse three times a day out of mine, that he has now seven Hoggs raised in my Estate that the Nigroes can't get a drop of Milk tho' there is a plenty even to spare Old Buidine & his [Moore's] Pigs every day. . . . I remember all the Bacon I laid in for Mill Wrights, Carpenters &c was also expended. . . .[75]

Jefferson also used informers: "Stanley [his overseer] has killed by his own confession 12 hogs, but as Jupiter sais [sic] 16. . . . The negroes say he has sold a great deal of corn." [76]

Muse, an exceptionally fine steward, was adamantly against this delicate question of the patriarch's right to know personally each slave as an expression of his authority. The relationship between a master and his field slaves should be only proprietary. Planters who made themselves the counsellors and advisors of slaves contributed to their dissatisfaction. His letter to Thomas Fairfax (whose family had once owned the entire Northern Neck as a vast proprietary grant) warned of the consequences of moderation and reasonableness with quarter "hands":

> I wish the two observations you make respecting the meadow & hogs was the only injury the Estate was to sustain from the last six months carrying on the business. I think the loss of 100 Acres land usually fallowed; Grain badly put in; Stock neglected; meadow rooten up with hogs; Creature[s] [be]ing in the orchard; Fences burnt; corn not gather'd at Christma[s] will prove in a few years

no small loss to the owner of the Estate. This Conduct has arose greatly from the authority taken from the overseer by hearing every tale that deceitful negroes will advance.[77]

"Your last letter," Fairfax replied angrily, "seems to Contain a tacit charge against me, I must not let it pass unnoticed. . . . You Say (in fact) that I have been in part the Cause of it, by giving ear to the tales of negroes which has lessened the overseers authority. No man," he continued, "who possessed the principles of Justice and humanity would ever deny those who are dependent on him (whether Slave or freemen) the privilege of making known their grievances to him." This enlightened patriarch sensed that his view was unique: "as to humanity toward Slaves, it appears to be an indefinite term in this Country and there are very few masters perhaps whose sentiments and mine woud agree upon this point. What I might Call a want of humanity, others might call a necessary Coercion." [78]

Fairfax's argument, as idealistic as his conception of slavery, is the more remarkable because it is addressed to a man who dealt directly with plantation slaves. It is also an eloquent argument and a fine example of the idealism of some patriarchs who, imbued with the natural rights philosophy of the Revolution, were determined to apply it to their relationships with slaves.

But the whites and blacks on the quarters saw the issue differently. One steward reported: "It gives me great concern to think a report of this Negro who is prejudiced to the highest degree that you should conclude the Negroes in Louisa have not been treated with the humanity that the *Brutes* are Intitled." Those who considered slaves as "brutes," as objects, were most likely to be the men who worked with them as their supervisors. Freemen who worked with those in bondage were convinced of the slaves' discontented, rebellious nature.[79]

The eighteenth-century Virginia planter was caught between his desire for self-sufficiency and his ultimate dependence on Great Britain. He was also forced to confront and forced to socialize a strange and threatening people, the Africans whom he imported and enslaved to support his way of life. The presence of these "outlandish" men, themselves soon caught between their old ways and the new colonial culture, created for owners another paradox. As an estate manager, the planter had to be a shrewd and calculating businessman who was able to rationally divide his authority among his supervisors on the plantations and quarters. But since the master's concept of authority was paternalistic, he felt that to be a good patriarch— wise, tolerant, and benevolent—he must retain complete control over all members of his extended plantation family. This situation left the overseer with little real power, the planter trapped between the contradictions inherent in his roles as estate manager and patriarch, and the plantation an especially vulnerable target for the field slaves' persistent rebelliousness and acts of sabotage.

2

Africans Become New Negroes

The available sources on slavery in eighteenth-century Virginia—plantation and county records, the newspaper advertisements for runaways—describe rebellious slaves and few others. The slaves described were lazy and thieving; they feigned illnesses, destroyed crops, stores, tools, and sometimes attacked or killed overseers. They operated blackmarkets in stolen goods. Runaways were defined as various types, they were truants (who usually returned voluntarily), "outlaws" (a legal term for "outlying" slaves who refused to give themselves up), and slaves who were actually fugitives: men who visited relatives, went to town to pass as free, or tried to escape slavery completely, either by boarding ships and leaving the colony, or banding together in cooperative efforts to establish villages or hide-outs on the frontier. The commitment of another type of rebellious slave was total: these men became killers, arsonists, and insurrectionists.

Patterns based on the slave's origin (birthplace) and position in the work hierarchy emerge from this wealth of detail. The sources themselves can be divided this way: plantation records deal primarily with field slaves and house servants, while most skilled slaves are described in newspaper advertisements for runaways. Native Africans and American-born slaves, plantation slaves (field and house slaves), and artisans reacted differently to slavery. Only native Africans who were new arrivals and referred to as "outlandish," ran off in groups or attempted to establish villages of runaways on the frontier. Most plantation slaves

34

(generally Africans who had been introduced into slavery and from then on known as "new Negroes") were merely truants, if they ran off at all. And American-born skilled slaves nearly always ran off alone into the most settled areas of the colony to pass as free men.

In assessing these observable differences in slave behavior, scholars usually ask whether a particular rebellious style represented resistance to slavery's abuses or real resistance to slavery itself. When slave behavior is examined in light of its political content, the most menial workers, the field slaves, fare badly. Speaking generally, their "laziness," boondoggling, and pilferage represented a limited, perhaps self-indulgent type of rebelliousness. Their reactions to unexpected abuses, or to sudden changes in plantation routine were at most only token acts against slavery. But the plantation slaves' organized and systematic schemes to obstruct the plantation's workings—their persistent acts of attrition against crops and stores, and cooperative night-time robberies that sustained the blackmarkets—were more "political" in their consequences, and represented resistance to slavery itself.

Yet arguments about the political aspect of slave resistance have only been part of a larger, and more misleading, scholarly controversy: the extent to which slaves "accommodated" to a "system" characterized as a type of "total" institution.[1] This conceptualization is anachronistic; it views rebellious slaves out of their historical context, and in concentrating on the whites and the structural features of the institution they created, it does not account well for: the insurrectionists, who resisted slavery totally; field slaves, who cooperated in acts of sabotage; and skilled fugitives, solitary, self-centered rebels who often ran away to hire themselves out, to become someone else's slave while enjoying a modicum of freedom, and at the same time, denying their former owners their highly valued services.

Focusing on the political dimension of resistance, nonetheless, may greatly expand our understanding of slave behavior, if we employ a method that shifts attention to the slaves themselves, and seeks to uncover the psychological implications of the rebellious slave's goals, and the significance of those goals for the slave and his society. A useful way of evaluating these issues is to distinguish between inward and outward goals. This typology is based on an evaluation of the direction or thrust of a particular rebellious action. That is, each style had direction in two ways: on the one hand, in a psychological sense of inward, internalized rebelliousness, or violence, that for the slave was self-defeating or even self-destructive, or an outward, self-enhancing, rebellious action; and on the other hand, direction in the sense of the setting and objectives for a style of resistance channeled either inward toward the plantation world, or outward toward a town, or out of the society altogether.

Plantation slaves most often directed their limited, sometimes self-defeating, acts against the plantation itself. Scarcely knowledgeable of the society beyond their world, too limited in such acculturative resources as conversational English to pass as free men in town, they reacted to their only "home," the plantation or quarter. Outlaws are an especially good example of inward-directed rebelliousness. Making little effort to save themselves by actually running away, they turned their rage back on its source; and before they were recaptured (or killed outright) they burned and pillaged their masters' property. Skilled fugitives, on the other hand, resisted outwardly in the sense of setting and goals: they were determined to get as far as possible from their masters and the plantation. Their flight from and repulsion of the plantation, moreover, were a fitting corollary to the psychological consequences of their training and work routines.

Styles of rebelliousness may be distinguished as inward and outward in a more subjective sense, one that focuses on the psychological implications of a pattern of resistance for the slave as an individual. The plantation slave's actions were typically short-range, direct attempts to deal immediately with his material environment: to fill his hunger, ease his fatigue, or to get revenge on an overseer or master. His punitive, sporadic, and sometimes desperate inward activities usually worsened his situation. He committed his transgression and then could do little more than wait to be discovered and punished. The skilled slave who frequently worked on and off the plantation, was usually better off. He rebelled to ameliorate his situation, and occasionally, to reject it outright. His resistance, which was seldom violent and directed inward on himself or the plantation, was aimed toward such long-range and intangible goals as more freedom of movement and leisure time than he normally enjoyed. As a runaway passing as a free man, hired by townsmen who asked few questions about his former owner, he often achieved these objectives. But it should be emphasized that many field slaves who resisted were especially successful because they did so cooperatively (Africans who were new arrivals also saw slavery as a collective problem). However, until the last years of the century, the skilled slaves cut off from the community of plantation slaves by their challenging and varied routines viewed resistance as an individual problem. Thus this typology, which examines rebelliousness from the slave's point of view, also illuminates the relationship between rebellion and adjustments to slavery by uncovering the fundamental determinants of slave behavior in the colonial period: the acculturative experience and task allotment.

Whether a slave resisted in an inward or outward way was chiefly attributable to these two interdependent variables. The slave's origin and degree of familiarity with English determined where he was placed in the work hierarchy. Conversely, job placement governed the rate and extent of acculturation (used interchangeably with the term assimilation). Resistance, the most thoroughly documented aspect of slave behavior, stemmed from the interaction of the two variables, the nature of acculturation and of the work routine.

The experience of acculturation [2] means that as slaves came to know varieties of whites and their ways, they acquired occupational skills, fluent English, and a distinctive, "sensible" manner in speaking situations. This acculturative process—usually accelerated when a man once exclusively a plantation slave acquired a work routine allowing him to travel outside the plantation "family"—also transformed slaves in a more basic, dynamic way. Relatively assimilated slaves (often referred to as artisans or skilled slaves), for example, were imbued with a pride and confidence that enhanced their ability to cope resourcefully with whites when they became fugitives.

Work was the second variable determining adjustments to slavery. So much of a slave's life was expressed in his job, that it is more appropriate to speak of his world of work, one that provided him with a particular outlook and self-view, and to recognize that a slave's task influenced the quality of his relations with other slaves and determined the frequency and intensity of his encounters with his master (a decisive factor in the adjustments of house servants). In the eighteenth century there were three types of task assignments: in the fields, household, and workshops. The actual location or setting of a slave's job was as important as his routine, or "bundle of tasks," because it controlled his degree of access to colonial values and ways requisite for outward types of resistance. Slaves assigned to the fields and household were confined and cut-off from the acculturative experiences that made slavery less oppressive and more manageable for those whose

jobs permitted travel beyond the plantation boundaries. So important
was the correlation between acculturation and the mobility factor, that
two types of semi-skilled slaves—watermen and waitingmen—whose
tasks required them to travel frequently, reacted outwardly to slavery.
More fugitives capable of passing as free men, in fact, came from these
occupations than from any others.

While the nature of the slave's work is the most apparent explanation for different adjustments, it is not a sufficient one. It does not account for the actions of the "outlandish" African who was recently
enslaved. The new arrival was a slave without a job. His unique behavior as a fugitive and a hesitant learner of English (the most important measures of level of acculturation) indicates that such facets
of his African upbringing as communalism provided norms for his
initial reaction to slavery. Only after the African became a "new Negro" did his job replace aspects of his heritage as a basic reference
point for his reaction to slavery. Jobs for all slaves were so fundamentally important that the very few Africans who acquired skilled
positions acted like American-born slaves: they too were assimilated,
mobile, individualistic, and outwardly rebellious.

The hypotheses are: that slavery in eighteenth-century Virginia
may also be construed as an encounter between two cultures, African
and English colonial; that one dimension of slave behavior in the colonial period was the slave's participation in an on-going process of cultural
change; and that as slaves acculturated they became outwardly rebellious and more difficult for whites to control. Given the correlation
between assimilation and outward forms of resistance, the Virginia
colonists' goals for their plantation communities and their slaves were
indeed contradictory. The desire to assimilate Africans as quickly as
possible in order to increase occupational specialization while maintaining stable, self-sufficient plantation communities, created a cruel
dilemma. Community and acculturation—the first a static design, the
latter a process—were not compatible. Assimilation into colonial society made a few Africans and many of their descendants outwardly rebellious and so, more difficult to control.

The acculturative process whereby Africans came to be "new Negroes,"
and a much smaller number assimilated slaves, was marked by three
stages. First, the "outlandish" Africans reacted to slavery on the basis
of the communal lives they had been living when enslaved. As their
prior cultural directives proved unworkable, they began as best they
could to bend such elements of the new culture as the English language, and in rare instances, technical skills to their advantage. Nearly
all Africans became field laborers, "new Negroes," who represented
the second level of assimilation. Since there seemed to be a "fit," or
degree of congruence, between their cultural background and the plantation's communal norms, few Africans ever became more than "new
Negroes." But those who did, the more educable and thoroughly assimilated Africans, were representative of the third level of acculturation. The latter were usually artisans, whose imaginative exploits as
fugitives dramatized the reciprocal relationship between the acquisition
of skills and more advanced assimilation. Artisanship and acculturation
made blacks individuals while enhancing their ability to cope creatively
with slavery. And individualism, already a basic ideal in colonial
American society, was not, as we shall see, a very highly developed
phenomenon in African tribes. Thus for the planter the acculturated
slave's altered perception of himself and slavery had some unforeseen
and undesirable consequences.

Newspaper advertisements for fugitive slaves are the most useful
and reliable source for demonstrating the effectiveness of the acculturation argument.[3] The advertisements are fairly objective, unlike such
narrative sources as Hugh Jones's. Slaveowners who used them were
neither explaining nor defending slavery, they simply—in sparse,
graphic phrases—listed their runaway's most noticeable physical and
psychological characteristics, while commenting on his origin, work,
and use of English. Since the notices also lend themselves well to a
quantitative analysis of such characteristics as height, posture, skin

color, habits of grooming and dress, and emotional peculiarities—for example, speech defects and uncontrollable movements of hands and face—they are indispensable for studying the change of physical norms, demographic make-up, and acculturation levels in the colonial slave population. For example: [4]

> RUN AWAY about the First Day of *June* last from the Subscriber, living on *Chickahominy* River, *James City* County. A Negroe Man, short and well-set, aged between 30 and 40 Years, but looks younger, having no Beard, is smooth-fac'd, and has some Scars on his Temples, being the Marks of his Country; talks pretty good *English;* is a cunning, subtile Fellow, and pretends to be a Doctor. It is likely, as he has a great Acquaintance, he may have procur'd a false Pass. Whoever brings him to me at my House aforesaid, shall have two Pistoles Reward, besides what the Law allows.
>
> Michael Sherman

Approximately 1,500 notices in newspapers published from 1736 to 1801 in Williamsburg, Richmond, and Fredericksburg were analyzed, including all notices in all of the various editions of the *Virginia Gazette* that are extant. These described 1,138 men and 142 women. Another 400 people were advertised as runaways taken up by constables or jailers. In this period only 138 fugitives, about 1 in 8, were advertised as born in Africa. These exceptions were usually two kinds: "outlandish" Africans, and the relatively acculturated slaves who were long-time residents in Virginia. "New Negroes," isolated on the quarters and in a phase of acculturation between the new arrivals and the assimilated slaves, are conspicuously absent from the notices.

Since the new arrivals and their masters had talked informally about Africa—an intriguing insight into the nature of procurement for both sides—the notices are filled with information about what Africans chose to tell whites about their lives before enslavement. Bonnaund told his master that he was from "the Ibo Country," where he "served in the Capacity of a Canoe Man." [5] Charles and Frank were also Ibo runaways, whose identities were conspicuous even though they were unable to tell their jailer whether or not they were Africans: their teeth were filed and chipped and their foreheads carved with ritual scars. While Frank's filed teeth were described as "sharp," Charles, who had "lost or broke off one or two of his fore Teeth," presumably tried to explain his ritual mutilations in what he already perceived to be a socially acceptable manner, said it was "done by a Cow in his country." [6]

Ritual scars were dramatic testimony to the West Africans' life before slavery. To see how these men may have stood out among all others in colonial America, compare reproductions of an Ife brass head and an eighteenth-century portrait painted, say, by Benjamin West or John Durand. On the one side, blacks have faces marked from ear to ear, hairline to throat, by deep striations proclaiming a heritage that was based on a fully ritualized cultural existence, and which sustained a society that functioned on a corporate and traditional basis. On the other side, whites are without scars or with "scars" outside themselves of velvet and lace at cuff and throat, feather fans and open books—symbols of a European culture which centuries earlier had reduced its ceremonies of human and social renewal to compartmentalized activities as neat as the sitting rooms in which they posed. Symbols too of a society—at least beyond the plantation—that functioned on an impersonal, civil, and individual basis. [7]

Many slaveowners had closely observed the Africans' scars and could describe them in minute detail. "He is marked in the manner of his country with dots under both eyes, and on the right side of his neck with something resembling a ladder." "He has a very noted mark carved on his forehead resembling a diamond, and some marks of his country on his temples"; or this variation: "he has a Flower in his Forehead made in the Form of a Diamond with Specks down to the End of his Nose." And "he has six rings of his country marks round his neck, his ears full of holes." [8]

These slaves had received their marks in ceremonies of pain, mystery, and celebration, which inculcated a distinctive sense of history (e.g. of reckoning time) and a sense of community, and made their initial adjustments unique among slaves. [9] On the personal level the rite was an unforgettable ordeal in which the emotional ties of a group of young adults were reoriented from their families to their village society. The ceremonies, calculated to burn the lesson of companionship and community into the very souls of the young participants, also left indelible scars that were visible. These "country-marks" announced: "I am because we are, and since we are, I am." [10] The West African scholar, John Mbiti, further explains that the rites united the celebrants with the rest of the community both living and dead, and "humanly speaking nothing can separate him from this corporate society." [11]

Thus, on the community level, the rites were a matter of survival. Most colonial slaves came from small-scale, technologically simple societies that lived in a precarious relationship with their environment. The facts of individual differences, of varied and uneven rates of growth among their young men of the same age, constituted a grave threat to the basic ordering of society, particularly during the grim and perilous days of the international slave trade. Individual preference and initiative, unnatural thoughts of self-improvement at the community's expense, all had to be redirected; thus the schema of the rites of passage. "The individual person or [age] group is cut off, isolated and then restored," writes the anthropologist David F. Pocock, "but never again to be the same; in this restoration individual distinctions and differences are translated into social ones." [12]

Philosophically, the coming of age ceremony was an integral part of the tribesman's conception of time. And the way the African slave marked time was at the core of how he made the world intelligible. Time in western technological society is a predictable and uniform movement; it is a commodity, too, that is utilized, measured in units, and so often bought and sold. For the African, however, time was created: it was based either on the major events of his life, such as coming of age, or at another level, on certain repetitive cyclic natural events, such as phases of the moon and the harvest seasons.[13]

The essentials of this non-western folk ethos, man-in-community and discontinuous time-reckoning, survived enslavement and became an integral part of the African's behavior as a slave. But only for a while. When his heritage proved unworkable, his job and other factors became reference points for his adjustment. Those Africans who initially reacted to slavery as runaways, and their later activities as learners of English, provide an opportunity to evaluate both their adjustment and the usefulness of the acculturation model itself for future studies of American Negro slavery.

"Outlandish" slaves, still to become "new Negroes," were unique among runaways in the colonial period. Whatever the precise meaning of procurement for the African as a person, his fellowship or affectivity, a core area of human behavior, remained intact as a slave. Africans, assuming that resistance was a group activity, ran off with their own countrymen, and American-born slaves including mulattoes.

In all of the advertisements there were only a very few groups of American-born slaves and these were made up of not more than three men. But there were five larger groups, all composed of Africans. A sixth group included two African men and their American-born wives, and another pair, an African and a white indentured servant. Africans were also the only fugitives in eighteenth-century Virginia reported to be in even larger groups, pursuing cooperative ventures (usually in their determination to return "home," as they said) or to be in the more remote areas of the colony. Step, for example, left Petersburg with a twelve-year-old girl. "He went off with several others," his master wrote, "being persuaded that they could find the Way back to their own Country." Six weeks later this group was discovered in Mecklenburg County on the colony's frontier.[14]

In at least one instance such a group was clearly organized to form a settlement of runaways. In a 1727 report to the Board of Trade, the governor, Sir William Gooch, mentioned fifteen Africans who left a "new" plantation at the falls of the James River to settle near the present site of Lexington, Virginia. Here they attempted to reconstruct familiar social and political arrangements. But shortly after building huts and sowing crops they were recaptured.[15]

In South Carolina recently imported Africans were even more active. What were merely tendencies among Africans in Virginia were definite patterns of behavior in South Carolina, where slaves made up about 60 per cent (as opposed to 40 per cent in Virginia) of the population. In sample runs of the South Carolina *Gazette* in the early 1750's and 1771 there was clear evidence of tribal cooperation in advertisements for the return of four "new Gambia men"; three Angolans, "all short fellows"; six other Angolans, purchased in the summer of 1771 and runaways by November, "so they cannot as yet speak English"; and four men from the "Fullah Country."[16] There were also several family groups that were advertised; one included an African husband and wife, a "country-born man and woman," and Jack, a young "mustee" man.[17] An advertiser for three men, an African from "Guinea," a slave from Angola ("a very good sawyer"), and a native American, said "they would either be on the Santee River, or higher up in the Back Settlements."[18] These Back Settlements, and Ponpon, an area about forty miles south of Charleston, attracted a number of fugitives.[19] While Virginia runaways seldom burdened themselves with anything more than the clothes on their back and

ran away just to escape, South Carolina Africans ran off with their
hoes, axes, bedding, and other equipment in order to replicate the
community life they lived before slavery, or to join the Indians, or
the Spanish in St. Augustine, Florida.[20]

If runaways were recaptured but not reclaimed their jailers published notices such as the following : [21]

> COMMITTED to the gaol of *Westmoreland,* on *Monday,* the
> 21st of *October* [1771] two Negro Men, the one a yellow fellow,
> with a remarkable flat nose, the other black, with filed teeth, about
> 4 feet 8 or 9 inches high eac[h]. They are both *Africans,* and speak
> very little *English,* so they are not able to tell their master's name.
> They had with them two muskets, and two small books, in one of
> which is wrote *Elijah Worden.* They are supposed to have run from
> *Maryland,* as there was a strange canoe found near the place they
> were taken. The owner is desired to take them away and pay charges
> the law directs.
>
> Edward Ransdell, jun. D.S.

The majority of Virginia slaves advertised as "taken up" had evidently
fled soon after their enslavement. Fugitive Africans who were recaptured—often cold and frost-bitten, nearly naked after long treks
and weeks in the wilds of the colonial South—could at most usually
only speak a few words of English: they are "all in rags"; he has
"nothing on but a blanket"; they are "entirely naked . . . and by lying
in the cold, their feet and legs have swelled very much, so that they
are not able to be sent to the [Charleston] work house." "He speaks
very bad English, but says his master's name is *William Cook,* as plain
as he can." [22]

The jailers listened carefully to the Africans' replies, and were sometimes sufficiently interested to record and print literally what they
were told. Consequently this data provides invaluable insights into
how Africans thought in their own languages while conversing in
English. Their responses also suggest that they looked upon slavery
as a temporary misfortune, that perhaps the jailer might help them
return "across grandywater" to their real homes in Africa. For example, when asked where they came from they took this to mean
Africa, not the colonies. He "only calls himself Peter [and] says he is
of the Bumbarozo Country." [23] Or, he "calls his Country Mundingo," [24] part of the Western Sudan. Most of the Africans who responded in this way, in fact, were from this area. Sarah, for example

(one of the very few African women who ran away in eighteenth-century Virginia and was later described in a newspaper advertisement), was a 14-year-old with severe "choking fits." She spoke English so poorly that she could not tell her master's name. She did, however, identify herself as a Mundingo.[25] But Africans who were long time residents in slavery soon learned the proper cues. Dick, a small fellow about 50 years of age, had roamed about the Stafford County seat for months before he was taken up, and was described this way: "by what little English he talks and by signs he makes, he belongs to one *William Helm,* as he expressed it, in *Maryland.*" [26]

The Africans' efforts to talk about what their new masters meant to them are perhaps also more understandable when seen in connection with their upbringing. In going from old to new authorities, Africans obviously made various adjustments; but one type of authority relationship which the African considered no longer valid when his master died is persistently alluded to in the advertisements. For example: the jailer of a South Carolina runaway advertised: he "says master dead"; [27] an Angolan, also taken up in South Carolina, made the revealing statement that his master was one William Anderson, "but [he] being dead, he cannot live with the family"; [28] James, with filed teeth and the slave of a Richard Adams, said that his master was dead "and his widow ha[d] gone out of the country"; [29] and a notice for two fugitives, who spoke "little English," said "their father's name is Davis but he is now dead." [30]

These two runaways had traveled a great distance for a considerable time. But their jailer had to estimate where they were from (he said either the Carolinas or Georgia), because he had to superimpose his reckoning of time on theirs. The Africans knew the proper words but still reacted to their old cultural directives. They had been, they said, "ten Moons from home." [31]

Occasionally in such conversations the two cultures' mythic paradigms for explaining location in time and space were set side by side. Sandy with filed teeth was asked how long he had been in the colony. He had, he replied, "made two crops for his master," and had been "absent from his service [for] two moons." [32] "All I can learn from her," wrote another jailer, "is that she belongs to one Mr. Ruff, who lives in a great town, by a grandywater." [33] Another African, who spoke "much broken," said he lived near "one Mr. Burley's where long leaf pine grows." [34] Although data of this type is fragmentary—

as is so often the case with historical reality for the "inarticulate"—it suggests that even though the African had partially adopted a new set of language symbols, his frame of reference had not changed. The "outlandish" slave's initial reaction to slavery as a runaway and his reluctance or inability to learn English demonstrate that at the dynamic level of his behavior, the level of philosophical orientation, he had remained an African.[35]

But in a year or so the "outlandish" African changed. As he became a "new Negro" he acquired English and new work routines which transformed his communal and outward style of rebelliousness. For the African, learning English was the key to this process of cultural change, for the norms of the slave society were mediated through his captor's language. In acquiring English the "new Negro" learned about slavery, and how whites expected field hands to act.

A record of runaway notices that included comments on the slave's proficiency in English indicates that the African's acquisition of his second language fell into two periods.[36] During the first few months after procurement, while some were trying to form settlements or return "home," Africans were unable to learn even a word of English. But after about six months, knowledge of the language increased sharply; and within another two or two and a half years most Africans were conversant in English. There are few notices of this type, however, because most runaways were not Africans and those who were represented either end of the acculturation scale: they were either new arrivals who spoke no English whatsoever, or assimilated Africans who spoke English fluently. For example, an October 1752 notice stated matter-of-factly, "they were imported in August and can't speak any English." [37] Another mentioned that five months after Charles's arrival he could only "call himself Charles which is every word of English he can speak." [38] Three runaways from an ironworks were "all new Negroes who had not been above 8 Months in the Country." Nonetheless one of them, Sambo, a small, thin, 30-year-old man, could speak English "so as to be understood." [39] Tom, a Mungingo, had been "in this Country about eighteen Months," his master reported. "He lived this Year under the direction of Mr. *Edward Giles,* and if he should be strictly questioned can tell either Mr. *Gile's* name or my Name." [40] Proficiency came after about three years of residence.

Age at time of importation, location (in or outside the plantation world), and job, in that order, were the most important variables with regard to the rate at which the African learned English. If the slave had been imported as a youth or had worked in an urban setting, for example, it was expected that he would speak "sensibly." A Fredericksburg merchant wrote a slave trader in surprise, that "although [Dobbo] has been constantly in Town [he] cannot yet speak a word of English," and was therefore an exceptional case.[41] Another master noted that his 30-year-old *"Angola* fellow" spoke "very good *English,* as he was imported young." [42]

THE FIELD SLAVES' ADJUSTMENT TO SLAVERY

Dobbo was an exceptional African; virtually all new arrivals were forced into field labor on the up-country quarters. These small, specialized plantations were a world of their own. Large planters divided their lands into small tracts called quarters. Usually from 500 to 1,500 acres in size, the quarters were economically specialized and isolated— separated from the activity and diversity of the home plantation, and surrounded by woods, swamps, rivers, and reserve land. There was a subtle compatibility among the quarter's essential components: the field slaves and overseer, the small flocks of fowl, herds of cattle and pigs, the coarse, makeshift slave huts and crude outbuildings amidst fields of tobacco, corn, small grain, and sometimes hemp.

Newspaper advertisements, plantation accounts (inventories and overseers' contracts), and wills portray the small-scale, economically limited, and sequestered quarter as environment, the setting in which the Africans as "new Negroes" began to assimilate slowly, and seldom very completely, into the society beyond their world. Advertisements and estate inventories often mentioned the number of slaves per quarter, and occasionally the land-man ratio. A 1777 notice read:

> A TRACT of good tobacco land in the county of Orange, about 8 miles above the courthouse . . . containing by estimation 1000 acres, with a plantation thereon sufficient to work 8 hands. A large swamp runs through the whole of this tract, where is a great quantity of limestone, also a great deal of fine meadow land on both sides of the swamp.[43]

The land-man ratio was high. Another notice described a "good" plantation of 1,400 acres on the Finnywood River and the branches

of Bluestone Creek in Mecklenburg County. It had land cleared for
10 to 12 hands. Another advertisement described a 1,000-acre tract in
Halifax County on the Dan River, which included 250 acres of low
ground "in good order for cropping, sufficient to work ten or twelve
hands to high advantage." [44] These figures are representative of notices
in the *Virginia Gazette* (all extant issues, 1736–79). All of the advertisements offering plantations for sale were tabulated, and the mean
number of hands per quarter was about eight.[45]

Although it is not possible to determine precisely the number of
slaves per quarter, probably the majority of plantations were worked
by about 10 hands or "shares," who represented about a third of the
full complement of slaves. The remainder were women and children,
who since they were not full time field workers, did not receive a full
"share" of the provisions. On the quarters, however, nearly all of the
women and children over about 12 or 13 years of age worked in the
field. Inventories for John Parke Custis's estate (1771 and 1774) are
among the most complete available, and particularly useful because
they list the workers' ages. On 9 quarters in York, New Kent, King
William counties, and on the Eastern Shore, nearly 45 per cent of the
slaves per quarter were 14 years of age or younger. Although 27
slaves were 50 or older (including an 85-year-old man), only John
and Arlington were listed without their ages, because they were "very
old & past Labour." There was no consistent ratio of men to women
per quarter: on 2 plantations there were twice as many men as women
(10 men and 4 women; 7 and 3)—excluding the young and old slaves
listed above; but on the Mill quarter there were 3 men and 8 women;
and on 2 others there were nearly equal numbers of men and women
(4 men and 5 women, and 7 each). Characteristically, Custis's craftsmen, such as carpenters and shoemakers, were only included in the
inventory for his "Great House." [46] This division of the work force
into small groups on the quarters was fairly representative. "King"
Carter, who used no less than 45 quarters in 1732, owned at least
6 that had fewer than 8 hands each.[47] Landon Carter employed 4
men at one quarter. His nephew, "Councillor" Carter, worked 5
Richmond County quarters from 1782 to 1791; one had 37 slaves,
but he had 2 quarters with 3 slaves each, and 5 more with fewer than
10 workers.[48]

These small allotments of land and slaves were probably related to
problems of supervision in the planter's absence. At least one slaveowner noted that his overseer could only manage about 10 slaves.

Slave gangs (or even concentrations of slaves in excess of 25 or 30 per quarter) are virtually non-existent in the records of eighteenth-century Virginia plantations.[49]

The quarter was simply composed of slaves, crops, and herds, and little more. John Hatley Norton's account with his overseer at Effingham Forest in Fauquier County included this inventory taken between 1782 and 1784.[50]

Negroes Taken March 18th 1784	*stock*
old Charles	Horses 10 (mostly mares)
Betty	
	Black Cattle (including)
Greenwich	"1 Red butt with a white face," and
Peter	"1 Pided Cow 8 yr old."
Frank	total: 33 No Cattle
Anthony	Hogs: 34
Timmy a boy	Sheep: 78
Sam a boy	
Cardis	
Milly	
Black Hannah	
Candis Child	
No. 12	

Acct. of Plantation Tools: 4 old Dutch Plows, 4 pr. Iron Traces, 1 pr. Iron Wedges, 4 Narrow Axes—two barrs Iron, 1 Broad Axx, 4 hilling hoes, 3 old Do. for Weading 4 old hoes M. Muse put here, 5 Mattocks of M. Muse 1 Grubing hoe, 2 Drawing Knives, 2 Chissels, 1 hand Saw 2 Augers, 1 adds, 1 froe, 1 Scthe, 3 Murren hides, Two of which are Calves Skins, 2 Spinning Wheels

Fowls in the Care of old Betty
10 guse, 6 Fatning for Mrs. Nortons Use
5 Turkies for breading
3 fatning for Mrs. Norton
5 Dungle hens
8 Ducks

In addition to plantation records and newspaper advertisements, overseer contracts also help to re-create the texture of life on the eighteenth-century plantation.[51]

Memo of an agreement Between Ralph Smith and Hugh George Witnesseth, That the said Smith has employed the said George the Year [1798] Present as an Overseer, and is to put Seven Hands

and four Work Horses under him and Tools sufficient to make a
Crop with, and is to Allow him the Eighth part of the Tobacco and
Tenth part of the Corn and Small Grain he makes, and is to find him
Bread Corn, Two Cows to give Milk, 100 lbs Beef at the Fall and
Twenty Dollars to buy Pork. . . . &c   To the performance of
which agreement we bind ourselves to each other in the Penal Sum
of One Hundred Pounds Virginia currency
Witness our hands and Seals this 8th Day of January 1798.

The field slave "is called up in the morning at daybreak, scarcely
allowed time to swallow three mouthfuls of homminy," wrote the
English traveler J. F. D. Smyth. Brief notations like this in travelers'
and plantation accounts and record books must suffice for data on the
field slave's material condition. Although the records are sketchy, his
diet, although probably adequate in bulk, was scarcely nourishing.
"Hominy," Indian corn, was the slaves' staple food.

Random accounts of quantities of corn allotted suggest that provisions were sometimes based on the worker's productivity. During
the Revolutionary War, "Councillor" Carter asked that "the stronger
Shears [shares] men & women" be given one peck of corn per week,
"the Remainder of the Black People they to have ¼ Peck per Week
each." By 1787 Carter, who was one of the least oppressive slave
masters, increased this slightly. He ordered 44 pecks of shelled Indian
corn as two weeks' allowance for 26 slaves, less than a full peck per
week per laborer. (One peck equals 14 lbs. of Indian corn.) [52]

Meat was seldom given to slaves. Smyth said slaves ate hoecakes and
little else; unless their master "be a man of humanity the slave eats a
little fat, skimmed milk, and rusty bacon." La Rochefoucauld-Liancourt
said that on large plantations the slave subsisted on corn and sometimes on buttermilk. They were given meat 6 times a year. Robert
"Councillor" Carter estimated that the common allowance for wheat
per hand per year was 15 bushels for those "negroes, who are not fed
with animal food" (e.g. meat). These slaves only received meat on
special occasions. Joseph Ball wrote his steward that slaves were to
"have ffresh meat when they are sick, if the time of the year will allow
it." The cuts were to be the least desirable, although not necessarily
the least nutritious. When calves were slaughtered, Ball ordered him
to give the field hands the "head and Pluck"; the "ffat backs, necks,
and other Coarse pieces" of hogs were also to be reserved for the
slaves. James Mercer directed his steward to give the slaves the innards
of chickens unless he sold them to the local Negro chicken merchants.[53]

Plantation slaves wore clothing usually cut from a heavy, coarse cloth of flax and tow originally manufactured in Osnabrück, Germany. Following the non-importation agreements of the late 1760's, coarse-textured cotton wool weave, "Virginia plains," "country linen," replaced "Osnabrugs." Unlike the colorful variety of many of the artisan's clothing, the notices for runaways after 1770 indicate that field laborers wore uniform pants and trousers. "They are well clothed in the usual manner for Negroes"; "clothed as usual" and "the usual winter clothing for corn field negroes" are representative descriptions from advertisements of that period.[54]

Black women who worked on the quarter wore clothing of the same weight and texture as the men. They usually dressed in a loose-fitting smock or shift, often tied at the waist; a short waistcoat was fitted over this dress. A Dutch blanket used for a sleeping robe and shoes and stockings completed the plantation Negroes' clothing allowance.[55]

Housing for slaves varied widely. But there are frequent references in travelers' accounts to clusters of slave cabins that looked like small villages, and, in plantation records, numerous directions from masters indicating a concern for warm, dry houses with floors, lofted roofs, and on occasion, fireplaces. Slave quarters, however, may have been a late development. Subscribers who used advertisements to sell plantations frequently mentioned "negro quarters," but usually only in those notices published in the last quarter of the century. The plantation's size, location, and wealth were not factors; nearly all had slave quarters. It is likely that the smaller planter's field hands may have slept in the lofts of barns, in tobacco houses, and other outbuildings before the war. Joseph Ball told his nephew that the slaves "must ly in the Tobacco house" while their quarters, 15 by 20 feet with fireplace and chimney, were "lathed & fitted." However, several planters, including George Washington, used a less substantial, pre-fab arrangement. These shacks were small, temporary, and were moved from quarter to quarter following the seasonal crop.[56]

J. F. D. Smyth was forced to take shelter one evening in a "miserable shell" inhabited by six slaves and their overseer. Unlike many slaves' houses "it was not lathed nor plaistered, neither ceiled nor lofted above . . . one window, but no glass in it, not even a brick chimney, and, as it stood on blocks about a foot above the ground, the hogs lay constantly under the floor, which made it swarm with flies." [57]

On the home plantations, "servants," like the crop hands, usually slept in their own quarters. A planter who moved to the valley in 1781 asked his steward to place the "house Servants for they have been more indulged than the rest" with the overseer and his family, "till Such Time as Warehouses can be provided for them." Slaves evidently rarely slept in the great house. A letter dated 1823 written to Dr. A. D. Galt of Williamsburg, mentioned that the writer's father could not find a house, "and the ones he has seen have not had separate quarters for the servants." They would then "have to stay in the basement or the garret rooms." This, she concluded, "[as] you know cannot be very agreeable to Virginians."

Some idea of a slave's yearly expenses is provided by James Madison's remark to a British visitor earlier in the nineteenth century. "Every negro earns annually, all expenses being deducted, about $257," wrote John Foster. "The expense of a negro including duty, board, clothing, and medicines, he [Madison] estimates from $12–13." [58]

The lean, spare character of the field slave's material condition was a function of his place in the servile work hierarchy. Most plantation slaves worked in the fields where their tasks were tedious, sometimes strenuous, and usually uninspiring. Although tobacco is a difficult and challenging crop, field laborers—especially the "new Negroes"—were forced into the most routine tasks of transplanting seedlings, weeding, suckering, and worming. Following the harvest their work days extended into the night, when they sorted, bundled, and pressed the tobacco into hogsheads for shipment. [59]

The slave jobber's work assignments were not as routine as the field laborer's chores. Armistead was hired out by his master to "act as a jobber, *viz.* to cut firewood, go to [the] Mill, work in your garden, and occasionally to work in your Corn-field." [60] Jobbers also mended stone and wood fences, patched and whitewashed the plantation's outbuildings, dug irrigation and drainage ditches, and the like. "Councillor" Carter hired John McKenney to "overlook" his jobbers in 1777. Their agreement read:

> the sd Jobbers to make a Crop of Corn Pumpkins, Irish Potatoes, at my plantation called Dickerson's Mill, that is, a full crop fr about 4 Shares—the sd Jobbers to raise Stone to build a tumbling Dam at Dickerson's Mill, they to make ye dirt Dam sufficient, there, and to do several Jobs at Nomony Hall in the course of this year. [61]

McKenney's wages indicate that this type of work was not well paid: he was "to receive f[o]r his services at the rate of 25s/6 per month, [is] to find himself, Board, lodging, Washing &c." [62]

But jobbers were scarcely better off than the field laborers, because they too did not travel outside the plantation. Nor did their menial tasks spur assimilation and a corresponding change in their view of slavery. Regardless of the specific nature of their tasks, the horizons and expectations of most plantation slaves were sharply limited by the plantation environment.

Their tiresome routines in the meager setting of reserve land, in meadow and woods, monotonous rows of tobacco, and temporary, ramshackle buildings, made the quarter a world of its own. But the isolation and work routines of the quarter provided slaves with a convenient means of expressing their unhappiness, so it was also a constant, nagging source of trouble for the planter. Blacks and whites alike knew that the plantation's efficiency and profitability could be seriously impaired simply by a "little leaning" on the slaves' part. "My people seem to be quite dead hearted, and either cannot or will not work"; "my people are all out of their senses for I cannot get one of them to do a thing as I would have it and as they do it even with their own time they have it to do again immediately." These words are Landon Carter's. A tough and competent man, Carter did not bend easily, but this note of resignation is heard early in his diary.[63]

Accounts of the field slave's performance are rare, but one of the best can be found in Jack P. Greene's fine edition of Landon Carter's Diary which tells a dreary story of the crop laborers' quiet and persistently non-cooperative actions. Slaves reported ill every day but Sunday when there were no complaints because they considered this "a holy day"; men treading wheat slept while their "boys," left to do the job, "neglected" it; the "crop people," forced to stem tobacco in the evening hours, retaliated "under the guise of semi-darkness [by] throwing away a great deal of the saleable tob[acco]"; men whom Carter harassed about weeding a corn patch feigned stupidity and leveled thousands of hills of corn seedlings. Carter's slaves, in fact, were so rebellious that he came to question the profitability of slavery. "It is the same at all my plantations," he complained:

> Although I have many to work and fine land to be tended, I hardly make more than what cloaths them, finds them tools, and pays their Levies. Perhaps a few scrawney hogs may be got in the year to be fattened up here. If these things do not require the greatest caution and frugality in living I am certain nothing can do.[64]

William Strickland, an Englishman who visited colonial America in 1800, concurred. As well as any traveler, he succinctly defined the character of the plantation slaves' rebelliousness in a letter to the Board of Trade:

> Any slave that I have seen at work, does not appear to perform half as much, as a labourer in England; nor does the business under which the master sits down contented, appear to be half of what we require to be performed by one. . . . If to this be added the slovenly carelessness with which all business is performed by the slave, the great number of useless hands the slave owner is obliged to maintain, the total indifference to, and neglect, not to say the frequent wilful destruction, of whatever is not immediately committed to his case. . . . And also the universal inclination to pilfering shown by them, I cannot do otherwise than acquiesce in the received opinion of the country, that slave labor is much dearer than any other.[65]

Lazy, wasteful, and indifferent work was a chronic problem on eighteenth-century plantations. Slaves understood that there was a great deal of time to waste, and little hope of improving their lot. "It will be better to have more eyes than one over such gangs," Landon Carter noted. Following another inspection he complained, "the old trade, take one hour from any Job and it makes a day loss in work." Most plantation slaves desired challenging tasks, but once they had them, they dragged out the job as long as possible. Herdsman Johnny, charged with breaking up the quarter patch at Sabine Hall, "does not intend to finish," Carter wrote, "by contriving that all his lambs should get out of the yard that he may be trifling about after them." [66]

Careful planters habitually spot-checked their slaves' productivity. Planters like Landon Carter and George Washington who demanded from their slaves punctiliousness, order, and a high output, were convenient and effective targets for the slaves' piddling laziness and wasteful procedures. A 1760 entry in Washington's diary noted that four of his sawyers hewed about 120 feet of timber in a day. Dissatisfied with this rate of production, and determined to apply gentle pressure, Washington stood and watched his men. They subsequently fell to work with such energy and enthusiasm that he concluded that one man could do in one day what four had previously accomplished in the same length of time.[67]

How many seemingly routine plantation practices were actually concessions to the unreliability of slave labor? For years Landon Carter refused to introduce plows and carts onto his quarters since he felt that these technological innovations would only serve "to make

Overseers and people extremely lazy . . . wherever they are in great abundance there is the least plantation work done." [68]

Feigned illness was another remarkably simple but effective ruse. When a slave asked to "lay-in," his master often suspected he was faking, but could never be certain. Too many had stood helplessly by while a strange and lethal "distemper," or "ague," suddenly swept through their slave quarters and carried off numbers of workers. Plantation records are filled with notes on these epidemics: "The mortalities in ties in my families are increased. . . . The number of my dead is now fifteen working slaves. I thank God I can bear these things with a great deal of resignation," or "a grevious mortality of my familys hath swept away an abundance of my people"; and, "we kept the plantations on James River to try to make Crops, but there broke out a malignant fever amongst the Negroes & swept off most of the able Hands; this threw all into Confusion & there has been little or no thing made since." [69]

Women who feigned illness were usually more effective than men. "As to Sall," James Mercer wrote his steward, "I believe her old complaint is mere deceit, if it is not attended with a fever it must be so unless it is owing to her monthly disorder & then can only last two days, and exercise is a necessary remedy." Washington complained of women who "will lay up a month, at the end of which no visible change in their countenance, nor the loss of an ounce of flesh, is discoverable; and their allowance of provision is going on as if nothing ailed them." Exasperated and uncertain about the health of a black woman, Betty Davis, he explained that "she has a disposition to be one of the most idle creatures on earth, and besides one of the most deceitful." When two of his slave women approached clutching their sides, Landon Carter told them to work or be whipped. He observed that they had no fever (the test of whether or not slaves were ill). "They worked very well with no grunting about pain." But Sarah, one of the women who had pretended to be pregnant for eleven months earlier in the year, soon ran off. When Wilmot used the same stratagem, Carter noted: "it cost me 12 months, before I broke her." This lesson was not satisfactory; for a third woman "fell into the same scheme," and "really carried it to a great length." So Carter whipped her severely; and she was "a good slave ever since only a cursed thief in making her Children milk Cows in the night." [70]

Plantation slaves who "hid out" in the woods and fields as runaways

represented a more serious breach of plantation security. They often
returned to the quarter in the evening for food and shelter, and were
an invitation to others to follow their example. But truancy was also
inward rebelliousness: it was sporadic, and it was directed toward the
plantation or quarter. Unlike the real fugitives, truants had no intention of leaving the immediate neighborhood and attempting to
permanently change their status. Truancy was so common that most
planters either did not make it a matter of record, or simply referred
to it in a random manner in their correspondence. "King" Carter
actually viewed it as part of his "outlandish" slaves' learning process:
"Now that my new negro woman has tasted the hardships of the
woods," he observed to an overseer, "she'll stay nearer to home where
she can have her belly full." [71] Planters accepted the fact that absenteeism, particularly in the evening hours, was scarcely controllable. In
response to Landon Carter's complaint that his pet deer were straying
in the Sabine Hall fields, John Tayloe wrote:

> Dear Col
>   . . . Now give me leave to complain to you, That your Patroll
> do not do their duty, my people are rambleing about every night,
> . . . my man Billie was out, he says he rode no horse of Master &
> that he only was at Col. Carter's, by particular invitation, so that
> the Entertainment was last night at Sabine Hall, & may probably
> be at Mt Airy this night, if my discoverys do not disconcert the
> Plan, these things would not be so I think, if the Patrollers did the
> duty they are paid for.[72]

Plantation slaves probably "rambled" to the "entertainment" in the
neighborhood several nights of the week; as long as they reported for
work the following day few efforts were made, or could be made, to
curtail this practice.[73]

Truants habitually remained very close to the quarter or plantation;
but this did not make it much easier for the planter to recapture them.
Evidently they were sufficiently clever (and the other plantation slaves
were sufficiently secretive) to keep themselves in hiding until they
decided to return on their own. Sarah ran off because Carter refused
to let her "lie-in" as ill. She spent a week in the woods and ate during
the evening hours while visiting the slave quarters. Simon, an ox-carter,
also hid beneath the vigilant Carter's very nose. He "lurked" in
Johnny's "inner room," and in the "Kitchen Vault." [74]

The outlaw, a far more dangerous type of runaway, used his

temporary freedom to inflict punishment on his tormentors. Outlawing a slave was a legal action, placing the runaway beyond the law, making him a public liability, and encouraging his destruction by any citizen. Those who killed outlaws did so without fear of legal prosecution; they also collected a fee from the public treasury and a reward from the slave's owner. The master's advertisements usually did not encourage the slave's preservation: George America was worth forty shillings if taken alive; five pounds if destroyed.[75]

Some slaveowners only threatened to outlaw truants. Recognizing the effective communication between slaves who remained on the quarter and their "outlying" brother, masters used outlawry as a warning for slaves to come in or suffer the consequences. Many did not return, nor were they satisfied with merely "lurking" about and "tasting the hardships of the woods" until hunger brought them back to the quarter. Outlaws destroyed. The omnibus slave codes of the century (four were passed from 1705 to 1797) described these desperate, courageous and "incorrigible" slaves in language which changed only slightly during the ninety years:

> WHEREAS many times slaves run away and lie hid and lurking in swamps, woods, and other obscure places, killing hogs, and committing other injuries to the inhabitants . . . upon intelligence, two justices (*Quorum unus*) can issue a proclamation . . . if the slave does not immediately return, anyone whatsoever may kill or destroy such slaves by such ways and means as he . . . shall think fit. . . . If the slave is apprehended . . . it shall . . . be lawful for the county court, to order such punishment to the said slave, either by dismembering, or in any other way . . . as they in their discretion shall think fit, for the reclaiming any such incorrigible slave, and terrifying others from the like practices.[76]

Newspaper advertisements provide a glimpse of why a few runaways were outlawed. John Smith outlawed Mann because he threatened to burn Smith's house; and John Tayloe's manager at the Occoquan Furnace reported that "Leamon's obstinacy in not delivering himself up when lurking a considerable time about the ironworks, and doing mischief, Induced me to have him outlawed; in which condition he now stands and remains." Other explanations were not as clear as these. Moses and his wife were "harboured" by some "ill disposed" persons in Williamsburg. His master advertised "such notorious offences are not to be borne with any degree of patience." Edward

Cary's explanation for outlawing Ben and Alice was even more cryptic. Cary was the chairman of the House of Burgesses committee that reimbursed masters whose slaves were outlawed as public liabilities. "As neither of those slaves have been ill used at my hands, I have had them outlawed in this county and for their bodies without hurt, or a proper certificate of their death, a proper reward will be given." [77]

Some potentially explosive outlaws stayed on the quarters and physically assaulted their overseers. One of Landon Carter's supervisors, Billy Beale, chastised a slave who was weeding a corn patch. Told that his work was "slovenly," the slave replied "a little impudently" and Beale was "obliged to give him a few licks with a switch across his Shoulders"; but the slave fought back, and he and Beale "had a fair box." Subsequently, the laborer was brought before his master; and Carter noted that "it seems nothing scared him." Direct confrontations such as these, between comparatively unassimilated slaves and whites, seem to have been rare; a few, however, are described in detail in the advertisements for runaways. Two fugitives, for example, a husband and wife, were recaptured by an overseer while crossing a field, and were "violently" taken from the overseer and set free by field workers. Another runaway, also a field hand, escaped by "cutting his Overseer in Several Pieces [places?] with a Knife." John Greenhow of Williamsburg lost a slave who "laid violent hands" on him; this man ran off with another field slave who had also beaten his overseer. [78]

Murders, small and unplanned uprisings, and suicides are instances of rebelliousness that was clearly inward-directed in a psychological sense as well as directed against the confines of the plantation. A September 1800 newspaper story graphically illustrates how even the most calculating, courageous, and murderously violent action could be, in a fashion, internalized violence: for after this slave methodically stalked and killed his master he simply "went home."

Captain John Patteson, a tobacco inspector at Horsley's warehouse in Buckingham County, punished his slave for "some misdemeanor"; and from that time, the slave told the court, "he ever after meditated [Patteson's] destruction."

> On the evening to which it was effected, my master directed me
> to set off home . . . and carry a hoe which we used at the place.
> . . . I concluded to way-lay him . . . after waiting a considerable

time, I heard the trampling of horses' feet . . . I got up and walked forwards—my master soon overtook me, and asked me (it being then dark) who I was: I answered Abram; he said he thought I had gone from town long enough to have been further advanced on the road; I said, I thought not; I spoke short to him, and did not care to irritate him—I walked on however; sometimes by the side of his horse, and sometimes before him.—In the course of our traveling an altercation ensued; I raised my hoe two different times to strike him, as the circumstance of the places suited my purpose, but was intimidated. . . . [W]hen I came to the fatal place, I turned to the side of the road; my master observed it, and stopped; I then turn'd suddenly round, lifted my hoe, and struck him across the breast; the stroke broke the handle of the hoe—he fell—I repeated my blows; the handle of the hoe broke a second time—I heard dogs bark, at a house which we passed, at a small distance; I was alarmed, and ran a little way, and stood behind a tree, 'till the barking ceased; in running, I stumbled and fell—I returned to finish the scene I began, and on my way picked up a stone, which I hurl'd at his head, face, &c. again and again and again, until I thought he was certainly dead—and then I went home.[79]

The most violent reactions to slavery were small, unorganized uprisings. A newspaper account written in 1770 reported a battle between slaves and free men, which suddenly erupted during the Christmas holidays on a small plantation quarter in New Wales, Hanover County. The reporter's explanation for the uprising was a familiar one. "Treated with too much lenity," the plantation slaves became "insolent and unruly." When a young and inexperienced overseer tried to "chastise" one of them by beating him to the ground and whipping him the man picked himself up and "slash[ed] at the overseer with an axe." He missed, but a group of slaves jumped on the white and administered such a severe beating that the "ringleader," the slave whom the overseer had whipped, intervened and saved his life. The overseer ran off in search of reinforcements; and instead of fleeing or arming themselves, the slaves tied up two other whites and "whipped [them] till they were raw from neck to waistband." Twelve armed whites arrived, and the slaves retreated into a barn where they were soon joined by a large body of slaves, "some say forty, some fifty." The whites "tried to prevail by persuasion," but the slaves, "deaf to all, rushed upon them with a desperate fury, armed solely with clubs and staves." Two slaves were shot and killed, five others were wounded, and the remainder fled.[80]

Some slaves took their own lives. The journals of the House of Burgesses contain 55 petitions from slaveowners who sought reimbursement from public funds for slaves who committed suicide. Most of these men were outlawed runaways who, since they feared trial and conviction for capital crimes, hanged or drowned themselves.[81] Since few petitioners reported the circumstances of a slave's death, the journals are not too informative. But one suicide, William Lightfoot's Jasper, was also described in a runaway notice:

> [A] well set Negro Man Slave, much pitted with the Small-pox; he was lately brought from *New-York,* but was either born or lived in the *West-Indies,* by which he has acquired their peculiar Way of speaking, and, seems to frown when he talks; he carried with him different Sorts of Apparel.[82]

If indeed Jasper was a suicide his decision to "dash his brains out against a rock" must have been sudden, for he took a change of clothing with him.[83]

But the field slaves' rebelliousness was not typically violent, self-destructive, or even individualistic. In fact they were much more inclined to attack the plantation in a quietly cooperative and effective way than were the slave artisans. Pilferage was a particularly rewarding and often organized action. "I laughed at the care we experienced in Milk, butter, fat, sugar, plumbs, soap, Candles, etc," wrote Landon Carter. "Not one of these ennumerations lasted my family half the year. All gone, no body knows how . . . thievish servants . . . Butter merely vanishing." Washington estimated that his servants stole two glasses of wine to every one consumed by the planter's visitors. His slaves made a practice of stealing nearly everything they could lay their hands on. Washington had to keep his corn and meat houses locked; apples were picked early, and sheep and pigs carefully watched.[84]

The following off-hand comments in records and newspapers indicate that much of this pilferage was not simply to satisfy hunger or anger. "Tell ye overseers to keep the keys of the folk's Cornhouse or else they will sell it, and starve themselves"; "bacon to spare will allow me a preference with the Country People, or rather Nigroes who are the general Chicken merchants"; and, "papermills I believe will answer well there . . . and I am sure the Negroes would supply them with Rags enough for Trifles"; and Washington's order that all dogs belonging to slaves be hanged immediately, because they "aid[ed] them in their night robberies." [85]

The slaves' traffic in stolen goods was extensive, relatively well organized, and carried on virtually with impunity. The problem was of such proportions that by the 1760's it led to several letters to newspaper editors and to a series of laws. "I suppose every family must have so sensibly felt this evil," noted one letter writer to the *Virginia Gazette*. He observed that in every part of the country, henhouses, dairies, barns, granaries, gardens, and even patches and fields were "robbed in every convenient moonshiny night." Another contributor noted that, in his travels about the country, he had heard "frequent and various complaints" of this "pernicious evil." There was "hardly a family that was not full of enjuries they had received from the numerous thefts of servants and slaves."

Many slaves were fences for stolen goods; they had licenses from "over-tender" masters to sell produce. Whites, too, cooperated with the plantation slaves; they were referred to in the newspapers as "common proprietors of orchards," "liquor fellers," and "idle scatter lopping people." One writer made the interesting observation that some slaveowners, with "a modest blush," were so ashamed to sell certain farm products that they gave them to their slaves to dispose of. "Pray why is a fowl more disgraceful," he asked, "in the sale of it at market, than a pig, lamb, a mutton, a veal, a cow or an ox?" [86]

Additional evidence of organized thievery as an outgrowth of the plantation slaves' culture and community is preserved in the Richmond County court records. Between 1710 and 1754 the justices tried and passed sentence in 426 cases. In 1750, although blacks made up 45 per cent of the population and there were nearly twice as many black tithes (1,235) as white (761), only 26 of these 426 actions involved slaves. (It should also be remembered that all slave criminals—with the exception of insurrectionists and murderers who were supposed to be tried by the General Court—were tried by county justices.) Only two trials concerned serious crimes. These were murder trials and both defendants were slave men. One was convicted of stabbing a black woman to death; the other, who later died in jail under very unusual circumstances, was charged with killing his master's young daughter. After his death, the court ordered his body to be quartered and displayed. Most slave crimes in this forty-four year period were petty thefts of the kind described earlier; that is, the charge was nearly always breaking and entering, and the slaves usually took a few shillings' worth of cider, liquor, bacon, cloth, or hogs. One typical case involved a slave who stole five sheets, a fishing line, and a bottle of brandy. Nearly all of these robberies were committed by one person; but the largest theft was conducted by a man and a woman. They took forty gallons of rum and fifty pounds of sugar. Evidently these thefts were well organized; the slaves usually selected such vulnerable targets as the homes of widows, ministers, warehouses, and slave quarters. Only on one occasion did a slave rob his master (who was Landon Carter!). The usual punishment for these crimes was between ten and thirty-nine lashes. For more serious crimes (including a conviction of perjury) slaves lost one or both ears. For capital crimes, slaves were often allowed to plead benefit of clergy.[87]

The plantation slaves' organized burglaries were similar to the rebellious styles of the mobile, comparatively assimilated slaves. These crimes required planning; they took the slaves outside the plantation, and evidently compensated them with money and goods which could be exchanged for articles they needed.

Most field slaves, however, never acquired sufficient literate and occupational skills to move away from the quarter and into the society beyond it. Most were Africans and they remained "new Negroes" all of their lives. There are, then, two possible aspects to the personal dimension of slave life on the quarter. First, from an outsider's point of view, the quarter was a stultifying experience which slowed and restricted the slave's rate of acculturation. Second, from the slave's point of view, life on the quarter was perhaps preferable to daily contact with his captors, because it allowed him to preserve some of his ways.

PLANTATION SLAVES WHO WERE "PRIVILEGED" HOUSE SERVANTS

Household slavery entwined the lives of whites and blacks. In the household more than anywhere else, there were direct and personal encounters that intensified the meaning of slavery for slaves and free alike. For the black servant these situations were often harrowing experiences which threatened to expose a nature sharply divided between enervating fear and aggressive hostility. His inward styles of rebelliousness and such related neurotic symptoms as speech defects were often manifestations of a profound ambiguity about whites and his own "privileged" status. For the white master the intimate presence of so many blacks subtly influenced domestic affairs, particularly his behavior toward his wife and children. The roles developed in household slavery restricted the master's actions toward his servants too. Once a style of discipline and correct order had been established, the master's reactions were often determined by what the slaves had come to expect of him. Highly sensitive to the patriarch's role, servants were quick to exploit any weakness in his performance. If the master was insecure, so were his dependents; but they also kept him that way by their persistent and petty rebelliousness. Household slavery then was the epitome of Professor Tannenbaum's dynamic view of human relationships in slave societies in which slavery was "not merely for blacks, but for the whites [and] . . . Nothing escaped, nothing, and no one." [88]

The greatly enlarged situational (or interpersonal) dimension of slavery in the household is fundamentally important for another reason. Our limited understanding of slave behavior is based almost exclusively on interpretations of these personal encounters. These interpretations, which argue that slaves became the characters they played for whites, that their masters' view of them as infants or Sambos became their self-view, must be used with extreme caution. The interpersonal encounter was only a fragment of slavery's reality for both whites and blacks. When slaves were among their own and using their own resources as fugitives and insurrectionists, it is abundantly clear that much of their true character was concealed or intentionally portrayed in a dissembling manner in the presence of whites.

The reciprocal—and often harmful—nature of human relations in the great mansions of his society was discussed by Thomas Jefferson in Query XVIII in *Notes on Virginia:*

> The whole commerce between master and slave is a perpetual exercise of the most boisterous passions, the most unremitting despotism on the one part, and degrading submissions on the other. Our children see this, and learn to imitate it. . . . The parent storms, the child looks on, catches the lineaments of wrath, puts on the same

airs in the circle of smaller slaves, gives loose to the worst of pas-
sions, and thus nursed, educated and daily exercised in tyranny, cannot but be stamped by it with odious peculiarities. The man must be
a prodigy who can retain his manners and morals undepraved by
such circumstances.[89]

In placing slavery in the context of "family" relations Jefferson
uncovered its essential nature: an intensely private affair for both
servant and master. But other parts of his statement warrant critical
examination. Servants did not typically participate in "degrading
submissions," nor were masters usually blustering despots. Their roles
were more intricate than that, and varied greatly in the patriarchal
households of William Byrd II, Landon Carter, and "Councillor"
Carter.[90]

"A perpetual exercise of the most boisterious passions."

William Byrd II was a well-educated, urbane man whose lordly disdain
for those dependent upon him was sometimes tempered by a lusty but
keen sense of humor.[91] He has left two Virginia diaries. The first one,
1709–12, was written by a proud man in his mid-thirties, married to
passionate and shrewish Lucy Parke Custis. Byrd contributed significantly to his wife's unhappiness, often handling the proud young
girl in an offhand and belittling manner. When the servants were
drawn into these domestic quarrels, they were sometimes cruelly
punished by the defeated party. In the second diary, 1739–41, his
blood had cooled. Married for fifteen years to Maria Taylor, a quiet,
efficient, and unassuming woman, Byrd was more secure about his
position in the family. Certain phrases recur in each diary. These
concern slaves and morning or evening salutations to God. In the
earlier diary the young planter usually closed an entry with a version
of, "I neglected to say my prayers, but had good health, good thoughts,
and good humor, thanks be to God Almighty"; or, "I rose at 5 o'clock,
danced my dance, read a chapter in Hebrew, and said my prayers."
Another recurring notation was a version of "Jenny and Eugene were
whipped"; or "Molly [Jenny, Eugene, Anaka, little Lucy] was
whipped for a hundred faults." In the later diary there are very few
reported whippings; most entries end simply: "I walked about the
plantation, talked with the people and prayed." [92]
In the first diary, Byrd's relationship with his servants was intimate.

There was a play element in many of their encounters. The slaves seldom won; they were repeatedly whipped; and on one occasion, Byrd's wife scarred "little Lucy" with a hot branding iron.[93] Since Byrd humiliated his wife as well as his servants, the interpersonal situations were often ludicrous, confused, and sad. "In the evening my wife and little Jenny had a great quarrel in which my wife got the worse but at last by the help of the family Jenny was overcome and soundly whipped." [94]

The encounters in the Westover household were intricate and game-like. This picture of a 16-year-old girl presented with an opportunity to defeat her mistress in an argument that terminated only when other family members extricated Lucy Parke and thrashed the slave, drama-tizes the complicated texture of lives in slave-society households, and the difficulties of stereotyping those lives.

Unlike most great planters, Byrd did not spend a great deal of time surveying his plantations. But while he was home time passed quickly because his favorite servants, who took liberties in the privacy of Westover that would have been inconceivable elsewhere, engaged in rounds of entertaining games. The slaves were clever; and Byrd, an able and vigilant opponent, was determined to curtail their devious and childish pranks: "Anaka was whipped yesterday for stealing the rum and filling the bottles with water." "Eugene was whipped for cheating in his work and so was little Jenny." At times it seemed the mischievous servants craved physical correction: "In the afternoon I beat Jenny for throwing water on the couch." [95]

Byrd's tempestuous marriage and his enjoyment of women, the excitement of their pursuit as well as love-making itself, enlivened activities in his household. One way he re-created the chase at Westover was to occasionally resolve his spats with Lucy Parke by "flourishing" her on the couch or pool table. Byrd however did not "roger" the servant women nearby; for if he did, it is assumed he would have said so in his truly secret diaries which proudly list his other conquests. Any fantasies Byrd may have had about his slave women were sublimated in the ritual games and whippings they used to establish physical contact, and in his keen observation of their marital and extra-marital sexual activities. Byrd, who had tumbled maids from London to Williamsburg, demanded fidelity among his servants. "In the afternoon I caused L-s-n to be whipped for beating his wife and Jenny was whipped for being his whore." [96] Or:

I threatened Anaka with a whipping if she did not confess the intrigue between Daniel and Nurse, but she prevented by a confession. I chided Nurse severely about it, but she denied, with an impudent face, protesting that Daniel only lay on the bed for the sake of the child.[97]

Byrd also liked to scrutinize Eugene, whose reactions indicated that household status for servants had more serious consequences than a few random beatings and scoldings. "Eugene was whipped again for his pissing in bed." Eighteen-year-old Eugene was a chronic bed-wetter, in fact, and after Byrd had whipped him and used the branding iron, he wrote: "I made Eugene drink a pint of piss." This type of "correction" obviously was not effective, but it does make an unforgettable comment upon the real nature of Byrd's view of Eugene. One June day in 1709, the young man ran away. Byrd's reaction was laconic, his explanation facile and insensitive: "my Eugene ran away this morning for no reason but because he had not done anything yesterday. I sent my people after him but in vain." [98]

Byrd's brutal humiliation of Eugene is partially understandable in the context of his society—one which legitimized such forms of violence as judicial torture. But these background factors do not illuminate the strain of perverse cruelty in Byrd's competitive reactions to the very few young black men in the Westover household; nor do they clarify such cloying, teasing games his servant women engaged him in, as watch-Jenny-throw-water-on-the-couch. Perhaps Byrd imagined that he and Eugene were engaged in a contest for control of the household women. If so this competitiveness would make more intelligible the relationships in Byrd's turbulent first marriage: his enthusiastic involvement in scenes with his wife, Anaka, and the ubiquitous Jenny; that girl's ability to argue with her mistress; and the uncivilized, unpatriarchal nature of Byrd's cruelty toward Eugene.

Further speculation along these lines should begin with Byrd's Commonplace book which underscores themes—his sexual prowess and his need to dominate women heroically—merely implied in his diaries. Like Richard Henry Lee's (see Chapter I), Byrd's daybook is filled with proverbs, poetry, and folk remedies for robust health, fat cattle, and bumper crops. There are also a few insightful entries on sex and domesticity. On the role of the mistress of the household, his view was that she should be barefoot and pregnant: "The Aegyptians of Old never allo[w]ed their Wives any sandals because they had no business to gad abroad, but to stay at home & take care of their Family." On Virility—the early Byrd catches the worm: "St. Martin abserved Such Strict Rules of abstinence & exercised Such austeritys upon himself [that] when the women came to lay him out after he was dead, they could hardly find any Penis." To these observations he added a recipe for an ointment "to procure Erection," another recipe for the same purpose, which was "drunk raw with Glorious success"; and a note on rams who "jump 50 or 60 sheep" in one night: "this denotes a prodigious natural vigor . . . how short do poor men fall of these Feats." [99]

"The parent storms, the child looks on."

Landon Carter, who was not as talented, cosmopolitan, or ambitious as Byrd, was obsessively preoccupied with the workings of his home plantation and the activities of all of its slaves. His direct supervision and surveys were in fact so extensive and exhaustive that virtually every slave at Sabine Hall was treated like a household servant. Consequently, his slaves—house, field, and artisans alike—knew his insecurities, and engaged in types of rebellious activities that gave the fullest expression to Carter's awkward execution of the patriarchal role, and the entire plantation family suffered.

Landon Carter was a deeply embittered man. "For some reason," writes Professor Greene, "he had failed—and he knew he had failed— to make any lasting impression upon his generation, to achieve that recognition among his contemporaries that would assure him a place in history." [100] Failure as a statesman underscored Carter's need to succeed as head of his large household.

Subordinates in this household were not playful as much as they were "impudent" and "unruly." When Carter's authority, self-respect, or dignity were compromised by their actions he quickly restored "order" by ritualized physical violence. But beating his servants did not lessen Carter's bitter disappointment in his son, Robert Wormeley. The planter spent his old age venting his anger and frustration in a running feud with his son. Painfully aware that Carter considered him a failure, Robert at one time sought his father's approval, which was not forthcoming because he lacked Landon's drive. Unfortunately for all, moreover, Robert and his family lived in the old man's household; consequently his behavior was often petty and self-defeating.[101]

The son's revenge was to waste himself by drinking, gambling, and squandering Landon's money—a type of negative rebelliousness that was especially effective because of Carter's drone-like preoccupation with plantation activities, and his sensitivity to insubordination. One "domestic gust," which Carter bitterly relived in his diary, began when his two granddaughters tattled on their brother. Robert's wife threatened to whip "young Landon." We can see the old man attempting to busy himself with his reading, yet incapable of remaining aloof since there was a lesson to be taught here. Landon sassed his mother, "telling her when she said she would whip him, that he did not care if she did." The boy's father, Carter's son, "heard this unmoved." So the patriarch assumed control: "I bid him come and tell me what he did say for I could not bear a child should be sawsy to his Mother." The boy ignored him; Carter grabbed his arm and shook him. There were words between father and son. The "gust" abated until breakfast, when the sulking youngster was twice summoned to the table by his father, then by his grandfather. Again, Carter, assuming command, was ignored. So he reached for his whip and "gave" the child "one cut over the left arm," and "the other over the banister by him." The outraged mother "then rose like a bedlamite," and "up came her Knight Errant"; there were "some heavy God damnings," but the son, the old man took pains to note, "prudently did not touch me. Otherwise my whip handle should have settled him if I could." [102]

Disappointment and frustration shadowed Carter even into his beloved kitchen garden. Here too he was clearly vulnerable because he had to deal with another man, in this instance, his slave gardener Toney. One morning after putting the slave to work fencing the plot, he rode out and inspected the job. Concerned even with the width of the gate posts, he dismounted:

> and showed [Toney] where the two concluding posts were to stand and the rest at 8 feet asunder from post to post . . . and I asked him if he understood me. He said he did and would do it so. I have been 2 hours out and when I came home nothing was done and he was gone about another jobb. I asked him why he served me so. He told me because it would not answer his design. The villain had so constantly interrupted my orders that I have given him about every jobb this year that I struck him about the shoulders with my stick. [103]

Predictably, Toney retaliated. The following morning he "laid himself up and complained of a pain in his shoulder, which did not raise the

least swelling," Carter noted. "The idle dog," moreover, refused to
come out and take off a lock that he had previously returned from a
locksmith, and that only he could remove. "I might as well give up
every Negroe if I submit to this impudence," Carter concluded.[104]

In a fashion, masters such as Carter influenced the very nature of
their servants' rebelliousness, because they themselves provided "privileged" slaves with the means by which they could sabotage the plantation operation. Most larger planters maintained a revolving fund of
odd jobs, piecemeal work, outside the field. Although low in prestige
and virtually without any meaningful personal compensation for the
slave, these tasks were eagerly sought after nonetheless by those who
wished temporarily to escape the dulling monotony of field work. From
the master's point of view, work in the garden, kitchen, or stable would
hopefully serve as an incentive for good behavior. From the slave's
point of view, the new task was truly appreciated; but once obtained,
the problem was to keep it. The servant's feelings were highly ambivalent, because the assignment also presented itself as an opportunity
for the slave to avenge himself. If the planter was present, so much
the better. Although he was demoted to the field, Johnny, Landon
Carter's herdsman, refused to be cowed. Carter was his audience.

> [He] was so pleased in being turned to the hoe that he came this
> morning at day break to tell me he was going and the rascal took
> his row next to hindmost man in my field. But to show him I did
> not intend the hoe to be his field of diversion I gave him the place
> of my fourth man and have ordered my overseers to keep him to
> that. I observed it made him quicken the motion of his arm which
> up here used to be one, two, in the time of a soldier's parade.[105]

Landon Carter was much too mistrustful, angry, and aggravated by
the slightest threat to his person to perform well as a patriarch. This
criticism of his son's handling of this role is informative, because it
points to a major source of weakness in Carter's own performance:

> And for my Sons people I suppose the same [one cotton shift per
> slave] altho' perhaps he may have ordered two shirts and shifts
> apiece for his people for he differs from me he loves to encourage
> people for doing nothing when for my part I think they ought to
> be severely punished.[106]

Unhappy with himself and unable to maintain easily his position as
head of the plantation family, Carter could not accept the fact that

competent patriarchs tolerantly overlooked much of their servants' in-
transigent behavior. A patriarch had to be discreet and discriminating
in his selection of the opportunities for "disciplining" slaves and in-
stilling in them a sense of "duty."

*"The Man must be a Prodigy who can Retain his Manners and
Morals Undepraved in such Circumstances."*

Robert "Councillor" Carter, Landon's nephew, was this kind of patriarch.[107] Unlike his uncle, "Councillor" Carter executed the patriarchal
role almost perfectly. He brought all of his slaves (even those who did
not live at Nomini Hall) within its purview, and he was singularly
successful as a master. His slaves were comparatively acquiescent and
productive, and they made him a great deal of money. Carter in fact
was one of the largest, wealthiest planter-businessmen in colonial
America. His religious views also set him apart from his contemporaries in Virginia; for his benevolent and compassionate relations with
slaves accompanied a prolonged religious experience that took him out
of the Anglican Church, into the Baptist faith, and at last into the
American New Church, a sect based on the writings of Emanuel Swe-
denborg (1688–1772). Shortly after abandoning the Baptist church
for Swedenborgianism, this surprising man manumitted more than
five hundred slaves.

"Councillor" Carter was even more exceptional because his slaves
gave him very little trouble. A clue to his unusual success is provided
by an insightful self-characterization which was recorded, from a break-
fast-table conversation, by his children's tutor: "It is just which
Solomon says, that there is a 'time for all things under the Sun; that
it discovered great Judgment to laugh in Season, and that, on the
whole, he is pleased with Taciturnity.' " [108]

Solomon's "taciturnity" was a fitting model for this self-effacing,
quietly confident patriarch. In sharp contrast to the erratic scenes
among whites and blacks at Byrd's Westover and Landon Carter's
Sabine Hall, there were few, if any, turbulent interpersonal confrontations at Nomini Hall. Too shrewd to put his personality on the line
when dealing with his servants, Carter relied on structure—a well-
articulated, completely understandable set of arrangements that allowed
him to extend servant status even to slaves on the farthest perimeters
of his extensive holdings.

One criterion for even moderately successful relations with plantation slaves seems to have been an ability to permit them to make proposals directly to the master on matters important to their lives. Carter dealt personally with all of his slaves, and he was remarkably receptive to their proposals about their families, jobs, and where they would live. His servants understood this procedure, and they seemed to recognize that at the very least it could bring them small benefits. Even the most dissatisfied group of slaves, the artisans, could often obtain the positions they wanted. One runaway carpenter, Sam, left his quarter in Prince William County and traveled to Nomini Hall in Westmoreland. He had been out for a week, and decided to bargain rather than to attempt to remain permanently free. He wanted to live with his wife, and Carter wrote the slave's overseer: "Sam thinks it a hard case to be separated from his wife—under Consideration Sam is not to return to Cancer." Leniency and "indulgence" were consciously spurned by most slaveowners; such treatment they believed "spoiled" slaves. But this permissive, empathetic way of dealing with slaves worked for Carter. If one of his people wanted to join a member of his family (as in Sam's case) Carter made efforts to bring them together. He also refused to hire out any slaves, since he would be unable to control their treatment and care. He once placed a slave boy in his blacksmith shop at the boy's father's request; and he refused to visit a fellow Baptist during cold weather, remarking, "I cannot think of exposing my Servants but where absolute necessity makes it necessary for them to turn out." Carter's reputation was well known to slaves on other plantations, of course. Runaways belonging to different masters claimed him on at least two occasions as their lawful owner when they were taken up and examined by jailers.[109]

Carter's way of talking about his slaves was as revealing as his methods. When an overseer beat two young boys, the mother of one reported the whippings, and the planter promptly warned the overseer: "I recommend moderate correction in every case and in the present case, I hope you will make proper allowance for the feelings of a Mother." [110] By the early 1770's Carter had completely taken over the responsibility of punishing slaves. There were few complaints from the overseers about this novelty. They realized that the planter's procedures worked, that his methods removed a great deal of the pressure and hazards inherent in managing slaves on the quarters.

But the Revolutionary era brought new realities that demonstrated

how fragile these arrangements were. During the war Carter characteristically appealed directly to his "people" at the Coles Point quarter,
asking them not to run off and join the British. For a year or so he
was successful; but when the British actually landed at Coles Point,
all thirty of its workers abandoned him for the uncertainties of life
aboard a British warship.[111] Carter's slaves were also different men
when they were set free. They began a series of destructive actions that
were bitterly described in an anonymous letter from one of Carter's
Frederick County neighbors, who wrote: if a man desired to "set fire
to his own building, though his Neighbour's is to be destroyed by it,"
unfortunately he was protected by the new Manumission Act of 1782.
The letter writer said he was not alone in his complaint; his "wishes &
ideas [were] those of a *vast* majority of the community":

> I have not heard a single instance among those you have freed
> meriting your liberality—they live generally by the plunder of grain
> & of the stock in their neighbourhood, & though some of them are
> hearty young Men, without any expense but their own maintenance
> . . . still worse effects; by mixing with those in bondage, much
> better off than themselves (for the Negroes in this County fare
> well) they disquiet their minds aid them in procuring false & stupid
> certificates of their being Mr. Carters free men.[112]

A patriarch like Robert "Councillor" Carter might insure a degree
of compliance from his slaves. But even Carter's exceptionally effective
procedures were successful only as long as the subtle equilibrium between his paternalism and the plantation setting was left undisturbed.
His slaves were comparatively acquiescent only while he was clearly in
charge as their sole leader, "benefactor"; they were his servants only
while their behavior was supported by the communal, well-organized
arrangements of the plantation world. Confronted by a new authority,
such as the British armies, or by the possibility of freedom, servants
readily displayed another side of their adjustment to slavery. The two
sides of the house servants' behavior, acquiescence and profound hostility often generating open rebelliousness, are more clearly indicated
in a discussion of waitingmen, and the selection of household servants.

"The Whole Commerce Between Master and Slave"

When a master made a slave his "servant," he considered the slave's
intelligence (usually defined as "quick," "brisk," or "active"), appear-

ance (size and probably skin complexion), age (youth, too, was an important factor) and a cooperative demeanor. These selective factors and some of the servant's many household responsibilities and chores are indicated in the following advertisements: "to be SOLD A YOUNG mulatto woman who is an excellent spinner on the flax wheel, a good knitter, can cut out and make up linen as well as any servant in Virginia"; "A Likely young Negro WENCH, about 25 years of age, she has a child of two months old, understands cooking, making paste, pickling, washing, ironing, cleaning house, and spinning. She is sober and honest." Another woman with an intriguing qualification was described as a strong, active, handy, and sensible Negro who could spin flax as well as cotton, wash and iron, and "she has never had a child." A man who was a cook was "under 40 years of age [he] can roast and boil very well, and understands made dishes, with baking of bread and pickling." Another man was "healthy and strongly made, fit for plantation service, but not calculated for a waitingman man or house servant, which is my only reason for wishing to part with him." John Tayloe's talented runaway, Billy, had not waited on the planter since "he is now grown to the size of a man"; and another servant for sale was "of a right size for a waitingman, and naturally very active." Deportment was an important qualification, for sellers as well as buyers. One man was advertised as "sold for no other fault than having lately disobliged his master, by going off some little time." [113]

For at least two owners, George Washington and Charles Yates, a prospective waitingman's behavior was decisive. Yates, a Fredericksburg merchant, wrote that his slave boy, Robin, had recently been sent to the West Indies. An action that "gave me some uneasiness," he said, "as I expected from his behavior in infancy that he would have turned out well & been servicable to me as a Valet." [114] Deportment was also an important criterion for George Washington who, a few months before his retirement from the Presidency, went over a list of prospective waitingmen for his steward's benefit:

> Sam has sense enough, and has had a little experience, but he wants honesty, and every other requisite; particularly industry— Cyrus . . . is strongly expected of roguery and drinking—otherwise he would do very well, as he is likely, young, and smart enough—the children of Daphne at the river farm are among the best disposed negros I have, but I do not recollect whether there be any of a fit size. [115]

Eventually he selected Cyrus and ordered his steward to "prime" him:
if he continued "to give evidence of such qualities as would fit him for
a waitingman, encourage him to persevere in them." Although at this
time Cyrus seemed to be "sober, attentive to duty, honest, obliging and
cleanly," Washington, like so many other planters, was most concerned with the real nature of his slave's deportment. If Cyrus "per-
severed," if the aforementioned attributes "should appear to be sincere
and permanent," he should be "taken into the house and clothes made
for him." "In the meanwhile," Washington added, "get him a strong
horn comb and direct him to keep his head well combed, that the hair
or wool may grow long." [116]

The quality of the waitingman's relationship with his master and
the nature of his duties were unique. His performance was continually
and critically assessed. His attitude was carefully scrutinized—he must
be "brisk" in anticipating master's whims, but never appear "bold"—
and on occasion he had to be a barber, "negro doctor," bootblack,
hostler, traveling companion, and in some instances, "right hand man"
about the plantation. Even a man who was free would encounter serious difficulties fulfilling all of these diverse roles to the satisfaction of
an eighteenth-century patriarch. For a slave to try to fulfill them while
maintaining a suitable demeanor was often an exercise in futility. Consider the tone and content of Joseph Ball's letter to his man-servant:

> Aron,
>   You were very Saucy while you were in England, and Resisted
> me twice. There must be no more of that; for if you offer to Strike
> your overseer, or be unruly, you must be tyed up and Slasht
> Severely and pickled: and if you Run away you must wear an
> Iron Pothook about your Neck: and if that don't tame you, you
> must wear Iron Spanaels till you Submit. [117]

A covering letter to Aaron's new master, Ball's nephew and steward,
proclaimed, "for he [Aaron] is my slave he must and shall be obedi-
ent." Then Ball asked that Aaron be used "kindly." On several occasions he sent clothing to Aaron in Virginia.

From Ball's point of view these gifts were an important element in
their relationship:

> for as you are my Slave you must and Shall be Obedient But if you
> be have yourself well, you Shall be used kind If I hear a Good

> Character of you, I will send you some of my best old Cloths; and
> other things. Take warning and don't Ruin yourself by your folly.
> I recd. your Letr. If you will be good I shall be yr. Loving Master.
>   Jos Ball [118]

"Benevolent" masters like Ball, who were so careful in selecting the
slaves they would have near them, did not really know their waitingmen as well as they thought they did. The very qualities masters believed were most desirable in those they would have as their traveling
companions, barbers, and the like, were the same traits and attitudes
that largely accounted for the waitingmen's success as fugitives. Once
on their own resources, many of these "active" men forged passes,
changed their names, stole horses and a change of clothing, and ran
off to a town to market their skills and guile as free men.[119] A few
detailed accounts of fugitive waitingmen illustrate how well some
coped with the pernicious nature of household status.

Consider John Tayloe's Billy, who was the subject of a curious
runaway notice printed in the Virginia *Gazette*. The planter began by
"tell[ing] the Publick" that there was little need for a particular description of Billy, since "for many Years [he] used to wait on me in
my Travels" and consequently "by his Pertness, or rather Impudence
was well known to almost all my Acquaintances." Tayloe then proceeded to describe Billy in considerable detail. "A very likely young
Fellow, about twenty Years old, five Feet nine Inches high, stout and
strong made," he had a remarkable swing in his walk. But what was
even more remarkable was his cunning: he had "a surprising Knack
. . . of gaining the good Graces of almost every Body who will listen
to his bewitching and deceitful Tongue, which seldom or ever speaks
the Truth." Of late his slave had worked at the planter's Neabsco Furnace: "from his Ingenuity, he is capable of doing almost any Sort of
Business, and for some Years past has been chiefly employed as a
Founder, a Stone Mason, and a Miller." Tayloe of course understood
the possible consequences of this type of training: "One of which
Trades, I imagine, he will, in the Character of a Freeman, profess."
He concluded with a warning that Billy would not attempt to conceal
himself but rather he would travel "towards *James* River, under the
Pretence of being sent by me on Business." [120]

James Mercer's notice for "my Man CHRISTMAS" describes an
even bolder and more confident man than Billy. Christmas was 30,
"lusty, well made, and genteel." He had waited on Mercer from his

infancy and could shave and dress "extremely well." His "complexion,
was rather light (his father being a light Mulatto), very pleasant, and
well featured." The waitingman also had two identifying scars: a
smallpox inoculation and "a large Cut on his Chin, the Effect of a
late Night Revel." Like Billy, Christmas was "very fluent of Speech";
he spoke "with great Propriety," and was so "artful" that he could
"invent a plausible Tale at a Moment's Warning." This servant was
so facile and deceptive, in fact, that Mercer concluded: "I suspect that
he will now pass unmolested under some Pretence or other, as a Freeman, which I presume will be most desireable to him. He has lived
little short of it with me." Christmas was still another waitingman who
had taken advantage of his position in order to change his status at
an opportune moment; "having been too much indulged, and being
very idle during my present Indisposition he has grown wanton in
Licentiousness, and several gross Acts of ill Behavior this Week past,
are now completed by an Elopement last Monday night." [121] Fifteen
years later, under virtually identical circumstances, the planter offered
to sell the waitingman. He "has treated me ungratefully in my late
Sickness & part we must" and "I fear he has injured his health," he
wrote his brother. He must stop drinking "but this he cannot do under
me." Mercer was still responsible for Christmas. He would "give" him
"choice in a master," and "presume[d] he wou'd prefer one of the
family." [122]

Romeo was another black man who came to be part of the historic
record when he ran away and was described in a newspaper advertisement. In 1789 this 24-year-old, "well-proportioned," six-foot-tall mulatto ran off with Juliet. He was a talented man who could read, write,
and "knew something of figures." Romeo was "acquainted with most
parts" of Virginia; he could care for a horse and his master noted that
he "waited tolerably well," but he was both "awkward and lazy" in
"respect to other work." Romeo's master was not completely unaware
of his companion's fear and anger: "when he walks he holds himself
erect . . . his upper lip turns up when he speaks or when he is
alarmed, and shews his teeth. . . . He generally appears thoughtful,
and is seldom seen to laugh." Romeo was his own man. He was, his
owner continued, "fond of prescribing and administering to sick negroes, by which he acquired the nickname Doctor among them," and
he had also "exercised his talents" by writing passes and certificates

of manumission for runaways. Shortly before his detection he ran off.[123]

Nassau was another slave "doctor" and waitingman who, like Romeo, suffered greatly because of his "privileged" status. But he too was often capable of harassing his master, Landon Carter. Nassau spent few of his waking hours sober:

> I have threatened him, begged him, Prayed him, and told him the consequences if he neglected the care of one of the sick people. . . . He knows he never gets a stroke but for his drinkings, and then he is very sharply whipped; but as soon as the cuts heal he gets drunk directly. I am now resolved not to pass one instance over and think myself justified both to God and Man.[124]

Carter's harangue is misleading: Nassau's relationship with the family was close, and his duties were varied. In addition to waiting on table, he was a barber, "doctor," and accompanying Carter on his inspections, "right-hand-man" at Sabine Hall. His master's tirades made this an unpleasant responsibility. Once Nassau was forced to strip the clothes from a slave who complained of such a sore arm that he "could not drive a nail"; on another, he was ordered to beat a runaway.

But Nassau was not consistently Carter's "my man Nassau." He used his influence to protect slaves. When a runaway was recaptured by his overseer "after a small struggle," Nassau decided to conceal the matter, realizing that Carter would not be inclined to beat a truant. Nassau's position as the plantation "captain" and intermediary was a precarious one; he was often caught between the slaves, who preferred him as their doctor, and Carter, who was notorious for the violent purges he administered. During one siege of illness, the planter and waitingman worked side by side for more than a week. Carter continually accused Nassau of concealing the nature of the slaves' illnesses; Nassau worked long hours principally bleeding slaves, and drank steadily. This scene ended when he ran off.[125]

One of Carter's remedies for Nassau's habitual drunkenness was Christianity. "[I] talked a great deal to him in [a] most religious and affectionate way. . . . I confess I have faults myself to be forgiven, but to be every day and hour committing them, and to seek the modes of committing them admits of no Plea of frailty; I hope then I may save his soul." [126]

Truly an admirable goal on Carter's part, this desire to save old Nassau's soul. But "religious and affectionate talk," and "praying him," did little to ease the painful impress of slavery: drunkenness was a fixed part of Nassau's character. So in 1768 Carter decided to send his waitingman to the West Indies, and advertised for another barber:

> My man Nassau, who I have with much care bred up to be of great service amongst my sick people, having fallen into a most abandoned state of drunkenness, and indeed injured his constitution by it, is become now rather a prejudice to me, as he cannot be trusted in the business he has been long practiced in. As I intend to indulge his appetite, which he cannot be cured of by any persuasion, I will, as soon as I can, send him to some of the islands, where no doubt he may get his liquor with less pains than he seems to take.[127]

Carter relented; but Nassau, like so many other waitingmen, was not easily intimidated. In the early 1770's he made half-hearted efforts to free himself. Twice he ran off following beatings. Then, in 1777, at the height of the war, he left with the intention of never returning. Carter understood the uniqueness of his servant's action on this occasion: "it is very remarkable, [he] has never absented himself for above a day or so," he mused. Unlike many house servants Nassau had broken through a mental barrier. He evidently carried off his entire wardrobe "except a Straw hat and a dirty shirt," and "even a set of raisors which he had purchased. . . . So," Carter concluded, "the trip must have been some time projecting." Nassau, who probably ran down to the Bay in order to board a British warship, was also outlawed.[128]

For many servants the problems encountered in adjusting to household status were especially critical because of an intimate relationship with their masters. Whatever the precise nature of this relationship, the slaves' emotional involvement was considerable. Close contact with the master, irrespective of what "good" treatment and "care" they received, was in many ways psychologically harmful. A study of the waitingman's problems of speech demonstrates that much of the servant's idiosyncratic behavior was symptomatic; that speech problems are another indication of the disturbed, neurotic nature of these fearful, hostile, and talented people; and that in the final analysis, a man-servant's speech impediments or facial tics were manifestations of roles contrary to their true feelings and impulses.

SLAVERY, THE INTERPERSONAL DIMENSION (I)

Masters advertising for runaway waitingmen often commented on their "noticeable" personality quirks, most of which were manifested in situations of verbal communication. "Sharp questioning," or "examination," as it was called, was a dreaded, painful process for slaves. Landon Carter's examination of a young slave girl during a familiar type of plantation family imbroglio is representative of these situational encounters. The girl and a field slave had evidently decided to rid the quarter of its overseer, John Selfe. The girl's complaint to the patriarch was bizarre: Selfe's wife had driven pins through her earlobes. Daniel, the laborer, asserted that Selfe had threatened him with a whipping for a mistake committed by Selfe's wife, who had evidently failed to lock the corn house. Someone had subsequently dumped a supply of corn off the quarter's landing. "These stories," Carter noted, "made me suspend my conclusion." [129] The girl was brought before him and was immediately ensnared between two choices equally undesirable. "This morning, seeing no Pinholes in that girl's ear only some blood about it, I asked her why she said the woman had run pins into it. She stood still for some time." [130] Then the torrent: the young slave was accountable to at least two other slaves:

> and at last [she] told me the overseer had whipped her about giving the Warehouse key to Jubas Harry; and her Granny bid her come and tell me that Selfe's wife had run pins into it; but begged Granny might not know that she told that she bid her say so, or she would whip her for it.[131]

White children, too, stood in fear before their fathers. "Councillor" Carter's tragically unlucky son, Robin, once wrote to his father: "this morning I waited on you in Your Library with an intention of asking you for some employment; It has and ever will be the case I am afraid, when before you; in my serious reflections, I have observed a stoppage in my Throat and intellect vastly confused." [132]

A master who wished to investigate an overseer's activities, as we have seen, often employed "trusted servants" as informers. These informers paid dearly for their special treatment; the confrontation with the master could be a stressful, confusing ordeal. In a long and peevish letter, James Mercer chastised his steward, for the "lice-ridden," famished appearance of two prized mares, "Fly" and "Kate." A slave carrying a report from a steward had intimàted that "Fly's" foal was also ridden too early, and that the overseer was responsible. Mercer explained his examination of James:

> any one who saw Fly when she went up & when she came down might venture to say she had stunk her foal without trusting to the Information of James—as to his lying about that Fact or about the two years old Coalt being rode, I know he informed me as well as he knew. I asked him certain questions, he did not know which way I wished him to answer, nor that my enquiries were towards complaining of Moore or any one else. I cannot therefore admit he cou'd be guilty of lying and do insist that he shall not be punished— nor can agree to such a precedent it must introduce—it will be hard & probably very unjust—to punish a Negro for answering any questions his Master puts to him as well as he knows.[133]

Many servants caught in James's predicament lost their semblance of accommodation and exhibited their turmoil in uncontrollable hand movements or peculiarities of speech. Nathaniel-Bacon Burwell described Essex in a runaway advertisement as "a tall slender Fellow" of "a discontented Countenance." Scipio, a valet for a French officer during the War, "affects to be very polite," his master noted, "and while talking looks very queerly out of his eyes." And Billy, who was extremely artful, had "a placid, agreeable countenance, bespeaking honesty and good conduct," also "spoke rather rapidly, using many words which occasion[ed] him to stammer." [134]

For many servants, confrontations with whites were frightening ordeals that could inadvertently reveal their true feelings. In these situations some waitingmen stuttered. Since this particular speech impediment, with few exceptions, afflicted only artisans, it will be dealt with in the following chapter; but some illustrations of house servants who were both stutterers and fugitives may further revise the traditional view that they were typically docile, accommodating Toms.

John Mayo's George, a runaway, was normally "of sulky looks and temper," except when he chose "to force a deceitful smile." He served as an apprentice to the barber's trade, dabbled in shoemaking, and "he is," Mayo reported, "a very complete domestic servant when he pleases." The slave also "stutter[ed] a little when about to speak." Major Anderson, a 20-year-old "dark" mulatto who could read and write "a little," was an "artful" man "capable of making an excellent house servant." He was also "a tolerable barber, underst[ood] the management of horses and drove a carriage well." When he spoke hastily, however, he was "apt to stammer." The most complete picture of a stutterer in these reports portrayed Jack Sunday, Richard Randolph's valet for many years at "Curls" in Henrico County. "Jet black," 35, 6 feet tall, and "very sensible," Sunday stuttered "a good deal, especially when in liquor." He and Peter, who was "rather yellow," and Randolph's "right hand man in the house for ten years past," ran off after Sunday was demoted and exiled to a staple-producing quarter in distant Cumberland County. Randolph made an additional comment concerning his stutterer's makeup: he noted that Peter had "not quite the understanding or spirits of the former [Sunday] but [that he was] much neater in his dress." [135]

In the familial and domestic world of eighteenth-century plantation society, the location of a slave's job was an important part of his activities as a slave. "Outlandish" Africans often reacted to their new condition by attempting to escape, either to return to Africa or to form settlements of fugitives to re-create their old life in the new land. These activities were not predicated upon the Africans' experience of plantation life, but on a total rejection of their lot.

Most Africans who did not run off at this point were placed on the isolated, up-country quarters, where they remained for the rest of their lives, slowly learning the ways of their captors. This task assignment affected "new Negroes" in two ways. First, the quarter limited their contact with persons who spoke good English and possessed job skills, thus reducing the possibilities that they would readily acquire skills that would widen horizons and move them out of the plantation circuit. Second, since the quarter was isolated, it directed the slaves' rebelliousness toward the plantation itself, rather than toward the less accessible outer world. The field laborers' acts of defiance produced a satisfaction which, though often short-lived, was direct, and brought a quick and visible relief to immediate pressures.

This inward-directed rebelliousness included attacks on crops, stores, tools, and overseers, as well as deliberate laziness, feigned illness, and truancy. While this type of behavior on the part of one slave was ineffectual, slaves understood that if together they did a "little leaning," the overall effect on the plantation's efficiency could be considerable. Only rarely did the quarter slaves reject slavery completely by resisting it outwardly.

A few Africans and many of their children did gain the requisite linguistic and occupational skills to make the move from the quarter to the slightly larger world of the great planter's house, or, rarely, into an even larger arena by way of literate and technical skills. For the house servants, most rebelliousness was still manifested in inward-directed ways: in games with the master, drunkenness, and "laziness." Unlike the crop hands, house servants were also subjected to frequent and often frightening confrontations with the master himself; some of them exhibited neurotic symptoms during these encounters. For the artisans and waitingmen, who—because they traveled extensively— were more able to see their relatively "privileged" positions in relationship to the possibilities of life outside the plantation, rebelliousness became a matter of escaping from slavery itself, of turning their hostilities away from themselves and the plantation. Both their jobs and their facility in speaking English gave them an assurance that they did not need the paternalistic protection of their masters or the plantation environment to survive within the society. On reaching a high level of understanding of their masters' ways, artisans too desired an "independence on every one but Providence"; and although they also sometimes exhibited fear reactions when confronting their masters, they were resourceful runaways, and by the end of the century, had become insurrectionists.

3

The Assimilated Slaves:
Slavery outside the Plantation Family

Skilled jobs that were varied, challenging, and mastered only by expertise and self-discipline were the vehicles for the learning process whereby acculturating slaves acquired their distinctive characteristics: work and leisure-time skills, fluent English, and a "sensible," "artful" demeanor when coping with inquisitive whites. Artisans usually worked at their own pace without direct supervision, spent considerable time by themselves or with other blacks; and as colonial society became increasingly understandable to them, gained a modicum of acceptance and freedom to move about, and in a limited way, to control their lives. They were allowed this margin of freedom of action because whites needed their skills, realized that training and craftsmanship could not be forced upon slaves, and generally treated blacks whose cultural and physical norms were more like their own in a less oppressive way. (Two assimilated types who did not enjoy this kind of work freedom, waitingmen and sailors, were not so adequately shielded by their otherwise relatively advantaged positions.) But there was another side to rapidly acculturating slaves. Some were noticeably unsure about their place and feelings toward masters who were permissive but often unpredictable; and artisans also found themselves working in different cultures while moving between the plantation and commercial areas—workshops, wharves, warehouses and inspection stations, industries, courthouses, and towns. Thus artisans were also bicultural, marginal men who sometimes manifested symptoms of a profound anxiety in interpersonal encounters with their masters.

THE ASSIMILATED SLAVE DESCRIBED: HIS TRAINING AND
TASK ASSIGNMENT

The spate of lottery schemes published in the late 1760's provides a
view of the assimilated slaves' many skills, and a rare measurement of
their value relative to that of other slaves.[1] The following "tradesmen,"
some of them sold with their families, are arranged in the order of
their cost, which was based on their age and degree of professionalism.

Table One: Slave Values in 1768–69

£280   1. Billy, 22 years of age, "a very trusty good forgeman, as well at the
finery as under the hammer, and understands putting up his fire;
and his wife, "a young wench," who works exceeding[ly] well both
in the house and field"

        2. Caesar, 30, a very good blacksmith; his wife and two children

£250   Sam, 26, "a fine chaffery man"; and his wife, a very good hand at
the hoe or in the house

£230   Isaac, 20, "an exceeding[ly] good hammerman and finer [a finisher
of iron]

£220   1. Joe, 27, "a very trusty good" forgeman

        2. Mingo, 24, "a very trusty good" finer and hammerman

        3. Abraham, 26, "an exceeding[ly] good forge carpenter, cooper,
and clapboard carpenter"

£190   Dick, a fine blacksmith and his tools

£180   Harry, a fine sawyer and clapboard carpenter; his wife and 1-year-
old baby

£170   York, a fine gang leader; his wife and child

£160   Jupiter, an unskilled man; and his wife

£150   Bob, 27, a very fine master collier

£120   1. Robin, a sawyer; and his wife

        2. Davy, 33, a mulatto carpenter

        3. Peter, 18, a trusty good wagoner

£100   1. Caesar, 32, a good bricklayer and sawyer

        2. Jemmy, "as good a sawyer as any in the colony," also "under-
stands clapboard work"

        3. Molly, 17, a very fine mulatto house servant, "understands all
kinds of needlework"

        4. Sarah, a very fine mulatto house servant, and a very good
mantua-maker [a loose gown or cloak]; and her child

£90   1. Will, a good hand at the whip-saw and scythe, "and any other
plantation business"

        2. Harry, a good sawyer, understands ditching

£85 Caroline Joe, 35, "a very fine planter"
£80 1. Eve, "used both to the house and plough"; and her child
     2. Jack, 40, a blacksmith
     3. George, 22, a good sawyer and carter
     4. Sampson, 32, skipper of a flat
£75 1. Rachel, 20, house business and a good hand in the field
     2. Ben, 25, a good house servant and carter
     3. Sarah and her child
£70 Dundee, 38, "a good planter"
£67 Lucy, 27, house and field worker
£60 1. Andrew, 30, a butcher and gardener
     2. Kate, 50, spinner and washer woman
     3. Toney, 6, a "very likely" Negro boy
£50 1. Moll, a good cook, can do all kinds of house work
     2. Tom, "an outlandish fellow"
£45 Cherry, 8, a Negro girl
£20 Lucy, "an outlandish Negro woman"
£15 Sall and Sue, both 3
£12 Harry, "an old Negro man"

Lotteries, slave slaves, and advertisements for runaways singled out, and made distinctions among, "tradesmen" on the basis of the degree of their professionalism. Among 20 slaves offered for sale in a 1787 notice were "some valuable tradesmen, such as a Blacksmith, Colliers, Cooper, Baker, Shoemaker [and] a Sawyer." [2] An iron foundry operator, advertising in 1769 for 100 slaves "collected from different estates at extravagant prices," mentioned "particularly among these slaves . . . a good blacksmith, many coarse shoemakers, several pair of fine sawyers and rough carpenters, a ditcher and tidebanker, cotton and flax spinners, valuable house servants of all kinds." [3]

Blacksmiths and carpenters, the most numerous and highly esteemed craftsmen, were usually rated as either semiskilled or skilled. "Coarse work," "house," "ship," and "negro carpenters" were noted in such advertisements as: "WANTED immediately, 3 or 4 good HOUSE CARPENTERS, also 4 or 5 NEGRO CARPENTERS"; or, for sale: "valuable Negro fellow, that understands HOUSE-CARPENTER work." A notice for six good smiths read: "they do all kinds of ship planters' work, shoe horses, &c. One of them has been used to gun work, and is a good nailer." Another described a runaway blacksmith as "so much of a Smith, as to Make the Nails and Shoe those he makes." The manager of the Ante Eutum Iron Works was even more discriminating. He would hire a slave blacksmith from a steward, "Provided you can assure me . . . he is capable of Shoeing a Horse, Steeling an Ax & laying plow Irons in case the other who works with him should be at anytime disabled. A mere Stricker," he cautioned, "you know can be had on much easier terms." [4]

Unfortunately, there is little information on the nature and quality of the education that accounted for the artisans' varying abilities and evaluations. While American-born slaves were occcasionally apprenticed, there are more references to slaves trained informally by local white and black artisans, who were brought onto the plantation to teach and supervise them. Robert "Councillor" Carter, who frequently hired white artisans for specific jobs rather than for an entire year, asked John Ballendine, a Northern Neck entrepreneur, for a Negro— "an Artist, not a Common Labourer"—who "underst[ood] building mud Walls." He paid Richard Oharrow (O'Hara?) a silver dollar and a pint of brandy a day, and the assistance of 4 slave carpenters for building a periauger (a long, narrow, shallow-draft boat). Carter occasionally used his own extensive resources. He ordered his Loudoun County overseer to convert a tobacco house to a spinning and weaving center, by filling its chinks, adding chimneys, purchasing six flax wheels, and "draught[ing] as many black girls as wheels." If the overseer's wife could not instruct them, he was to hire a woman who knew how "to make good linen, I mean such linen as is commonly called Lanabrigs & Rolls." Robert McKilldoe and his family received 40 pounds of pork, 30 barrels of Indian corn, and 1,000 barrels of tobacco in 1780, when McKilldoe agreed to "work with & look after [John Tayloe's] carpenters and joiners." Tayloe also had accounts with William Walker, a fuller, for "looking after the Spinners and weavers at Landsdown," and Robert Hall, carpenter, "to work with them [his carpenters] as Occasion may require." [5]

Records of slaves formally apprenticed are rare and seldom more than a notation: "An additional audit and settlement of the estate of Robt. Poole, decd. To a Fee paid a Cooper learning his negro Amos the Cooper's Trade, £1.10..7." Among scores of newspaper advertisements (1736–1801) offering slaves for sale, only a very few mentioned blacks apprenticed to ship-carpenters, and to a bricklayer; 2 slaves "bred to the business of a cabinet maker"; and 2 more "brought up to the coach and chair, harness and shoemaking business." The man who offered the "six good smiths," said they "served regular times to the trade." Professor Thad Tate has found a few instances of Negro apprentices in Williamsburg. In 1772 William Digges, Jr., of Yorktown apprenticed 2 slave boys to Matthew Tuell, carpenter; and in the same year, an unidentified advertiser offered to buy 2 boys for the specific purpose of apprenticing them. Only 3 of more than 1,000 (1736–1801) advertisers for runaways mentioned slaves who had been formally trained. Billy, a 24-year-old mulatto, had "served a regular apprenticeship to the rope-making business, & was considered a very good workman"; and Gerrard, an exceptionally competent blacksmith, ran off after completing his apprenticeship in the Falmouth-Fredericksburg area.[6]

From the 1760's on, a few small industries and special agricultural projects—namely, leather-, salt-, rope-, iron-works, and Andrew Estave's public vineyard outside Williamsburg—purchased and trained slaves. Some of these men were unusually specialized and provided their owners with a degree of self-sufficiency comparable to the large plantations. William Pearson, a Williamsburg tanner, employed slave shoemakers, a carpenter, a cook, and a spinner, as well as tanners; and James Hunter, a large foundry operator, used slave house-carpenters, coopers, several blacksmiths, a miller, bricklayer, a wheelwright, a ship's-carpenter and caulker, and 3 watermen ("one of whom has gone [as] Skipper of the Sloop for some Years past, and is well acquainted with the Bay and most of the Rivers in Virginia and Maryland").[7]

Generally, before the Revolutionary War businesses were small and more than adequately supplied with slaves from probate and debt proceedings. In the 1760's, this supply was increased, as many tidewater planters switched to general farming and wheat growing, and hired out slaves they could not profitably employ. Even parish slaves were drawn into commercial areas during this time of economic change. In 1789, the Norfolk Borough Parish hired out to a butcher and other shopkeepers 9 adult slaves, including 4 mothers and their 15 children. But during this time, most mobile, skilled slaves belonged to large planters, who lent or hired them out to kin and neighbors and only occasionally to industries.[8]

The Revolution changed this picture considerably. Manufacturers, striving to meet wartime needs for cloth and munitions, rapidly expanded the market for slave hiring. Prior to the war, for example, ironworks owned their own slaves; but after 1776 such large foundry operators as Isaac Zane of the Marlborough Iron Works in Frederick

County, David Ross of Bedford County, and James Hunter, at the falls of the Rappahannock River, became the largest employers of slaves who were hired. Generally, wartime entrepreneurs wanted young slaves for three to five years, and for little or no cash outlay. Advertisements in the late 1770's, for example, were placed by the "Williamsburg Manufactoring Society" for "5 or 6 likely NEGRO LADS from 15 to 20 years of age, and as many GIRLS from 12 to 15 years"; by David Ross, for young and likely boys between 15 and 20 years; and by two Fredericksburg businessmen, "promot[ing] the manufactory of linen, duck, cotton, and woollen cloths." Instead of offering immediate payment for white or black boys and girls, "from twelve years old and upwards" to serve 5 years, these advertisers appealed to the planters' patriotism and desire to off-set the expense of unproductive slave youngsters. They reminded the "Gentlemen who are friends of their country" that their slave women were prolific: "by assisting us with a few of their supernumerary little negroes [they] rid themselves of that charge," and eventually would profit by their slaves' education as stay- and harness-makers. White boys and girls, they continued, are taught to read and write, and boarded and clothed in a "decent manner." "Negroes are boarded and clothed clear of expense." [9]

The question of how hired slaves were treated surfaced during the Revolutionary period in contracts between businessmen and planters and in advertisements. The planters usually required industrialists to feed, clothe, and pay the taxes on their slaves. One owner advertised: "These Negroes will not be suffered to go further than the counties of Stafford, King George, or Spotsylvania." [10] Another stipulated security and the "well-feeding" of his slaves.[11] While entrepreneurs were receptive to the planters' new sensitivity to the most conspicuously inhumane aspects of slavery, they also realized that owners sometimes hired out their most troublesome slaves, and that in many cases, slaves who traveled were inclined to run away. In 1788 James Harris, a manager for the navigational project at the falls of the James, advertised for "a number of able-bodied LABOURERS for the use of the canal, and will warrant their being well-treated." [12] One year later he ran the identical notice with the exception of his insistence that slaves he hired be "men of good character." [13] While requesting a highly specialized slave blacksmith, the manager of the Ante Eutum Iron Works warned: "if he is addicted to running away I would not wish to have any thing to do with him." [14]

THE CHARACTERISTICS OF ASSIMILATED SLAVES WHO WERE "ADDICTED TO RUNNING AWAY"

The acculturated slaves we know best were the most successful rebels of the century; slaves sufficiently gifted to cope with freedom, with whites, and with themselves while on their own resources. They were among the 1,138 men, described in the newspaper advertisements for runaways between 1736 and 1801, of whom clearly 60 per cent or 668 were comparatively acculturated, using the criteria for measuring cultural change as mentioned previously—the slave's task, facility in speaking English, and a distinctive, "sensible" demeanor (itself a function of his clear and fluent English). Fugitive artisans were described in the notices in two ways: first, their masters openly praised their character as well as their highly esteemed skills, and then evaluated their motives as rebellious slaves, and their most illusive, but essential quality: an intelligent, adaptive manner in speaking situations. Second, assimilateds revealed themselves by such by-products of their training as reading, writing, conversational English, and musical and religious interests. These abilities, which protected the assimilated's individuality and enhanced his ability and desire to function on his own, were also the basis for his outward—that is, creative, imaginative, and personally rewarding—styles of resistance. Together these characteristics made him a special type of slave, but for convenience the effect of each is examined separately in the following section.

Mobility

Mobility for the rapidly acculturating slave created a sense of slavery and a self-view that developed outside the plantation "family." Artisans escaped the imprint of plantation norms and their masters' values because they were mobile in another way too: as young men they often had two or three owners. Why such highly valued slaves as these were sold is difficult to explain. But they were a reliable source of quick and high profits in a declining tobacco economy; and their inclination to run away and pass as free men may also explain their change of owners. The very few slaves belonging to "Councillor" Carter who ran away and did not return voluntarily were immediately sold, for example. A correlation between multiple owners, mobility, and running away can be drawn from the notices, too. By 1770 virtually every other advertisement listed at least one previous owner, in order to suggest where the fugitive might be. William Garthright, Jr.'s, Sam, a mulatto, had belonged first to "one Mr. *Stubbs* of *Gloucester* county, who kept a ferry upon *York* river, afterwards to Major *Finnie,* near *Williamsburg;* and was lately the property of Mr. *Peter Russell,* of *New-Kent* county, and I expect he is gone towards his old walks." Peter, a remarkably versatile carpenter, cooper, bricklayer, and plasterer, ran away from John West of Charles City County. Formerly he had belonged to the Willis family, Gloucester County, who "gave" him to Mrs. Kennon, who sent him to her husband's iron mine in Buckingham County. When Peter was returned to the tidewater, he ran away.[15] "Full-faced" Tom left a Caroline County plantation in 1772. Earlier he had been purchased from the Reverend John Dixon of Williamsburg. His present master listed his old haunts:

> I have reasons to believe that he will endeavour to secrete himself either at the town of *Falmouth,* in *King George* County, at the glebe in *Kingston* parish, in *Gloucester* County, at Colonel *Humphrey Hill's* quarter in *King & Queen,* or at Mr. *John Hill's* quarter, near *Aylett's* warehouse in *King William,* as he has many relations at each place.[16]

Mobility and freedom from exclusive control by one master were common denominators for acculturated slaves. Even the most menial semiskilled laborer—if he possessed a marketable skill—spent considerable time outside his family, working among different slaves in unfamiliar settings. Richard Henry Lee's account for one of his itinerant slave jobbers read:

> Congo worked 13½ days for me White-washing &c. the last of October & 1st of Novr. 1781—Congo worked for Mr. Londale at Westmr. Courthouse about 5 months of Summer Spring & Fall 1781. Also he worked 7 days for Richd. Muse in Octr. 1781.[17]

Mobility for the slave diminished his fear of whites and their world by narrowing the differences between him and free men. For the society, the slave's mobility and cultural change had serious repercussions: it weakened slavery's hold on the very slaves who were most able to resist it effectively. While traveling and working in the rich and challenging linguistic environment of the towns and seaports, slaves came to understand the nuances and shades of meaning, the conventions and norms, of colonial society. More specifically, they acquired a competent, assured command of English that gave them—depending on their master's point of view—a "sensible" or "artful and cunning" demeanor. For the whites who saw the assimilated largely in the context of their verbal exchanges, the slave's conversational English and an intelligent demeanor were inextricably linked.

Discourse and demeanor

Craftsmanship, Erik Erikson reminds us, tends to become crafty.[18] The acculturated slave's "smooth-tongued," confident way of handling whites in their own language was the key both to his special qualities as a slave, and to his master's efforts to portray these qualities in fugitive slave advertisements. These comments were of two types: a description of the runaway's clarity of speech, and a more inclusive statement on his discourse as an indication of character.

While these characterizations were graphic, useful indices of acculturation levels, they were based on little more than the master's understanding of the slave in speaking situations. Some portrayals, connecting the skilled slave's unique education with his rebellious style, were deft and evidently essentially correct: Davy was a "great hypocrite, of mild expression," who showed his teeth when he laughed. Another man was identified simply as a "fair spoken, deceiving slippery chap." Other descriptions were more leisurely—but invariably based on the transactional setting. Harry's master knew his slave intimately. He had a sharp chin, thin visage, and a "soft voice and a bashful manner when spoken to." A small hand and foot, a neat leg, too, and a very handsome even set of teeth; when Harry spoke it was with "a down cast look under his upper eye lids, three-fourths open." Some masters clearly understood the connection between mobility and self-assurance: "He is well acquainted in many parts of the Country, and [is] an artful insinuating fellow." "He is very apt to give surly Answers, and is in general an obstinate Fellow, he having been allowed for Several Years past to hire himself out." [19]

These characterizations were intended to warn gullible whites, as well as to identify the runaway attempting to pass as a free man. "He is so smooth and plausible in speech," one owner cautioned, that those who do not know him would "suppose him to be honest." Tom, from

St. Andrews' Glebe, Stafford County, was so "sensible, cunning, and smooth-tongued," that the "person who takes him up, should be very careful of him." Brunswick, who had run off several times, often "appears rather silly, which induces those that has had him in custody to indulge him, by which he effects his escape." [20]

But artful dissemblers required a receptive audience, and they were seldom disappointed. Assimilated slaves so often successfully passed as free men because whites were susceptible to their ruses. Why this was so is another issue; perhaps the colonists unwittingly acknowledged and approved the fact that at last among the strange and threatening plantation slaves a significant number had come to learn white ways and could now play their social games with artistry. When Jamy was whipped by an overseer he became one of the very few men from Sabine Hall who actually ran away to "turn [a] free man." Jamy's manner, supported by unnamed whites, was also remarkable: "a most passionate, lazy rascal," Landon Carter noted, "and I always find he is more as he works abroad, for the people treat him so much like a gentleman, that he can't fancy himself otherwise when he gets home." Slaves like Jamy, who used whites as foils, recur persistently in late eighteenth-century notices: Bob—"artful, designing, and exceedingly smooth-tongued"—was a ferryman for many years who, from his acquaintance with gentlemen, had "assumed an Immoderate Stock of Assurance." [21]

Slaveowners also made more obvious and direct statements about the fugitive's speech; they evaluated its comprehensibility. In the dynamic environment of speech and languages—which provides the most adequate examples of the bicultural setting in eighteenth-century Virginia—Negro speech often confused whites. The medley of dialects and languages spoken in the colony before the war included a patois which all slaves used to protect themselves and their culture. The Virginians were fascinated with their slaves' speech; and before 1775, when most slaves were still changing their traditional ways, nearly every other notice for Africans and country-born alike included such comments on the runaway's clarity of speech as: "he is remarkably sensible and plausible in his discourse"; "remarkably sensible [and] fluent of speech," or simply, "he speaks plain." [22]

Leisure-time Activities and Skills

Some slaves had sufficient leisure to develop and increase the literary and musical skills that were initially by-products of their training. There were reports of fugitives who could read, or write, or both, which they did to the continual frustration of their masters. William Macon's complaint was typical: "[Peter] by some means has learned to write a little, and has frequently wrote passes for himself and other Negroes to go a little distance, and I am apprehensive he has done the like again." [23]

Fugitives who chose to burden themselves with excess baggage nearly always took their musical instruments rather than a change of clothing or a set of tools. Among all slaves advertised as runaways there were 23 fiddlers, 11 violinists, a drummer, a French horn player, and 2 men who played the banjo.[24] This instrument was always referred to as a "banger," which described the way it was played. Although it could be strummed, the banger's flexed wooden frame covered with hide made a fine percussion instrument for slaves who evidently preferred to strike rather than pick it. The only drummer reported was from the West Indies: Damon, who spoke "a smattering of French," and "beat the drum tolerable well which he [was] very fond of." [25] (His master's appreciation and matter-of-fact observation might encourage us to re-examine the notion that African drumming was systematically suppressed by North American slaveowners.) Some other fugitives sang or whistled. A shoemaker who could read plain print sang "the new tunes by note" while working at his bench. Peter Brown, a painter and carpenter, whistled and sang.[26] Harry sang "Scotch songs"; and Joe, whose master noted sarcastically that he was fond of exhorting his brethren of the Ethiopian Tribe, liked to sing hymns.[27]

Artisanship stretched the minds of assimilated slaves and taught them how to cope with whites. One runaway's master expressed the issue directly: Harry "is seldom long in a place before he puts his engenuity in practice." While many slaveowners could only portray slaves like Harry as "cunning" or "artful"—to say more was to recognize what they were doing to black men as slaves and to recognize that slavery was not their natural condition—others were more explicit, appreciative, and accurate. The mulatto carpenter, John Wilson, who could read, write, and "cipher very well," was described by his owner William Black as "very well qualified to attempt passing as a freeman." [28]

The Whites' Evaluation of the Assimilated's Skills and its Impact on his Outlook

The slaveowners' strong and positive evaluation of the artisans' character and abilities further indicates the way work affected the assimilateds' social character, personality, and overall sense of worth and dignity. Gerrard's owner said he was a blacksmith "perhaps inferior to none." Billy, an ironworker, stonemason, and miller, "From his Ingenuity [was] capable of doing almost any Sort of Business." A young seaman who had made two voyages before he was 17 was "remarkably smart and sensible." And a mere ditcher was described as "very sensible & fair spoken, understands his business perfectly well." Others included "a very knowing fellow," "strong-headed sensible," "a very ingenious fellow and a fine shoemaker," and "very ingenious at any work." [29] These slaves represented only a few of the sixty-three occupations of fugitives listed below:

Table Two: The Assimilated Slaves' Jobs

Thirty-two per cent (359 of the 1,138) fugitives were listed as skilled. Almost 50 per cent of this group (168) were tradesmen; one in four (89) were house servants, nearly the same proportion (85) were slaves who "went by water," and 17, slightly less than 5 per cent, worked in small-scale extractive and craft industries (forges, mines, ropewalks, etc.).[30]

N.B. Among the 30-odd artisans skilled in more than one trade (usually in combination with carpentry or shoemaking) were 19 not listed below, among whom were: a butcher, scytheman, coarse carpenter, a currier, a whiskey distiller, and a flax spinner.[31]

Artisans ("Tradesmen")
blacksmiths; one also a carpenter (20)
shoemakers (47)
    shoe- and harness-maker (1)
    shoemakers who were also skilled as carpenters, blacksmiths, house
    servants or watermen (18)

woodworkers; about one-sixth of all skilled fugitives (60)
    carpenters (18)
    sawyers (14)
    carpenters and coopers (12)
    coopers (9)
    carpenters and sawyers (4)
    ship's-carpenter (1)
    carpenter and joiner (1)
    sawyer and clapboarder (1)
wheelwrights; all skilled in other crafts (3)
    wheelwright, house-carpenter, joiner, and carpenter (1)
    wheelwright, carpenter, glazier, and painter (1)
    wheelwright, house-carpenter, and sawyer (1)
wagonmakers and wheelwrights; one also a blacksmith (2)
bricklayers (2)
miller (1)
millwrights (2)
tailors (5)
weaver (1)
pressman (1)
painter and carpenter (1)
house-carpenter, cooper, bricklayer, plasterer, whitewasher, and
gardener (1)

Slaves who Worked on the Water
watermen (55), 14 per cent of all skilled slave runaways, including those
designated:
    flatboatman (1)
    skippers of flats (2)
    pilots (2)
    ferrymen (3)
    sailors (30)

House Servants
waitingmen (37), 10 per cent of all skilled fugitives
hostlers (11)
jockeys (4)
barbers (3)
cooks (2)
gardeners (3)
hostler and jockey (1)
servants in inns and taverns (2)

coachmen (2)
unspecified house servants (24)

Fugitives from Small-scale Extractive and Craft Industries

ironworkers (6)
    Hunter's Iron forge (1)
    Jerdone and Holt's Providence Forge, New Kent County (1)
    John Tayloe's Neabsco Furnace, Maryland; also a runaway, listed
    as an artisan, from his Prince William, Occoquan Iron Furnace (2)
    Mossy Creek Ironworks, Augusta County (1)
    Isaac Zane's Marlborough Furnace, Frederick County (1)
laborers, public Armory, Westham, Henrico County (3)
miners (3)
    Moses Austin and Co., lead mine, Augusta County (2)
    William Kennan's Mine, Buckingham County (1)
ropemakers (3)
    Chatham Rope Walk, New Kent County (1)
    Campbell Rope Walk, Norfolk (2)
saltmakers (2)
laborer, Dismal Swamp Land Company (1)
canal worker, Richmond City, J. Ballendine and T. Southall, managers (1)
warehouseman (1)

Several of these men mastered more than one trade and displayed a
rare enthusiasm for their accomplishments in spite of slavery and the
attitude of whites. Dick, 30, was a slim, active blacksmith, who was
also "a Compleat Wheelwright . . . and likewise a good Cooper,
Sawyer, and House-Carpenter," who had also been "employed in small
Craft by Water." Caesar, a strong-headed, sensible man, was a sawyer
and carpenter who enjoyed working in the harvest. "It is likely," his
master wrote, "he will be seen at the time of cutting small grain, as he
is extremely fond of that business, and generally gets from 6 to 8
shillings per day by it." Charles Green's master, John Tyler of Green-
way, was effusive in his praise for a slave who had just run away.
Green, a "yellow man," was an excellent hostler "in the general Way,"
and a "remarkable good Race-Keeper and Rider." In his younger days
he was well known on the turf, and had ridden mounts "at all the race
grounds of consequence" for one of the colony's big horsemen, Littlebury Hardyman. He was in fact "handy about every kind of business
a house or field servant can be employed in." Tyler concluded with an
observation of the differences between life in the North and South in
the 1790's. If Green chose to "make his living in the line of his old

profession," he would probably remain in Virginia or travel south to the Carolinas. But if he intended to pass as free·"by his other qualities," he "should go to the North." [32]

Notices for two men who were also thoroughly familiar with colonial culture warrant fuller treatment; these documents underscore the unusual complexity and inner strength and resourcefulness of some assimilated men, the problems of typifying slave personalities, and they re-emphasize the extent to which "the slave" we have come to know was largely a creation of the shared values and attitudes of whites and blacks in interpersonal encounters. David, a very cunning, artful mulatto, had hair "of the Negro kind," which he kept very high and well combed. "He has always been my Waiting Man when I went from home," his master wrote. He is also "a good Waiter, Driver, and Hostler. [He] understands something of Gardening, of combing and dressing Wigs and Hair, [he] can Plough, work at the Hoe and Axe very well, and is, on the Whole, a very clever, active, brisk Fellow." [33] Peter Deadfoot, another mulatto, was hired out as a sawyer in Loudoun County; returned to his master's quarter in Stafford, he left for Philadelphia, using a forged pass and the name William Swann. His master advertised that he was a genteel, handsome fellow, tall, broad-shouldered, slim, clean-limbed, and active. But Deadfoot, usually "very sensible" and "smooth-tongued," evidently harbored ambivalent feelings about himself and a master who allowed him to live as he did. For he was apt to "speak quick, swear, and with dreadful curses upon himself, in defense of his innocence, if tasked with a fault," his master noted, "even when guilty." This mulatto's world of work—his proud desire to accomplish a task faultlessly and thus through his craft realize a measure of control—was indeed remarkable. His skills? He was:

> an indifferent shoemaker, a good butcher, ploughman, and carter; an excellent sawyer, and waterman, and understands breaking oxen well, and is one of the best scythemen, either with or without a cradle, in *America;* in short, he is so ingenious a Fellow, that he can turn his hand to any thing.[34]

But, most important, Peter Deadfoot had a "great share of pride." [35]

"Pride," "Ingenuity," and "an Immoderate Stock of Assurance"— are not customary present-day views of the impact of slavery on slaves in North America. The bicultural assimilateds paid a severe personal price as harbingers of the historic changes that in a few generations transformed their people from the African prototype, the "wild" and "barbarous" man of ritual scars and mythopoeic notions of time and space, who had been so conspicuous in the early years of the century. For the "pride" of the acculturating man, a transitional figure between the plantation and commercial cultures, had another side: rage and a fear of whites.

SLAVERY, THE INTERPERSONAL DIMENSION (2)

Challenged to communicate before their masters (in the ways whites would have them communicate) some slaves stuttered. An analysis of the situational dimension of this speech defect provides the clearest view of the assimilated's divided self and cultural marginality. Among the 1,138 fugitive men, 49 (or 4.3 per cent) were advertised as stutterers. This group bore few signs of ill-treatment accountable to poor medical care, occupational accidents (highly prevalent among slaves of all kinds), or physical abuse. Only 1 man was scarred by a whip; less than a fourth, 11, had prominent complications of health; these few included 3 smallpox victims, 4 who were bowlegged, a man with an injured hand (cut by the stroke of a sickle), another with an eye covered with a film, and a fugitive in a truss protecting a rupture. [36]

All the stutterers were American-born except for one native African who spoke "pretty good English." While 17 per cent of all runaways were mulattoes, 25 per cent of the stutterers were mulattoes. Another 15 per cent were "yellowish-complexioned." Light-skinned slaves then, made up 40 per cent of the group. The jobs for 60 per cent were listed: 18 of the 19 so listed were skilled, and more than half of this number were either sailors (not simply watermen) or waitingmen. One of the sailors was a "very good seaman and rigger"; another, while still a cabin boy, had been to "England, Scotland, Ireland, New and Old Spain, Portugal, and the East Indies." The 5 servants combined many skills; they were waitingmen as well as hostlers, a jockey, a cook, and a preacher. The remaining non-field stutterers were equally divided between the highest and lowest skilled positions. Laborers included 2 saltmakers, a ropeworker, a sawyer, and a warehouseman; craftsmen included 2 coopers, a tailor, and a pressman for a Richmond newspaper. [37]

Masters generally agreed with one another when they tried to explain their slaves' problems of speech: slaves stuttered when replying to their owners' "sharp questioning." These men—who were neither learners of a second language, nor physically clumsy or disabled—exhibited symptoms of extreme anxiety when answering their masters. Advertisers were quite explicit about both the cause and extent of their slaves' handicap. Five said that "close questioning" accounted for speech defects; five mentioned slaves who stuttered when "surprised." "Fear," intoxication, speaking hurriedly, and "confusion," were cited in that order of frequency, as explanations for others. Some men, of course, were not as affected as others. Sam had a smooth tongue, "but snuffle[d] a little"; Major Jackson was "apt to stammer" when he "attempted to speak Hastily," but generally he spoke "low and inwardly." [38]

But with some, however, the affliction was more severe. John had "a custom of repeating his words when he [spoke] with a kind of stammering that appears rather affected than natural"; Will was "apt to stammer when surprised or questioned sharp"; and Frederick, 16 and a jockey, stammered "much when affrighted [but] at other times speaks plain and fast." For a few, replying to the master induced profound conflicts and anguish. Jacob had "a Stoppage in his Speech," and when "strictly examined or suddenly asked a Question," he could not "directly give an Answer." Ben, a waterman suspected of joining Governor Dunmore's regiment of runaways, stammered in his "common Discourse," and if spoken to unexpectedly, he could not return an immediate answer. Fox, a "bright"-complexioned mulatto with bowed legs and a down look, stammered when not surprised, but when "closely attacked" he was much worse. [39]

A few men also exhibited uncontrollable hand movements and tics. Pompey, a short, thick-set tailor, was "very apt to wink his eyes quick, contract one corner of his mouth, and stammer in his speech when under any apprehensions of fear." [40] Jem, like Pompey, was about 35, a tall, large, and square-built man; he stuttered, "and when challenged with a fault, or surprised [he made] an extraordinary motion with his hands, which he could not avoid." Some wore their inner turmoil on their faces. "When surprised" Will's eyes turned red. Jacob had a "staring look when confused"; and the portrait of Daniel was that of a haunted man: his back much scarred with old whippings; "when he looked at a person his face appeared much awry." For a few, answering whites was plainly terrifying. Bob, who could not converse "very plain" when spoken to, exhibited "a remarkable turning of his eyes

and winking, with some hesitation before he replied"; and George Turberville's Vincent cleared his throat and spoke "rather in his throat
than on the tip of his tongue, particularly when alarmed." [41]

Too much liquor, like "close questioning," also tapped the residue
of pain, fear, and hatred that festered in many slave men. These descriptions were also invariably based—not on the effects of alcohol on
health or work habits—but on its influence upon slaves in speaking
situations. [42] These slaves, clearly aggressive and hostile men, were also
sufficiently close to free society and their masters to tell them what it
was like to be drunk and a slave. Any deferential pose quickly gave
way to a purer pattern of behavior at these times. Isaac, normally a
"well-disposed Fellow, rather plausible and insinuating when sober,"
once "in Liquor," was "stubborn and inclinable to be impudent"; Ab-
ner was "quarrelsome when in Liquor"; and Thomas Jefferson's
Sandy, the mulatto shoemaker and jockey, was "greatly addicted to
liquor, and when drunk insolent and disorderly." While drunkenness
tends to leave most people either quiet and withdrawn, or outgoing
and loud-spoken, acculturating slaves when drunk and addressing their
masters—with no reported exceptions—were always "bold," "obstinate," "daring," "impudent," or "turbulent." [43]

We need to know more about the owners whose fears and inade-
quacies helped create the settings and scenes in which slaves were intentionally dissembling, aggressively drunk, or exhibited involuntary
quirks and gestures. Every master and his slaves worked out their own
arrangements about the basic requirements for everyday existence—
essential questions about the slaves' food, clothing, possessions, visiting
privileges, and days-off. These were woven into the texture of their
personal interactions. Perhaps neurotic slaves and insecure masters
were concentrated in a few households. A notice for a blacksmith, Will,
placed by the same George Turberville who advertised for Vincent
(who cleared his throat before he spoke), said that Will spoke slowly
and "generally with a grinning smile especially when answering a
question." One master of a slave who stuttered "much when he [was]
scared" was notorious; his murderously violent nature was an established fact. This man was Colonel John Chiswell of Williamsburg, a
well-known tidewater aristocrat who, before he took his own life, was
the defendant in a controversial murder case. [44]

In order to come to some tentative conclusions about the nature of
the interpersonal dimension of slavery for men who exhibited notice-

able problems when communicating with their masters, it is useful to compare the stutterers' occupations with those of fugitives in general. Missing from this group were the most prestigious and numerous craftsmen—blacksmiths, shoemakers, and carpenters—who characteristically worked by themselves, at their own pace, and with a minimum of direct and persistent supervision. The only possible connection between the two occupational groups heavily represented among stutterers, the waitingmen and sailors, on the other hand, is precisely this factor: the nature of the work environment with regard to mobility and frequency of contact with whites. Both sailors and waitingmen were forced continually to deal with whites in radically different environments. Waitingmen performed a number of tasks ranging from the inane to the highly challenging; and as plantation captains, they had to be adept and resourceful in two cultures: the plantation and the town. Sailors obviously spent most of their time outside the plantation. But evidently they found life aboard ocean-going vessels with crews—presumably mostly white—highly stressful, and between voyages when they were with their masters—or when they ran off—they too may have experienced difficulties in going between their masters' world and their normal work setting.

The high percentage of mulattoes among stutterers offers a further clue to the source of the affliction. While nearly half of all mulattoes who ran away were skilled, only 20 per cent (4 of 14) of the mulatto stutterers possessed relatively advantaged positions. If they were their masters' children, or the offspring of plantation overseers who still had direct control of them because they were field workers, the mulattoes' failure to obtain the jobs they believed were theirs could have been an important source of the profound conflicts manifested in speech defects.

While present-day research on the etiology of stuttering is inconclusive,[45] it is well-known that many who are so handicapped do not exhibit the symptom when singing or reciting in unison. Those slaves who experienced severe problems of speech also did so only on occasion—as their masters were so careful to indicate. It is highly unlikely that the slave preacher, Anthony, for example, stuttered when he addressed gatherings of his own people. Perhaps his quirk or defect, which was situational and displayed only when "sharply questioned" by his master, was part of a reaction formation. That is, like so many other rapidly acculturating artisans forced to answer their masters, he exhibited on these occasions a type of protective behavior, leaning over backwards, that was opposite to his inner emotions and desires.

It is useful to ask what the fugitives' communicative problems revealed about their self-view. In personality theory the point is often made that the ultimate determinant of behavior—at the very core—is the self-image or self-concept.[46] What took place in the stutterer's head —often a slave quite determined to do his job well—when he was made accountable in one way or another to an insecure master (whose own petty frustrations stemmed from the inevitable paradoxes of the plantation world itself) is difficult to say. We may hazard however that while these bicultural slaves were less oppressed, their masters' treatment was ambiguous; and their problems began at this point. The very jobs that brought pride and other incalculable psychological protections against the abuses of slavery, also sensitized the slaves to what they really were: marginal men,[47] often light skinned, who enjoyed a quasi-free status that was only tenuously sustained by skills, performances, attitudes, and most importantly, by constant vigilance over feelings the discovery of which would jeopardize the slaves' positions and possibly their lives. These men were also acutely aware of their inability to punish directly "the man" who held power; and "the man" with whom they were forced to deal continually, as "privileged" slaves. This group's elite status did little to assuage the galling, painful impress of slavery; in fact, it intensified it. Above all, these men were burdened by fear. They were fearful and watchful, especially before their masters. Eventually many channeled some of their anger and resourcefulness into attempts to pass as free men, and occasionally to leave the colony.

Escape from what? Both slave and master were imprisoned in the slave society. The slaveowner was incapable of acknowledging the slave's humanity; the slave was imprisoned by his status no matter what it brought in the way of "privileges" and responsibilities. He remained a black man in a white man's country:

> Yes it does indeed mean something—something unspeakable to be born, in a white country, an Anglo-Teutonic, anti-sexual country, black. You very soon, without knowing it, give up all hope of communion. Black people mainly look down or look up but do not look at each other, not at you, and white people mainly look away.[48]

Neither the anger, in this instance James Baldwin's, nor the theme, the depersonalization of black people in this society, is recent. Themes of facelessness, or "invisibility," prevail in Negro literature. With few exceptions these themes deal only with black men; black women escaped the more oppressive ravages of slavery.

Slavery for Fugitive Women

Without exception the 141 women advertised as runaways from 1736 to 1801 were virtually free of the neurotic symptoms that characterized so many slave men.

Slaveowners knew their slave women better than they knew the men. While only about half of the slaveowners who publicized runaway men hazarded a guess where they were going, two-thirds of the owners of fugitive women mentioned their destination. Most of the women in the notices worked in the plantation house rather than in the quarters and in the fields; we would expect their masters, then, to have more opportunity to know them well.

No woman who ran away stammered or exhibited uncontrollable movements of hands or face. While several men drank to excess with predictable results, only one woman was an occasional drunk: Phillis, who belonged to "Councillor" Carter, when intoxicated entertained others with "indecent" and "Sailors' Songs." The very few women who manifested remarkable behavior in speaking situations included Hannah, who when angered flashed a "very passionate temper." She was 19, a servant, who also "talked very much and very fast" when angered. Sarah's serious illness was evidently physiological in nature: this small and courageous girl was 14, "somewhat slender made," and very black. When taken up she could not remember her owner's name, although she readily identified herself as a Mundingo. Sarah, unclaimed as a runaway, was sold for her jail fees and "turned loose at *Smithfield,* without any thing being further done." Taken in by "sundry families, as an object [of mercy]," she became "much troubled with choaking fits, which deprive[d] her of the use of her limbs, as well as her senses." [49]

Although nearly all fugitive women were comparatively highly assimilated, their families remained important to them; but the opposite, as we shall see, was often the case with acculturated slave men. One fourth of the women left to visit their husbands, parents or children; another two-fifths went to town to pass as free; and very few (as compared to 15 per cent of the fugitive men) ran off to leave the colony and escape slavery completely. It should be remembered, however, that it would be extremely difficult for a woman to pass as free and live and work in a society in which women in general did not go about alone. Consequently, more than a fourth of all fugitive black women were accompanied by men, both white and black (and sometimes by their own children). And of the fifteen who left with men, three ran off with whites.[50]

The other men who figured prominently in the notices for runaway slave women were their masters who knew some of them intimately. William Allegre's "very black," six-foot woman held her head "pretty high" when she spoke and had a large scar, "as long as One's Finger above her Breast." Lucy had a scar "under her left breast"; and Milly, with grey eyes and "very large Breasts," was also "a sly, subtle Wench, and a great Lyar." Cicley's master, a wiser man after his slave woman ran off, warned: "Beware to secure her Well, for she is very wicked and full of flattery." Another, a mulatto woman with "some pretensions to freedom," somehow obtained a pass from a justice of the peace "in order to seek for witnesses to support her claim" and never returned. Her owner wrote: "she was a sensible wench and may impose on the credulous as a free woman." There was little love lost between Hannah and her master, who wrote that Hannah, the daughter of Sykes's Doctor, had a "middle stature a good Deal like her Father, the well known Fiddler." After she had twice run off in a six-month period her master, the proprietor of Bland's Ordinary in Prince George County, sought to humiliate her by cutting her hair "in a very irregular Manner." She still ran off; her owner's advertisement read in part: "she is very insinuating, and a notorious Thief" who will "endeavour to pass as a free Person, or frame some plausible Excuse for her Absence." [51]

Some slave women continued to use men—and to be used by them—even while at large as fugitives. Patt, who ran off during the War, was "harboured" at the troop barracks in Albemarle County. Nanny ran off with a group of comedians that visited the capital in 1768; and Kate, who was at times rather impertinent, had previously run off with the master of a ship sailing for the West Indies. This time she was "lurking about some of the shores, in order to get off." The most interesting, sociable woman was Mary, 26 years old, whose plan for freedom did not affect her feelings as a mother. She ran away with her two children, "one a boy sucking at the breast named BILLY, the other a girl named LIDIA, about 9 years old, of a yellow complexion like the mother." Mary, "very sensible and artful," also "like[d] much to be in the company of white people," her owner reported, "and can go very well dressed, having carried a variety of clothes with her." She had been seen at Carter's Nomini Hall, but she was surely on her way to Norfolk "or some other maritime town," as "she likes much to be on board of vessels, and in the company of sailors." [52]

Only three native African women were included among the 142 advertised. The first notice was not placed until 1772, when the slave trade was rapidly drawing to a close. It described a "spare made" girl "of good Features," who did not speak English. She left with her husband; her owner wrote: "I imagine she is entirely governed by him." One African woman who did not run off with a man was a rather tall and poorly clothed woman who spoke "bad" English, and "was remarkable for talking to herself." She also had scars down both cheeks [country marks?] and one on an arm, "occasioned by a burn." [53]

The overall condition of this woman was exceptionally bad.[54] In general, with regard to problems of health, noticeable personality quirks, and a subjective evaluation of their cooperative relations with others, including members of their own families, fugitive black women were an even more superior group of slaves than the men. Descriptive terms that recurred in their notices—"genteel," "neat," and "bold"—convey a strong impression that these women were exceedingly clever, aggressively resourceful slaves.

WHY SLAVES RAN AWAY

Slaves as well as their masters provided information on their motives and activities as runaways. While masters were often misleading when they tried to portray a fugitive's character, they were sometimes remarkably well informed about his whereabouts; because by the time they advertised they had often received information from other slaves, townsmen, and officials who had dealt with the runaway.[55] Recognizing that this feedback made advertisements more effective, owners inserted it presumably intact along with their own knowledge into the runaway notices. The advertisements then in two ways convey an unusual impression of the slave's freedom and the planter's isolation:

first, this style of resistance forced the master to realize that the slave had a life of his own, which was scarcely apprehensible in their inter-personal encounters. Second, news of the runaway's adventures in distant and unfamiliar places further underscored the master's seclusion and limited authority. Knowing where a fugitive was in this extensive agricultural society, in which communications were so primitive, did not mean that he could be easily recaptured. To learn where the slave was, that he was participating in unheard of activities, and yet to be unable to recapture him, must have been a peculiarly frustrating experience for many a white: "He ran from his overseer about 18 months ago and has passed for a free man ever since"; "there is a wench at Mr. Thomas Husk's between the Rappahannock and Potomack rivers who calls herself free Milla, who may probably be the same [slave as advertised]"; "I advertised [Stepney Blue who ran off with a free Negro woman] some Time ago in this Paper, and have not been so fortunate as yet to get him but have been informed that he has been lately employed by some Gentlemen in Fredericksburg, as a Freeman." [56]

Fugitives had three significantly different objectives. First, many visited relatives and wives on other plantations. This represented little more than truancy. Since masters kept themselves well informed of their slaves' friends, relatives, wives, and lovers, they usually recaptured runaways who visited without much difficulty. Second, an equally large number of fugitives went to town to hire themselves out and pass as free men. Their position was often tenuous; they were still productive and only partially free in a slave society; and some were retaken. Yet a reasonably large number were successful, because for a variety of reasons the many whites who "harboured" them were willing to challenge the slave code at its weakest point. Third, a smaller number of slaves completely rejected slavery by boarding vessels and leaving the colony, or by running into the North Carolina piedmont, where most whites were non-slaveholding farmers, or into Pennsylvania after 1775, when slavery was gradually outlawed in the North.

Slaves who allegedly ran off because they were whipped, demoted, or "seduced" away, do not fall into these categories; but they do provide additional insights into the assimilated's self-view.

A very small number ran off because they were demoted or whipped. Only a few runaways had whip marks healed or fresh. It seems slaves

who resisted slavery as runaways were not likely to get themselves
into situations where they could be beaten. Ben left when his late
master's widow "used him ill," and when he was taken up he refused
to tell who she was or where she lived. Peter, a "sly, artful rogue if
not watched," had had several owners. His present master reported:
"He often told the other Negroes that if I ever used him ill he would
go to his old mistress. . . . [for] She never sold him . . . but only
lent him during [her] pleasure, and that he would go to her and be
protected." [57]

Because some fugitives were often more concerned with the conditions of their enslavement than with freedom itself, Peter's comment
to his master to treat him properly may not have been as capricious
as it seems. Two Caroline County mulattoes, bound to age 31, forced
premature manumission by repeatedly running off.[58] And Bob and
Duke also ran away, not to escape but to bargain with a recalcitrant
master, in this instance, John Tayloe's son, who explained his slaves'
action:

> I well know they have no cause to complain of ill treatment in any
> respect whatever, and am satisfied that the object of their going is to
> compel me to hire or sell them, as many applications have been
> made, I will do neither till they return to a sense of their duty. I
> have reason to suspect they are harboured and employed by some
> ill disposed persons.[59]

When Richard Randolph's valet, and right hand man in the house
for ten years, was sent to a distant quarter in Cumberland County, he
promptly ran off with another ex-servant. Their demotion was a recent development, because Randolph noted, "they may have some of
their old liveries." John Tayloe's Billy was another servant who lost
his household status when he became a full-grown man. He became a
stonemason and miller at the Neabsco Furnace, which seemed to have
a great deal of trouble with talented runaways. A sudden break in the
career of an emancipated black man, Sam, "who was reduced to slavery again," encouraged him to run away. He had lived in the frontier
county of Dunmore, where he purchased his freedom in the early
1770's, and in 1774 he joined Governor Dunmore's expedition against
the Ohio Valley Indians. Returning home, he attempted to "inveigle
away a number of negroes to the new or Indian country (where he had
been most of last summer)." While the colonial slave society was no-

Table Three:
Where Fugitives Went:
Slaveowners' Estimations of Their Runaways'
Motives and Destinations *

Acculturated Runaways

Destination	Number	Per cent
Visiting	100	15
To town, to pass as free, or to obtain employment	205	31
Out of the colony/state	121	18
Other destinations	5	1
Motive or destination not stated	238	35
Total acculturated	669	100

Unacculturated Runaways

Destination	Number	Per cent
Visiting	38	32
To town	10	8
Out of the colony/state	7	6
Other destinations	2	2
Motive or destination not stated	62	52
Total unacculturated	119	100

Degree of acculturation not indicated

Destination	Number	Per cent
Visiting	60	29
To town	18	9
Out of the colony/state	31	15
Other destinations	2	1
Motive or destination not stated	101	46
Total	212	100

* This tabulation does not include the 138 native African runaways.

Origin
Of the 1,138 slave men who were advertised as fugitives between 1736 and 1801, twelve per cent, 138, were Africans, 88 percent were American-born. Included in this group of 1,000 were 25 slaves from the West Indies, 200 mulattoes, and 147 described as "yellow"-complexioned.

Degree of Assimilation
Two-thirds, 669, of the American-born fugitives were comparatively assimilated; 119 were relatively unassimilated. Of the Africans, 25 of 138 were comparatively acculturated. As for the remaining 212 slaves, their descriptions were too brief to determine their understanding of colonial society.

toriously lax about enforcing codes for runaways, slaveowners quickly closed ranks against blacks who would settle runaways in a western preserve. When Sam was discovered, his neighbors insisted he be reduced to slavery again. He ran away a few months later.[60]

A few explanations for runaways were unique. A wagoner's master wrote that he could "assign no Reason for his [slave's] running away, but quarreling with his Wife." Tom's master reported: "[He is a] . . . simple fellow [and] I am persuaded he was enticed away by Sam." James Southall, a Williamsburg shopkeeper who became an important entrepreneur after the war, advertised a small Negro boy at his home, "abandoned by some Person unknown." [61]

Freedom was not the immediate objective of a third of the slaves advertised: these ran off to rejoin members of their families. The owners' understatements indicate a depth to slave family life—and the whites' tacit recognition of that life—that up till now has not been dealt with in interpretations of American Negro slavery. "His parents are free and live in Port-Royal"; "His Parents now belong to Francis Nelson"; "he is about Mr. Samuel Thomae's [sic] in Warwick county, where he has a father and grandmother"; or: "supposed to be harboured by Colonel John Snelson's Negroes . . . among whom he has a Wife, or by his Brother, John Kenny, a Mulatto Slave belonging to Mr. Thomas Johnson of Louisa." [62]

Jobs
359 of all American-born slaves, or 35 per cent, were skilled or semi-skilled; a remarkable 19 of 25, or 78 per cent, of the West Indians; and 16 Africans were skilled, or 12 per cent.

The Argument
Assimilated slaves, those not as bound to the communal setting of the plantation, would tend to run away from the plantation, toward towns, to pass as free men, to get jobs, or leave the colony; unassimilated slaves would tend to stay within the plantation context, visiting relatives, or "lurking" about their own and other plantations.

Conclusions
The data supported the argument. Over half of the assimilated fugitives went either to town or out of the colony, while only one-seventh of the unassimilated slaves did. On the other hand, a third of the unassimilated runaways visited, while only one sixth of the assimilateds did so. Those slaves whose masters gave no indication of their level of assimilation behaved much like the unassimilated runaways, with the exception that a much higher proportion, one fourth, went to towns or out of the colony. It was also evident that masters knew their assimilated slaves better than they knew the others. While they had an idea where 7 in 10 assimilateds might be going, they only guessed at about half of the unassimilateds' destinations. All of the results were based on percentages since the assimilateds, of whom there were 669 as compared to 119 unassimilateds, were numerically predominant in every category.

Sometimes advertisers only made implicit reference to their runaway's tragically fragmented family life. Curry Tuxent, a mulatto, left the Eastern Shore and crossed the Bay to the lower James River area in pursuit of "a parcel of Negroes lately purchased by Sir Peyton Skipworth from the Estate of Robert Bristow, Esq." But others were more directly informative. The children of "Negro Tony" and "wench Phillis" were widely scattered. Before he ran off, Tony had belonged to two owners, Captain William Payne of Lancaster County and Thomas Chilton of Culpeper. He met his wife Phillis who, we are told, was also born in Lancaster County, and later belonged to Chilton. Here they raised a family whose members were soon "sold and dispersed through Culpeper, Frederick, and Augusta counties." "If they are not in Lancaster," their master concluded, "I suspect that they are in . . . [Augusta], as the fellow always expressed an uncommon desire to return there." Three slaves, two men and a woman, reputedly had several partners, of whom their masters were surprisingly well-informed. One man was "supported and concealed" in Prince George County "by several Negro Women whom he calls his Wives, his greatest Favourite amongst them belongs to Mr. *Robert Bates.*" Cambridge, a waterman who previously had three owners, ran away from the schooner *Sharpe,* "is so well known," his master wrote, "[he needs] no other description, as he has a Wife at almost every landing on *Rappahannock, Mattapony,* and *Pamunkey* Rivers." His owner dutifully listed his waterman's three previous owners and said "I beg all who have settled on the above rivers to have their negro quarters searched for him."

Masters revealed themselves while commenting on their slaves' personal lives. William Black advertised for an African blacksmith whom he allowed to visit his wife sometimes for a month. Molly's master mentioned that his servant, a neat, healthy, and industrious "wench," had been hired-out "for some years" in Fredericksburg. Her husband lived there and when she was returned home, obviously against her will, she ran off. Her owner was astonished: "She was never known to misbehave or run away until removed from there." [63]

The fugitive's determination to maintain a semblance of family life was partially responsible for North Carolina's reputation as a haven for fugitives. Since Virginians, black and white, played a leading role in populating the colony during the middle decades of the eighteenth century, it was perhaps inevitable that slave families would be broken up, thus providing an additional incentive for some to run south. The colony also attracted an exceptionally skilled group of slaves who were as interested in working in a less restrictive environment as they were to rejoin members of their families.

In addition to the evidence in official records, slaveowners indicated on thirty-six occasions before 1775 that their slaves were bound for North Carolina, while the number of slaves fleeing toward the frontier, Maryland, or Pennsylvania during the same period was six. Royal governors, beginning with Sir Francis Nicholson in 1691, made "almost constant complaint" to their counterparts in North Carolina; and in 1715 that colony responded with a law providing a fine for "entertaining" fugitives: "10 shillings per day to the master, together with all costs of returning the servant." [64] But runaway codes were generally unsuccessful throughout the century, and this one was no exception. North Carolina's ability to absorb and to "lose" slaves for long periods of time is illustrated in the experiences of two fugitives, Bob and Billy.

John Tayloe's Billy, who was 30 and played the violin, ran off to North Carolina in 1768, where he "travelled without much interruption" with a pass given him by "some good natured person." This slave's craftsmanship undoubtedly aided his ruse. The colony's basic industry was forest products, and he was a ship's-carpenter.[65] Bob, an exceptionally talented man, left William Trebell's plantation near Williamsburg on a Saturday night in April 1767. His master's notice mentioned that he had previously run away and was absent for three years. Before he was recaptured in Hertford County, North Carolina, he had lived with a small inland farmer, one Van Pelt, on the Chinkopin River. Bob, who had passed as a free man, "Edmund Tomar," could read, write, and he "pretended" to make shoes; he was a sawyer, carpenter, currier, and a "very good sailor." Trebell made a casual reference to an even earlier absence of eight years' duration(!) when the runaway had evidently used his skill as a seaman, and had either been hired out or illegally passed as free in Charleston, South Carolina. Literate, skilled, and in so many ways a more experienced and well-traveled man than most white Virginians, this fugitive's services must have seemed an irresistible temptation to a subsistence farmer like Van Pelt. One strong indication that "Edmund Tomar" and Van Pelt had an "understanding" which was mutually beneficial was that Bob's master said the slave's new wife also lived on the Chinkopin River.[66]

Many free people in North Carolina seemed willing to use someone else's slave with few questions asked. Instead of viewing runaways as felons, many whites, for a variety of reasons, sought to employ them. The colony was also readily accessible to fugitives, who consistently used the entire southside area east of the piedmont as an escape route south. This vast and relatively uninhabited region, clogged with muddy creeks and rivers, provided a welcome cover for slaves hurrying out of the populous tidewater. Here a runaway could travel by day as well as by night as he fled toward eventual freedom and employment in North Carolina. Fugitives ran down the banks of the great inland rivers, the Staunton, Blackwater, and Nottoway, to the Roanoke and Meherrin-Chowan rivers and thus into the eastern piedmont counties of Bute and Halifax.

The economic and social condition in North Carolina was very different from that in the rich and cultured tidewater area of Virginia, resembling the less-developed piedmont far more in its basic character.[67] Families with few slaves predominated, even in the most prosperous region around the Albemarle Sound; and non-slaveholding farmers abounded in the inland area which attracted most Virginia fugitives. The economy, based on the production of such forest commodities as shingles, barrel staves, tar, pitch, and turpentine, was impeded by a shortage of skilled and semi-skilled laborers even more severe than in Virginia. For three-quarters of the eighteenth century highly skilled fugitives, including carters, ship's-carpenters, sawyers, gardeners, a millwright, a waitingman, and a blacksmith, followed Billy and Bob to North Carolina.[68]

Whites Who "Entertained" Blacks

In Virginia, hiring fugitives was also highly prevalent and a significant demonstration of the whites' confidence in the security of their slave society, and in the open, ill-defined nature of slavery itself in the last decades of the eighteenth century.

Nearly every other runaway notice warned "ill-disposed" whites about "harbouring" fugitives. But many Virginians, probably even those who felt slavery was morally wrong, employed runaways (perhaps as a subversive as well as lucrative form of protest), satisfying their self-interest as well as their moral scruples. "I do declare," wrote one advertiser, "if any Person entertains the said Slave that I will prosecute them with the utmost Severity, unless they immediately deliver him up." [69] Another advertisement read: "N.B. Any persons harbouring or dealing any manner with the above mentioned negro [a shoemaker also 'very ingenious in woodwork of any kind'] will be prosecuted to the extent of the law; more particularly those who have been guilty of the same heretofore." [70] The merchant John Aylett purchased a cook, Rachel, from the estate of the horse breeder, Littlebury Hardiman. He waited three months for her delivery and then published the following: ". . . since which I have not seen her. . . . I am determined not to dispose of her, and will sue any person who entertains her." [71] John Mercer had a similar problem with Joe, a coachman, purchased in January, who had run off three times by September. Mercer was understandably exasperated and suspicious: "I have great Reason to believe that he is privately encouraged to run away, and then harboured and concealed, that I may be induced to sell him." [72] Mercer's suspicions were well founded; with each of Joe's departures several offers to purchase the slave were made by Mercer's neighbors. [73]

A fugitive's skill increased the probability that he could hire himself out as a free man with few questions asked. An advertisement for two runaways, "excellent harvesters and watermen," read: "I hereby forewarn all masters of vessels, and other persons from hiring them, either of them." Overseers were also cautioned: "both will attempt to hire themselves in time of Harvest as free men, they being both good Cradlers, and will probably work . . . to get cash to carry on their rascality." Bob's master put the matter directly: "he is a very good blacksmith, and as supposed, is harboured by some white man of that trade." [74]

Some whites openly aided fugitive slaves. Will, another slave who traveled to North Carolina, using a pass "signed by a white man," "made a pact" with an Irishman, "who talks big and loud, and is of a mean character." After "some Dealings" between Will and the Irish servant and his family, they all crossed into North Carolina at Jefferson's Ferry on the Roanoke River in August 1771. "No doubt," the slave's master warned, ". . . [they] will endeavour to make him pass for a Freeman." [75]

This particular tactic was used by the underground railroad fifty years later: whites—who were sometimes fugitives too—posed as gentlemen waited on by the black runaway. Margaret Grant, a mulatto, an "artful hussy" who could read and write, ran off with an English convict-servant, John Chambers. She disguised herself in a suit of men's clothing and "attended" him as a waiting boy.[76]

Instances of slaves and free men running off together or cooperating in crimes were not infrequent. At least four men ran off and joined white women, three of whom were identified: Anne Ashwell, a prostitute; Elizabeth Beaver; and Mary Marshall, an Irish servant.[77]

Some whites allegedly carried off slaves. For many reasons, slave-owners preferred to see others as principally responsible for their slaves' desire to be free. Consider the reasoning behind the following advertisements: William Graves's for Jamie and Toby, both 15, read: "I am apt to believe they were stolen away, as they have never been heard of since their elopement"; Tom's master mentioned that his slave was on an errand and had not "since been heard of. . . . It is supposed the said Negro Boy, is decoy'd away"; Daniel's owner was even more explicit: "It is suppos'd that he hath been seduced and carried away by Some of the Back Inhabitants travelling that Way." [78]

Ship captains and white watermen were the worst offenders against the fugitive slave code; they made a practice of dealing with runaways. Once the slave was aboard, his bargaining power was negligible, but the captain's alternatives were attractive. He could make the fugitive a crewman, a subterfuge that would allay the fears of both officials and fugitive; and, if the latter became uncooperative, the captain could sell him in a port-of-call.

Some of the most interesting slave men and women made use of white watermen. Abel, for example, who was 40, a mulatto, and scarred in the face with a brick thrown by another Negro, was an "excellent and well-known pilot" on the York River and the Bay. He played the violin, and he had traveled to England where he had learned to drink. Since his return, his master noted, Abel had become "very fond" both of liquor and writing forged passes. Twice whipped for "this bad Behavior," his wounds were still fresh when he ran off. Although Abel was also described as "a very great Rogue," "several people living on Wormeley's Creek, York River," disagreed: they said that Samuel Meredith, a Northern Neck gentleman, "was not worthy to be his Master." The slave was last seen with a white lad in a two-masted schooner, sixty leagues south of Cape Henry.[79] Frederick McFarlan, another mulatto, left his Stafford County quarter on the Potomac River, crossed the peninsula through King and

Queen County, to the town of Port Royal on the Rappahannock. Here he applied for a job to the skipper of a sloop. But this man, "being apprehensive he might not be free," refused to employ him. McFarlan was patient, and the skipper, as usual, did not report him to the officials, although he eventually wrote McFarlan's master to say that "a few days afterwards" he saw the slave board a vessel, which was loading salt at Falmouth and was bound for Nansemond County in the southside. Frank, a mulatto, was suspected of "sculking about" Indiantown on the lower Pamunkey River where his wife lived. He had twice run away and his master wrote, "had always got aboard some vessel or other and worked as a freeman." [80] The account of Edward Ker's mulatto, Isaac, who was taken aboard by a New England ship captain, Lynde Valentine, is especially informative. "By an Extract from the Customhouse Books," Ker discovered that Valentine was the master and owner of the sloop *Sally* which was built in Massachusetts in 1767, registered in Rhode Island, May 19, 1767, and cleared Port Accomac, May 9, 1772, for Antigua. Ker was convinced that his slave was aboard and that the captain would "make for some *Dutch* or *Danish* Port, particularly *Santa Croix,* and there offer the Negro for Sale." [81] Peg, 16 and a likely mulatto, lived at Brooke's Bank in Essex County: when "taxed for committing any fault . . . appear[ed] to be greatly surprized, and . . . [was] apt to cry." "She was born where I live," her master wrote after she ran off, "and never was 5 miles from home." Peg had hailed a ship one day from the Banks of the Rappahannock. Her master could not believe that she ran off on her own; he argued this point in his newspaper advertisement. "I am inclined to believe she was prevailed on to go off, as she went away without the least provocation, and never was guilty of the like before." His monologue continued:

> The same evening she went away she was seen to go on board a sloop at *Layton*'s warehouses; when she hailed the sloop, she told the skipper, who was a white man, that her name was *Dinah,* and that she wanted to go to *Norfolk,* or to be set ashore on the other side of the river: The skipper sent his flat and two negroes and carried her on board, about sun-set. This information I had from the sailors on board captain *Martin's* ship, who saw all that passed.[82]

In the 1790's the conviction that slaves were incapable of enjoying freedom or even understanding what it was like took root after a decade of the amelioration of slavery. As southern abolitionism died out, the notion that slaves could not be free became widespread. So did its corollary, that slaves who ran away were activated by the ever-present "ill-disposed person" or some other outsider. This change too was seen in a fanciful blockprint that appeared (to replace the familiar figure of a slave hurrying down a road with a knapsack tossed over his shoulder) : a picture of a demon with a trident hovering above a slave toiling dutifully in the field, the demon filling the slave's head with "unnatural" thoughts of freedom.[83]

ON THE ROAD AND IN TOWN

Once on their own and under way, fugitives often used tactics which were aided immeasurably by their expert and facile command of English and by their "smooth-tongued" guile, and which were as amusing as they were successful. In response to an inquisitive white a favorite technique was to feign "passing the roads in publick, on pretence of being about business," pretending to be searching for some of master's horses, or, "pretend[ing] to belong to some person with . . . wagons" returning from Maryland. A variation of this ruse often occurred in town : John Hatley Norton's Mingo, reported to be in the port town of Hampton, "pretended he was sent down to wait on a Gentleman." [84]

At least two masters refused to be taken in by their fugitive's cunning. Joe, an "artful chap" hired out to a Richmond resident, ran off and "caused a report to be circulated" that he had been seen in Philadelphia, when in fact he was running in the opposite direction. William Dandridge, his master, realized that since Joe had lived for several years in the capital, he would probably be hidden there by his many acquaintances; if not there, he would be "secreted" about Weir Creek in New Kent County. In 1768 Louis Burwell's Jack Ash feigned a suicide; but Burwell was unconvinced by the "evidence," which included Jack's clothing, left "near the Waterside, I suppose to prevent any Inquiry," Burwell wrote, "as he might think I should suspect he had drowned himself." Ash survived this adventure and ran away again in 1805 at the age of 50, when he was given leave to visit his wife and failed to return.[85]

The pace of some runaways was quite leisurely. Inquisitive whites

—if they bothered at all—were seldom a problem. Frederick, a jockey who stuttered when frightened, left his master's home in Surry County and three days later stopped at Mr. Andrew Mackie's in Isle of Wight. When he was stopped and questioned, the poised 16-year-old said he belonged to one Mr. Adam Fleming of Norfolk and had been sent "express" to Cabin Point, but, unfortunately, he had since lost his horse. Mackie "gave him an open line to pass." Bob, a tall mulatto ferryman, and Bristol, an African, "as ignorant as the other is artful," also used the southside as an escape route. They left Swan's Point in early April 1774 and three weeks later arrived in Williamsburg, one of the most popular destinations for fugitives. Taken up and examined by John Hartwell Cocke (soon after elected to the Surry County Committee of Safety), Bob convinced the official that he and Bristol were on legitimate business. Bob was the same ferryman who had "assumed an immoderate Stock of Assurance" from his "acquaintance with Gentlemen"—like Cocke. The latter, "indulged by the Plausibility of their Story," not only set them free, but gave them a pass dated the day they were questioned.[86]

Passes were seldom an obstacle for fugitives. Free people who were inclined to stop and check them were either put off by a forgery or by the slave's guile. John, a large, stout man, left Caroline County bound for Baltimore or Philadelphia, and crossed the Rappahannock River at Fredericksburg. The ferryman, mildly suspicious, or perhaps simply making conversation, asked John where he was going. That the fugitive's response did not elicit an immediate request for his pass is amazing in view of his reply that "he had hired his time [which was illegal] for the year and was going to the Federal City to seek Employment." The ferryman later reported to the runaway's owner, John Minor, who was opposed to slavery, that the slave "had a paper in his hat which he supposed to be his pass." Many slaves evidently knew which white men, especially among watermen and officials, were lenient enough or sufficiently gullible to let them pass as free. If a fugitive was audacious, the possibility was excellent that he would be given "an open line to pass," and an opportunity "to travel without much interruption."[87]

Most fugitives, such as John Minor's John, sought liberty of a special variety: freedom in an urban setting which allowed them to hide in a town's slave community, obtain work, practice a skill, and generally act like free men. Some slaveowners were not totally unaware of these desires; approximately one in three advertisers mentioned that their runaways were bound for a port to obtain either work or passage out of the colony. Fugitive artisans, then, usually ran from their home plantations to the major navigable rivers, turned east and south, and proceeded, usually by foot, sometimes by boat or horseback, "down-country" into the tidewater. Throughout the century their goal was either the capital, a port, such as Dumfries, Urbanna, York-town, or Norfolk, or a town at the head of navigation, such as Fredericksburg or Richmond.

No other town proved to be more hospitable than Williamsburg, where mobile slaves used their connections.[88] Daniel, a waitingman, was protected for ten days in the capital before he was seen leaving College Landing, bound for Portsmouth in a craft "conducted by negroes." Another fugitive, taken up in the town, escaped again within a few hours of his return, but before he left he told his master that he had "dealt very freely in Williamsburg in the oyster and fish way— in their seasons." This slaveowner's advertisement was typical: he asked "the favor of all that deal in that way with Negroes, to observe the above description, and detect the villain if possible." Joseph Scrivener, a dealer in West Indian, Spanish, and Portuguese goods, wrote from his shop on Duke of Gloucester Street that his mulatto carter was "either lurking in this town, or about the Capitol landing where he was bred." [89]

Fugitive women found Williamsburg to be even more hospitable. In the 1770's nearly one woman in six advertised as a runaway was suspected of being "entertained" in one way or another in the capital city. Like the men, they were evidently harboured within the Negro quarters on Queen's Creek or out on College Landing Road. But the more daring women remained in town. Jenny, a whip scar on her cheek, 23 years old and from Green Spring, was the second woman reported to be "dressed in the habit of a man." In Williamsburg, she had lived on occasion with a blacksmith, but most recently, and "for some time," with a Mr. Robert Ryland. Her owner's threat was the usual: he was "determined to prosecute any person whatever who shall harbour or entertain her." Venus, 17 and remarkably strong, hid out "in the kitchens and quarters about the city"; and Nanny was secreted at the very source for ensuring the swift apprehension of fugitives, the newspaper press. She was seen with her husband who worked for John Dixon and James Hunter, editors of the *Gazette*.[90]

Fugitives used towns of any size, especially those on navigable water. Slaveowners took this for granted: "Pretty saucy" Sarah was reported "in the neighbourhood of *Blandsford* or *Petersburg,* as there are runaways always thereabouts." Jacob, a mulatto waterman passing as "Reuban Anderson," returned to his master who lived in Richmond and boasted to "the people" that he had readily passed as a freeman "about *Richmond, Newscastle,* and *Fredericksburg."* Pedro, a waitingman of good address who had belonged to Patrick Henry, had also lived in Richmond some years and was reported as a runaway near that city, "as he is well acquainted with most of the negroes of that place." A shoemaker hired out to a resident of Hanovertown also boldly made his living "trading with a small cart" in Richmond or Yorktown. Even a small frontier town like Halifax had an enclave of free blacks who aided slaves as fugitives and later as insurrectionists. In 1767 Benjamin Harrison wrote that Aaron was "entertained by some free mulattoes near Halifax town." [91]

The underground communities of free and quasi-free blacks in Petersburg, Richmond, and Williamsburg were nearly as useful to the fugitives as the white townsmen, artisans, and watermen. Town blacks effectively dispensed food, shelter, jobs, and information. Ben, for example, left his master at the Campbell County courthouse and ran to Petersburg where he hired himself to an enterprising free mulatto, one Curties, who ran a boat service between that city and the new capital at Richmond. On board, Ben was known as "John Cussens" and worked for another free mulatto, Captain Dikes. Sam, a mulatto sailor, ran off in 1771 after distributing stolen broadcloth to his crew "in order to bribe them to Secrecy." On Christmas day in Norfolk he told an inquisitive white that he was part of a crew lately wrecked on the sea coast nearby. With such a story, his master warned, "some Person in Want of Hands might be induced to engage him." There is a remarkable similarity between this story and John Emanuel's, a sailor who passed for a number of years as a freeman in Norfolk. While accompanied by "a little Negro," Jack Cawn, "Son of one Fanny Cawn, now living in Norfolk," he was eventually committed up the James River in Chesterfield County in August 1774. "He says he was brought into this Colony by a Spanish Vessel," his jailer wrote, "which was cast away on our Bay . . . that they were taken from the Wreck and carried into Norfolk." [92]

Many runaways were successful for a considerable period of time, and some passed as free even though their real status must have been obvious to their white neighbors. Dick, a mulatto carpenter from Amelia County, ran off to Portsmouth in May 1774, where he was employed by several different persons. Captured in Norfolk he was brought up the James River to Charles City County, but he escaped and returned to the coast. In the summer of 1775 he enlisted as a soldier, "Will Thompson," in the Princess Anne County militia; but when his company came to the capital, he was again discovered and re-taken. He soon broke out of the public jail—in order to return to a crop of corn he had left in Princess Anne. Or, his jailer wrote, "the runaway may board a ship and leave the colony." [93]

Some fugitives exceeded this man's record by several years. That they could have done so without the open cooperation of the white community is simply impossible. Jude, a bowlegged carpenter and waterman who passed for seven or eight years in and about Hobb's Hole (Tappahannock), confessed when he was finally taken up, that he had a master; but was soon reprieved by a man from whom he promptly fled. Another slave from Isle of Wight also passed several years in Essex County as a freeman; and a South Carolina fugitive, a mulatto named Louis Patterson, who spoke French but only "broken English," lived in King and Queen County for twelve years! [94]

In the last quarter of the century, the free community was so un-concerned about fugitives that even a few plainly "outlandish" Africans successfully passed as freemen. James, a small, black waterman, could not speak English plainly, yet he evidently had no difficulty obtaining a job and remaining on his own, even though his master knew ap-proximately where he was. "He was lately employed on an Oyster Boat on *James* River near [Bermuda] *Hundred,*" his master wrote. Another African whose ancestry was verifiable because his ears were bored for earrings and his English was poor, was sufficiently re-sourceful to pass as a free Negro for several months before he was jailed.[95]

Post-war economic and demographic developments increased the rate of acculturation among all slaves. Among runaway Africans who reflected this change was Bacchus, 19, who equated freedom with England, not Africa. His master reported that he and a 27-year-old black woman were on their way to Great Britain. And Prince, a waitingman six feet tall, stout, full-eyed, who "talked fast" was "well acquainted with most of America." "I expect," his master continued, "he will endeavour to get to Howe's army, and he has once attempted to join Dunmore." [96]

After acquiring a strikingly altered perception of slavery, the goals of the acculturated African fugitives were virtually identical to those of the American-born slaves. They too ran off alone and into the most heavily settled, commercial areas of the tidewater region. The few Africans who reached this level of acculturation were usually well-traveled men like Prince who could now, in interpersonal situations, play the word and role games which so many American-born slaves were known for. Ayre, slim and light-complexioned, who spoke with a remarkable twist of his mouth, was described in this way: "although an Affrican, he affects to pronounce English very fine, or rather to clip it." This man could also read and write, so his master warned "it is more than presumable he may have forged a pass," and he will probably travel "where he pleases as a free man." [97]

The experiences of these Africans were as much a commentary on the openness of colonial slave society, as they were on the African's ability to remain intact as a person and cope with slavery, while his heritage eroded away.

Given the picture of these bold and imaginative fugitives, hiring on as free sailors and watermen, living with black and white townsmen, and trading from their small carts "in the oyster and fish way," the following conclusion is inescapable: while whites repeatedly passed stringent laws against fugitives—and just as readily ignored them—they did not consider this particular breech of security a very serious one. Evidently they did not believe that assimilateds would endanger them in any meaningful way. This was the situation on the eve of Governor Dunmore's Proclamation and Gabriel's Rebellion.

The personal significance of the assimilated's routine, which has not been adequately explored up to now, may be an important criteria for re-assessing the usefulness of the Tannenbaum-Elkins thesis: that the presence of such institutions in Latin America as Roman law and the Catholic Church made slavery milder and emancipation and integration less violent and tragic experiences than in our own country.[98] Unlike the Catholic societies of Latin America, craftsmanship in Protestant Virginia was a highly esteemed calling to which few whites and many American-born blacks responded. Moreover, while Latin American slave artisans often operated from large urban enclaves of blacks (e.g. Cuba) that sheltered old ways and impeded cultural change, the artisan's task in eighteenth-century Virginia separated him from the bulk of slaves, the plantation norms, and even his master's values. Until the very end of the century his job, to a degree, made slavery tolerable; but in Latin America skilled, urban slaves were often leaders in insurrections that were much larger and more numerous than in our own slave society. For the artisan in Virginia who, when he resisted, was typically a fugitive but not an insurrectionist, his job was truly a world of work in the meaning the sociologist Robert Blauner used when he described the inclusive nature of the free industrial worker's routine: "the nature of a man's work affects his social character and personality, the manner in which he participates or fails to participate as a citizen in the larger community, and his over-all sense of worth and dignity." [99]

In comparing slavery in the Americas at this more manageable level—that is, a study of one slave type, the artisan, and one problem, the relationship between cultural change and slave behavior—the question is not so much why slaves here lost their heritage so much more readily, but why their acculturation, like many other processes of colonial settlement and growth in North America, progressed so much more rapidly than in Latin America. Our colonial societies, unlike the feudal regimes of New France and New Spain, consistently rewarded adaptability, achievement, and change (values intrinsic to the Virginia artisan's world) while in many ways punishing typically African characteristics. In the North American plantation societies assimilated slaves were among the chief beneficiaries of the English colonist's cultural chauvinism: they responded to language and occupational training and used this learning to make slavery more manageable.

But the assimilated's status was also a source of pain. To what extent his speech defects and aggressive behavior when drunk were manifestations of his separateness and alienation from his own people and from himself (as well as being symptoms of his fear and hatred of whites) is a question brilliantly illuminated by George Memmi and Frantz Fanon.[100] They see the assimilated properly: in the context of the "contact situation" between the rulers and the ruled, between the colonists and the mother-country, between the folk of technologically simpler village society and the armed citizens of European industrial society. In this context the assimilated is essentially a marginal man:

striving to emulate his oppressors' ways, because he craves their respect and approval, he ultimately is forced to understand that he has been tossed a bone or two—while denying his own customs, his people, and finally himself.

In order to expand our understanding of slave behavior it would be very profitable for future historians to see slavery also as a contact situation, and some slaves as marginal or transitional types. But the view of the assimilated set forth by Memmi and Fanon is of limited value when applied to the artisans of late eighteenth-century Virginia. At this point in the history of the black man in North America—although the issue is principally one of emphasis—the positive features of assimilation far outweighed the negative ones. The planters, who based their way of life on slaves who acculturated and became occupationally specialized, gave to these slaves real privileges and responsibilities that significantly changed the psychological implications of slavery. Even though artisans sometimes exhibited manifestations of profound anxiety when speaking or drinking, they were certainly not immobilized by self-hate, a central feature of the Memmi-Fanon concept of cultural marginality. The ease with which they set aside the slave role once on their own as fugitives, the resilient, imaginative way they coped with whites—conning watermen and officials into giving them passage or an "open line to pass"—is testimony to the way their routines shielded their humanity.[101]

But the assimilateds were loners. Their predisposition to act on their own as fugitives was a most fortunate one—settlements of runaways never succeeded in eighteenth-century Virginia. But when this elite group tried to organize a large-scale resistance in 1800, their separateness resulted in a tragic debacle. Before examining Gabriel's Rebellion, it is necessary to deal with the complex changes responsible for the artisans' new outlook: that slavery should be resisted collectively.

4
War, Economic Change, and Slavery

Throughout the eighteenth century slave rebelliousness was usually sporadic and solitary, and the Virginia slave society was permissive and open. Before the Revolution, whites, confident of their ability to control most types of rebellion, viewed only the occasional outlaw as an exceptionally dangerous slave.

Two unprecedented events, Governor Dunmore's Emancipation Proclamation, November 1775, and Gabriel's insurrection, September 1800, changed this attitude by introducing to whites the possibility of organized rebellion by armed Negroes. Dunmore's Proclamation accomplished little for either the British or the slaves. Blacks fought under white officers in an army that was critically undermanned and poorly supported by the home government. The royal governor's "Black Regiment," little more than a group of fugitives temporarily welded together to perform a desperate holding action, was largely a creation of the planters' imagination and their newspaper press.

In dealing with this minor aspect of the Revolution in Virginia, it is more profitable to ask why slaves did not see the British invasion as an opportunity to escape or rise up. In effect, the war and the Proclamation itself were premature. The first widespread, large-scale slave insurrection in Southern history waited for conditions, latent in 1775 but manifest at the turn of the century, which perceptibly altered the lives, values, and expectations of so many slaves and whites.

A SOCIETY "ILL AT EASE"

Virginia society in 1800 was "ill at ease," wrote Henry Adams in his history of the administrations of Presidents Jefferson and Madison.

Fundamental demographic, economic, and religious developments in the state in the last quarter of the century lent substance to Adams' insight.[1]

Economic developments were the most obvious indices of change.[2] From mid-century, as we have seen, the colony's agrarian order was in serious difficulty. Many planters, determined to free themselves from debt and a slavish dependency on British manufactures, turned to the production of wheat, hemp, flax, cotton, and diversification through home industries. Their slaves who became occupationally specialized were the basis for these changes in the pace and direction of the economy. Slaves also came off the plantation to work in nascent textile, ship, salt, rope, and furnaceworks that were stimulated by the non-importation agreements of the late 1760's.[3] In the tidewater, once the wealthiest region with the largest slave population, the war years intensified an economic crisis under way since the 1750's.[4]

British depredations in 1775, 1777, and 1781 in this region completed a despoliation begun earlier by soil exhaustion, poor husbandry, and wasteful, indifferent cultivation by slaves. The removal of the seat of government to Richmond in 1780, following the tide of emigration and economic opportunity to the north and west, postponed the revival of Williamsburg until the establishment in this century of the Rockefeller-endowed Colonial Williamsburg Restoration Project. But the area has never recovered its past glory. The spectacle in the post-war capital was disillusioning: Carter Braxton wrote to a friend who was returning there after a long absence, "you would wish yourself away again. Your city deserted & declining, every old Family showing the greatest want & distress—The War had its evils but they were trifling to those we feel now." "Now" was 1784.[5]

The 1780's brought further indications of economic reorientation: prices inflated, currency depreciated greatly, and trade with England was re-established with few of the benefits enjoyed before independence. Although signs of the decay and failure of familiar but outmoded vocations were more pronounced than indications of revitalization, the new wartime industries were sources of future economic health and vigor; and the sharp post-war depression was brief and did not affect all sectors of the economy.

Signs of economic growth and transition were most noticeable in the Northern Neck. Spared the ravages of war, this region became the most dynamic section of the state, and attracted the investment interests of Robert Morris, the Philadelphia businessman and "Financier of the Revolution." [6] Munitions and artillery works in Fredericksburg and Alexandria, for example, continued to expand following the peace treaty. Winchester at the bottom of the valley, Alexandria at the falls of the Potomac, and Baltimore became an export center for the Potomac River valley, one of the world's leading wheat-producing areas. Cattle raising, fruit production, experiments in soil conservation, and novel crop techniques were now pursued more systematically. In the midst of this subregional economic resurgence were two of colonial America's wealthiest planter-businessmen, George Washington and Robert "Councillor" Carter. Advanced methods of farming, which included crop-rotation, the replenishment of the soil with marl and manure, and agricultural diversification, had been in practice at Mount Vernon and Nomini Hall for at least a quarter of a century.[7]

Demographic and cultural changes complemented these economic developments. Migrations in and out of the state, the end of the African slave trade, and a great increase in the number of urban freedmen accelerated acculturation of all slaves, altered the pattern of slave ownership, and the proportion of native Africans and "new Negroes" to assimilated American-born slaves.

By the late eighteenth century the heaviest concentration of slaves was no longer in the oldest areas of settlement. By the time of the Federal Constitutional Convention in 1787, slaves were concentrated in a "black belt," running through new, expanding commercial areas like Richmond, and encompassing piedmont and tidewater counties lying below and along the fall-line. While slavery was practically nonexistent in frontier counties, slaves represented slightly more than 50 per cent of the population in the piedmont counties of King George, Spotsylvania, Louisa, Goochland, Cumberland, Amelia, Nottoway, and Brunswick, and 60 per cent of the population in all the tidewater counties on the Rappahannock River south to the James. But the once wealthy and influential counties of Middlesex, James City, and Charles City suffered a decline in slave population which corresponded to this older area's diminished economic potential.[8]

Convinced that these demographic and economic developments indicated a worsening situation, many Virginians emigrated to the territories of Kentucky and Tennessee. The tobacco they cultivated in the upper South soon came to rival amounts produced in the "Virginia District" (southside, the southwestern piedmont, and the inland areas of northeastern North Carolina), the only region of extensive tobacco production in the new state following the war.[9]

The path of westward emigration was crossed by a southward, inland immigration of farmers, many of whom were lately of Europe, familiar with general farming techniques, and mildly opposed to slavery. Beginning in the 1740's, interrupted temporarily by the Revolution in 1776 and the War of 1812, and increasing in volume well into the nineteenth century, these settlers poured out of Maryland and Pennsylvania, down both sides of the Blue Ridge Mountains and into Virginia. The backcountry settlers, who demanded land, navigational projects, and political representation, more than offset the large numbers leaving the state; from 1775 to 1800 the population increased from about 500,000 to 886,149.[10]

Carried on flats or walking in coffles, black men initially accompanied their "families" on these migratory treks. Later they made up the embryonic interstate slave trade. The introduction of the Whitney cotton gin and the extensive use of long-staple or sea-island cotton seed soon turned this stream of manpower into a veritable floodtide; and by the first decade of the nineteenth century, slave raising and interstate slave trading became a business in many areas of Virginia and North Carolina.[11]

A presumably less tragic fate awaited slaves and freedmen who remained in Virginia. If a barometer of the relations between races in slave societies is provided by views of manumission (a process which reflects a people's belief in its ability to absorb ex-castes into its ranks), the last quarter of the eighteenth century may well have been one of the most relaxed and tolerant periods in race relations in Virginia before the emancipation. In the decade following the 1782 act, facilitating individual manumission without recourse to legislative enactment, more than 10,000 slaves were freed. Virginians, who never again demonstrated a receptiveness to freedmen as on this occasion, also made significant attempts to ameliorate the slaves' condition. It was probably not merely a coincidence that these changes came at the same time when most native Africans were aging or sufficiently acculturated to off-set a cultural chauvinism on their masters' part which had been sharpened by the revolutionary struggle with England.[12]

Paradoxically, while whites were easing the transition from slave to free status, they sought to further restrict those who remained in bondage. In 1795 the slave code, for the fourth time in the century, was revised to stringently regulate ship captains who harboured runaways, hiring-out procedures, and slaves who met for religious services. In Richmond, where a few years later the apathy of the free community toward the slave code nearly resulted in a major disaster, the mayor insisted that the new laws be published. "With the hope," he wrote, "to check many evils and abuses practiced in this City." [13] As usual the statutes were soon violated with impugnity by whites and blacks alike. Consequently, the insurrectionist, Gabriel Prosser, and his lieutenants made extensive use of rivers and watermen, bogus passes, whites who sold them supplies, and religious revivals in order to plan the wholesale destruction of the new capital city.

The whites' disregard for even the most essential security precautions was a dangerously outmoded custom, because with the passing of the steady importations of Africans, the slave population came to be made up of mostly American-born slaves. In the final decade of the century twice as many blacks as whites, or nearly 50,000, were added to the population. After 1775 the traditional work settings for both Africans and American-born also changed, although it is not possible to say precisely to what extent. For the Africans, the isolated up-country quarter was no longer such a characteristic feature of the agricultural life because of the decline of the tobacco market, the despoliation of the tidewater, and the switch to wheat and general farming north of the James River in both the tidewater and piedmont. (Many large planters such as "Councillor" Carter broke up their quarters and leased them to tenants; and in the Northern Neck tenantry actually increased after the war.) For the American-born skilled slaves, the new agricultural practices and the industries developed during the war combined to offer them more opportunities as hired slaves in commercial areas.

Another indication that customary ways were no longer workable is provided by newspaper notices for fugitives who ran away after 1775. In the last quarter of the century (see Table 4) runaways changed their usual courses, instead of running south to work or visit they ran north to be free in areas where slavery was gradually outlawed. The notices also provide a provocative glimpse of a formidable and bold runaway rarely seen in the years before the war. The Revolution itself and the Great Awakening brought into Virginia novel cultural traditions which the skilled slaves imitated to add style to their clever ways of dealing with whites. One indication of the subtle but im-

Table Four: The Change in the Fugitives' Motives and Destinations in the Revolutionary Period

Owners offered essentially three explanations for their fugitives' actions: visiting, going to town, or leaving the colony. The war changed these goals considerably. Before 1775, 11 per cent of all masters who assigned goals for runaways said they were going to North Carolina; after 1775 this dropped to 3 per cent; before the war only one master (a negligible percentage) offered Maryland and north as a goal; after the war, this response increased to 7 per cent. The war made for other significant changes: more runaways stayed in the colony, for example, 32 per cent left before 1775, 19 per cent after that date. Visiting increased too, from 29 per cent (nearly 1 in 3) to 38 per cent (nearly 2 in 5); last, after 1775 there was a slight increase in the number of slaves who went to town to work and pass as free. The runaways' goals, how frequently that motive was listed in the advertisements, and what percentage it represented of all goals assigned both before 1775 and after are listed below in that order (the figures in parentheses refer to specific responses within a heading and are not included in the sub-totals).

	Before 1775		After 1775	
	Incidence of motive	% of all motives	Incidence of motive	% of all motives
What masters said the fugitive would do :				
Visiting "he will return to his former master" or, "he will return to where he was bred" "at Col. _____'s quarter of plantation; and harboured thereabouts by relatives (a spouse, parents, brother or sister)"; or runaway was later seen with a woman presumed to be his wife	91	29	106	38
To town to "pass as free" or "gain employment"	124	39	122	43
Out of the colony to North Carolina, "Carolina" or southward;	(37)		(8)	
Northward (usually Pennsylvania, sometimes Maryland);	101	32	55	19
"he will board a ship in order to escape"; "he will attempt to join Gov. Dunmore."	(1)		(19)	
Total number of motives offered	316	100	283	100
Total number of male runaways (not including native Africans)	539		461	

portant change in their manner as fugitives is that they now displayed an openly militant nature where, previously, "artful" inconspicuousness had been the norm. French officers and gentlemen, and Baptist and

Methodist ministers were especially popular with slaves sufficiently mobile and adaptable to imitate their ways and put them to their own use. The runaway, Scipio, for example, "pretended" to know something of the French tongue, which he had "gained some knowledge of while serving as a valet to a French officer during the War." Joe Cully, a mulatto, would attempt, his master reported, "to pass as a Frenchman and alter his tongue to a broken [a second] language." [14]

The revivalistic Christianity of the late eighteenth century also encouraged some slaves to be unusually conspicuous and outspoken. They made the fundamentalist style and creed a part of their outlook and their ruses. Nearly all fugitives described as religious ran off after 1770; they were literate, and they manifested this new militancy: Charles, yellow-complexioned, and an artful, cunning sawyer and shoemaker, read well, and was a great preacher. Titus, 40, six feet tall, large face and very broad nostrils, limped and "stoop[ed]" much in walking. His back "retain[ed] the mark of the whip." He was "uncommon[ly] sensible and artful for a negro, fond of preaching and exhorting, being, as he says, of the Baptist persuasion." Adam, a very tall, bearded mulatto cooper, could also read and write "a little (generally a very small hand)," forged passes and "pretend[ed] to be a New Light." [15]

The war, the end of the slave trade, and the Great Awakening [16] accelerated economic and cultural changes underway in Virginia since the 1750's. The increased demand for skilled slaves in commercial areas, the Manumission Act of 1782, and the appearance of the slave preacher were only a few signs of important modifications of a society once almost exclusively agricultural, colonial, and aristocratic. Governor Dunmore's Emancipation Proclamation and Gabriel's call to arms, representing new types of slave resistance—outward, but also more organized and large-scale—followed these developments and dramatically exposed some of the yet untested features of a society "ill at ease."

GOVERNOR DUNMORE'S EMANCIPATION PROCLAMATION

British administrators and Virginia slaves had been well aware of one another throughout the eighteenth century. As the Revolution approached it became increasingly evident to the slaves that the British were white men with a significantly different view of slavery than their masters. Rumors of the Somerset Case, for example, encouraged slaves from even the most remote areas to run away and attempt to secure passage to England.[17] (News of Lord Mansfield's decision, that in effect set free all Negroes brought to England as slaves, reached the colony by the summer 1772.) When Bacchus ran away from Augusta County on the frontier, his master advertised that he would attempt "to board a vessel for Great Britain . . . from the knowledge he has of the late Determination of Somerset's Case";[18] and another notice for a runaway slave couple mentioned that they too were on their way to Britain, "where they imagine they will be free (a Notion now too prevalent among the Negroes, greatly to the Vexation and Prejudice of their Masters)."[19]

But the English officers overestimated the strategic implications of the slaves' unrest. In a 1772 report to the Secretary of the colonies, Dunmore wrote:

> in case of a War which may probably often happen with Spain or indeed any other power, that might make an attack upon this Colony, the people, with great reason, trembled at the facility that an enemy would find in procuring Such a body of men, attached by no tye to their Masters or to the Country, on the Contrary it is natural to Suppose that their Condition must inspire them with an aversion to both, and therefore are ready to join the first that would encourage them to revenge themselves by which means a Conquest of this Country would inevitably be effected in a very Short time; it cannot therefor but be a Matter of the greatest concern, to find proper means of averting a Calamity so alarming.[20]

This report anticipates the Governor's reaction to revolutionary violence in the colony. Following the Powder Incident (April 1775) he warned the mayor of Williamsburg that he would "proclaim liberty" for slaves and reduce the town to ashes if the planters resorted to "civil disorder." A few months later Dunmore's threat became strategy with the publication of his "damned," "infernal," "Diabolical" Proclamation.

Contemporary and present-day accounts vary considerably about how many slaves eventually joined the British. According to Professor Benjamin Quarles in *The Negro in the American Revolution* (Chapel Hill, 1961) about 800 joined. Three weeks after the Proclamation Dunmore used between 300 and 400 runaways at the Battle of Great Bridge in Norfolk County.[21] Whites on both sides over-reacted to the crisis because armed and organized blacks were involved. The governor strutted:

> This is a fine country to act in, and food of all kind in great abundance. . . . A winter campaign would reduce, without the smallest doubt, the *whole of this southern continent to a perfect state of obedience*.[22]

Inflated by a few cheap victories in the form of small-scale, amphibious guerrilla raids on the colony's unprotected coastline, Dunmore exaggerated the importance of his victories: "The *negroes* are also flocking in from all quarters, which I hope will oblige the rebels to disperse, to take care of their families and their property." [23] Fugitive slaves continued "to flock" to the British ships even though Dunmore's raids became increasingly smaller in scale and fewer in number. By the first of the year he sheltered about a thousand slaves: "had it not been for this horrid disorder," he wrote during a smallpox epidemic in June 1776, "I should have had two thousand blacks; with whom I should have had no doubt of penetrating into the heart of this Colony." [24]

Many planters essentially agreed with the Governor. Edmund Pendleton wrote to Richard Lee three weeks after the publication of the Proclamation: "letters mention that slaves flock to him in abundance; but I hope it is magnified." George Washington warned that "if the Virginians are wise, that arch traitor . . . Dunmore should be instantly crushed, if it takes the force of the whole army to do it; otherwise like a snowball rolling, his army will get size." [25] The Proclamation's appeal led others, such as John Francis Mercer, to question their treatment of slaves. This Northern Neck planter, who later represented Maryland at the Federal Convention of 1787, wrote to his steward:

> let me tell you, that I think it highly prudent, to even relax if that would engage the Negroes to stay—this Country has become the Seat of War . . . it is probable it will Continue so. In that case unless the Situation of these poor devils is rendered at least supportable, the natural Consequence will be that we shall be left without.[26]

Many were not certain about their runaways' real intentions. Landon Carter commented sarcastically: "if he was a fellow very remarkable for enduring labour, I should have thought he was gone to increase *the black regiment* forming in *Norfolk* harbour; but really he is too weakly and idle to be desirous of going where he must work for his freedom, as it is called." But Robert Brent, a wealthy Northern Neck Catholic whose estate was destroyed by the British, did not doubt his runaway's intentions: his flight "was long premeditated. . . . I am apprehensive he may prove daring and resolute, if endeavoured to be taken." Brent noted too that his slave's "elopement was from no cause of complaint . . . but from a determined resolution to get liberty, as he conceived, by flying to lord Dunmore." [27]

Since the Governor abandoned the tidewater region for the relative security of his ships after mid-December 1775, slaves who sought his protection had to obtain boats and sail into the rivers and the Bay. Driven by promises of freedom these runaways proved to be desperate, frightened men, and their efforts to reach the British were often disorganized, frantic, and disastrous. Nine runaways, two of them women, for instance, attempted to sail in a small open boat from the Eastern Shore to Norfolk. Floundering ashore at Old Point Comfort, they were pursued and fired upon: "two of the fellows were wounded," the *Gazette* reported, "and it is expected the rest will soon be made examples of." Early in the following spring, three slaves boarded a Virginia vessel in the belief that it was one of the British tenders; and before they were "undeceived," they "declared their resolution to spend the last drop of *their blood* in lord *Dunmore's* service." [28]

The heavy volume of runaways continued throughout the war years. Many slaves enlisted as a means of escaping detection while they awaited an opportunity to continue their flight to freedom. A mulatto, Anthony Ferriah, received a "great part of the bounty" (for enlisting) and promptly deserted. Lewis, who passed as a free Negro "Lewis Roberts," in Williamsburg, "was heard to say he would take a man's place to go to the northward." At least one slaveowner recognized that the army, any army—French, American, or British—was often a vehicle to freedom. Jacob Wray, advertising for his slave in 1778, noted: "expect he is smart enough to go off and [en]list." Some masters responded to this special wartime problem by allowing slaves to replace them as enlistees and then reneging on their promise to free them at the completion of their service. In 1783, therefore, a law was passed enjoining slaveowners to free those slaves who had served as substitutes.[29]

In the 1780's several runaway slaves used the French contingents, whose officers often protected them by refusing to return them to their lawful masters. This problem was of such proportions that Governor Benjamin Harrison wrote to Count Rochambeau complaining of the "contraband" slaves whom the French had taken up. The Count considered all black refugees as freedmen; Harrison thought all blacks were slaves: "I have," the Governor wrote, "to request the favor of your Excellency to give immediate orders for the securing all the Negroes without distinction that are amongst your troops." [30]

Even though Dunmore's raids were of minimal economic and military importance, they provided the Virginians with an opportunity to reveal their real feelings about Negroes. Obsessed with the notion of slaves armed by "outsiders" with guns and unnatural thoughts of freedom, the ex-colonists unleashed in editorials and letters-to-the-editor a torrent of virulently anti-Negro propaganda. "What a hopeful crew has his lordship invited to become his lifeguards! Many a *less noble* man would hardly have admitted such caitiffs into his service as shoe-blacks." The runaways were known variously as the "Speckled regiment," "renegadoes," and "black bandetti." [31] One particularly ugly commentary read:

> We hear that lord Dunmore's *Royal Regiment of Black Fusileers* is largely recruited . . . who, after doing the drudgery of the day (such as acting as scullions, &c. on board the fleet) are ordered upon deck to perform the military exercise; and, to comply with their *native* warlike genius, instead of the drowsy drum and fife, will be gratified with the use of the sprightly and enliving *barrafoo* an instrument peculiarly adapted to the martial tune of *"Hungry Niger, parch'd Corn!"* and which from henceforward is to be styled, by way of eminence, the BLACKBIRD MARCH.[32]

The *Gazette* editor's own contribution to an "incensed" public, discussed the Governor's "diabolical schemes against the good people" of Virginia, and warned that his readers would not soon forget that the Governor "had taken into his service the *very scum* of the country." [33]

As the war ground on, the whites' attitudes became more fearful, their arguments more strident and extreme:

> The second class of people, for whose sake a few remarks upon this proclamation seem necessary, is the *Negroes*. They have been flattered with their freedom. . . . To none . . . is freedom promised but to such as are able to do Lord *Dunmore* service. The aged, the infirm, the women and children, are still to remain the property

of their masters, masters who will be provoked to severity, should part of their slaves desert them. Lord *Dunmore's* declaration, therefore . . . leaves by far the greater number at the mercy of an enraged and injured people. But should there be any amongst the Negroes weak enough to believe that *Dunmore* intends to do them a kindness, and wicked enough to provoke the fury of the Americans against their defenceless fathers and mothers, their wives, their women and children, let them only consider the difficulty of effecting their escape, and what they must expect to suffer if they fall into the hands of the Americans.[34]

This crude threat against those whom the runaway left behind says a great deal about the real, the fundamental, sensibility of some members of the Revolutionary generation on the issue of slaves and slavery. The writer continued and asked the Negroes to consider what would happen to them if the British were victorious; he also asked the slaves to bear in mind their masters' efforts to ameliorate their condition:

Long have the Americans, moved by compassion, and actuated by sound policy, endeavoured to stop the progress of slavery. Our Assemblies have repeatedly passed acts laying heavy duties upon imported Negroes, by which they meant altogether to prevent the horrid traffick; but their human intentions have been as often frustrated by the cruelty and covetiousness of a set of English merchants, who prevailed upon the King to repeal our kind and merciful acts, little indeed to the credit of his humanity. Can it then be supposed that the Negroes will be better used by the English . . . No, the ends of lord *Dunmore* and his party being answered, they will either give up the offending Negroes to the rigour of the laws they have broken, or sell them in the West Indies, where every year they sell many thousands of their miserable brethren, to perish either by the inclemency of the weather, or the cruelty of barbarous master. Be not then, ye Negroes tempted by this proclamation to ruin yourselves. I have given you a faithful view of what you are to expect; and I declare before GOD, in doing it, I have considered your welfare, as well as that of the country. Whether you will profit by my advice I cannot tell; but this I know, that whether we suffer or not, if you desert us, you most certainly will.[35]

Another version of this curious, twisted, and revealing appeal to slaves read: "if they were reminded of their duty as enjoined by the Apostles, *Servants obey your Masters* . . . they would be contented with their situation and expect a better condition in the next world." [36] The peculiar logic exhibited in these public addresses seems strangely out of place in the Revolutionary era; and indeed such watchwords as *"Servants obey your Masters,"* intended for an audience of whites not blacks, were characteristic features of the ante-bellum pro-slavery argument. A speech such as the one quoted above, arguing that import duties on Africans illustrated the slaveowners' desire to ameliorate the blacks' condition, was scarcely intended for potential runaways. Confronted by the pressures of war and the vision of armed slaves in their midst, the Virginians began explaining slavery to the world in an attempt to explain it to themselves.

Dunmore's brief pursuit of the war along Virginia's unprotected coasts was unimaginative and conducted on a limited scale. Cramped by an orthodox mind, he could not comprehend the scope of the Revolution in Virginia. The ex-colonists' objective to "circumscribe within narrow bounds" Dunmore's "sphere of mischief" was soon accomplished. When a virulent smallpox epidemic ravaged his sorely pressed force on Gwinn's Island, he sailed from Virginia and did not return.

Hundreds of slaves, however, responded as runaways to Dunmore's Proclamation, and when the British returned in 1777 and 1781 even more joined them. But the question of how many slaves ran off during the war years is simply part of a larger issue, namely: the slaves' reaction to the idealism and rhetoric of the Revolutionary era. Although whites habitually attributed the slaves' discontent to external provocation—a reflection more of their own needs than those of their slaves—the blacks were actually moved deeply by the natural rights philosophy. In sum, the presence of the British, wartime disruption in general, revolutionary rhetoric, as well as the aforementioned economic and demographic changes, all worked to heighten the slaves' receptiveness to plans for an organized, large-scale endeavour to "free themselves." When rebellion came, it originated among the artisans working in the most dynamic area in the new state—the new capital at Richmond.

THE NEW CAPITAL AS SETTING FOR THE INSURRECTION

As the setting for the most sophisticated and ambitious slave conspiracy in our history, Richmond was the embodiment of the social and economic changes in postwar Virginia.[37] The city was founded by the enterprising William Byrd in 1737 at the head of navigation on the James River. For most of the century, the town had been little more than two tobacco warehouses and inspection stations, Rockett's and Shockoe's; and for a time its rival was Manchester (Rocky Ridge), the colony's leading slave market, which stood immediately across the river.

About 5,300 people lived in Richmond in 1790. At this time its few rutty, muddy streets were cut by many streams, gullies, and swamps, which have long since disappeared beneath the streets of the present-day city. The most important stream, Shockoe Creek (now a railroad bed and Interstate 95), divided the city into "new" and "old" Richmond. North of Shockoe Creek stood the new section, which included the Capitol (its bare red brick walls were still unstuccoed), the governor's house, and the Armory—all primary objectives for the insurrectionists. A commodious wharf stood where the Shockoe flowed into the James, and beyond it was a fashionable elm-lined promenade. Townsmen raised their first public building, a long, low market, on the north slope of the creek. An expansive, grassy "common" ran down in front of the market to the water, which the "common laundresses" used for drying their laundry. South Richmond, the older section and warehouse district, was and still is the site of the Henrico County courthouse and St. John's, the venerable Episcopal Church. This section, called "Rocketts," was a poorer, more boisterous area. The capital's present-day black community lives there. Gabriel, then, knew it well; it was his first objective, because its congested rows of wooden sheds could be easily set afire.

The town's thriving merchant class was largely composed of Scots, whose shops clustered around either end of Broad Street (even now the capital's principal thoroughfare) and at 1st and 12th streets. Great wagons from Staunton and the Valley, loaded with such country produce as flour, butter, hemp, wax, tallow, flaxseed, lead, feathers, deer and bear skins, furs, ginseng, and snakeroot, entered the town from the west at the head of Broad Street. Some wagoners sold their goods out on the avenues, but most of them went down town to the docks and the new canal.

The James River Canal Company, sponsored by George Washington and other gentlemen, was capitalized at $10,000. The entrepreneurs' objective, to make Richmond the entrepôt for backcountry commodities, was set in motion by a canal project, which included a channel seven miles in length around the falls and a series of sluices and dams up the Kanawha, that opened the James to Lynchburg. This great waterway was completed in 1795, and it was originally constructed for a special type of boat, the batteau, which was long, narrow, and capable of carrying from seven to ten hogsheads of tobacco. The river, as usual, was a vital basis for communication among slaves, and during Gabriel's Rebellion several "batteau men" carried the news of revolution to the Tuckahoe Coal Pits and the Arsenal at Point of Fork.

There were additional signs of a boom in the 1790's. The first bank was chartered in December 1792 with $400,000 in stocks, and a coach line (four horses per coach) was completed. The Southern Stage ran from the capital to Wilmington, North Carolina with connections by packet-boat to Charleston, South Carolina. The city also offered several good bars, including the Eagle Tavern, four flourishing newspapers, and a new local military order, "The Richmond Light Infantry Blues."

Religious, political, and fraternal activities enlivened this dynamic town. In the era of the French Revolution the Masonic Order was powerful, fashionable, and very conspicuous. In a glamorous ceremony, on the 18th of August, 1785, the Richmond Lodge of Masons No. 13 officiated, with all due pomp and ceremony, at the setting of the first stone for the State Capitol. Present among the Masonic officials were men who would later become state and national leaders: James Mercer, Edmund Randolph (the city recorder), and John Marshall. Indeed, the French Revolution, which even influenced clothing styles in the new town, increased the political awareness in the people of Richmond. Since the city was a Federalist stronghold in a Jeffersonian tide, most citizens wore black ribbons or cockades in support of President Washington's Neutrality Proclamation. But the more vocal anti-administration people wore the tri-color.

The Methodists were another conspicuous, outspoken, and controversial group which reflected the times. This irrepressible denomination was the most active religious group in the 1790's. Although they used various stables and warehouses as churches, the out-of-doors was more conducive to their style, and they really preferred the steps of the courthouse or Capitol for their shouting and singing sessions. Thomas Lyell, "a young man of good talents and great zeal," and the incomparable Jesse Lee made this sect the fastest-growing in the area while calling down the fire on hundreds of Richmond folk. The congregation, composed almost equally of whites and blacks, reluctantly came in from the city streets in 1800 when their church was completed.

It was also in 1800 that Gabriel Prosser planned the destruction of Richmond, which had continued to grow and thrive. It was described in that year from the vantage point of Colonel John Mayo's Bridge—the same Colonel Mayo whose waitingman, George, was one of the first slaves implicated as an insurrectionist.

> [Richmond] contains about 300 houses. The new houses are well built. A large and elegant state-house or capitol has lately been erected on the hill (Shockoe's). The lower part of the town is divided by a creek, over which there is a bridge which for Virginia is elegant. A handsome and expensive bridge, between 300 and 400 yards in length has lately been thrown across the James River at the foot of the Falls by Col. John Mayo, a respectable and wealthy planter, whose seat is about one mile from Richmond. The Bridge connects Richmond and Manchester and as the passengers pay toll it produces a handsome revenue to Col. Mayo, who is the sole proprietor. The Falls above the bridge are seven miles in length. A canal is cutting on the North side of the river, which is to terminate on a basin of about 2 acres in the town of Richmond. The opening of this canal promises the addition of much wealth to Richmond.[38]

5

Religion, Acculturation, and American
Negro Slave Rebellions: Gabriel's Insurrection

❋

In the summer of 1800 a group of slave-artisans organized an attack on Richmond.[1] Because their plan was essentially an expression
of their class and its understanding of the values and norms of the
American Revolutionary era, Gabriel's Rebellion was exceptionally
political in character. It never took place; and the following chapter is
divided into a narrative conveying the significance of the conspiracy
for its participants, and an examination of its preconditions and setting, in order to illuminate the sources of its failure.[2]

"A SOCIETY TO FIGHT THE WHITE PEOPLE FOR [OUR] FREEDOM"

At the gallows in Richmond, Friday noon, 12 September 1800, Colonel
Mayo questioned the slaves who were awaiting execution for their
part in Gabriel's Rebellion. Mayo asked about his own slave, George,
a fugitive and a waitingman, who was implicated in the conspiracy.[3]
George was a special slave, an assimilated, a type we have previously
encountered in runaway notices. His read:

> One Hundred and Fifty Doll[ar]s
> REWARD
> *For stopping the Villian!!!*
> RAN-AWAY on the 25th of July last from the subscriber, near this
> city
>
> GEORGE
>
> A likely stout made mulatto man, 24 or 25 years of age, five feet
> eight or nine inches, with a conspicuous [sc]ar under his left jaw,
> occasioned b[y] a defective tooth, a large scar on the back of his
> right hand from the cut of a knife—and a small one inclining

> obliquely downwards, in the middle of his forehead, occasioned by
> some accident when a child—stutters a little when about to speak,
> a bushy head of hair—legs rather small from the constant use of
> boots, and of sulky looks and temper, except when he chooses to
> force a deceitful smile—He has served an apprenticeship to the
> barber's trade—knows a little of shoemaking, and is, when he
> pleases, a very complete domestic servant.
>   . . . As he has several times travelle[d] with me into the North-
> ern states, it is possible he may obtain a forged certificate of freedom,
> and endeavour to go that way.[4]

As a fugitive and insurrectionist, Mayo's George typifies the men who
participated in Gabriel's Rebellion: born in Virginia (not Africa),
highly assimilated, well traveled, and versatile in a variety of skilled
tasks.

Mayo also asked about his friend and neighbor William Young,
whose slaves instigated the rebellion. Although Young was merely neg-
ligent (it was necessary for him to publicly defend himself in the
Richmond newspapers), his actions called in question the practices of
other slaveowners, who on this count were as guilty as he was.[5] This
carelessness was indicative of the permissive, confused, and disordered
state of slavery in the final years of the eighteenth century: careless
and permissive because whites usually ignored such critical features of
the slave code as the system of written passes for slaves who traveled,
prohibitions against selling to slaves, and the supervision of their gatherings. Slavery was also in a confused and indecisive state, because in
this period of revolutionary and religious idealism reform ameliorated
the slave's condition but seldom made him a free man. Such examples
of "humanitarianism" as the liberalized manumission procedure, a
restricted slave trade,[6] and the encouragement of the sale of slaves in
families (mothers and their children only) did not placate some slaves.[7]
Governor James Monroe's remarks to the Governor of South Carolina
were representative of the slaveowners misconceptions about the effects
of liberalizing slavery without abolishing it outright. "It seemed
strange that the slaves should embark in this novel and unexampled
enterprise," Monroe reported, "for their treatment has been more
favorable since the revolution."[8] Indeed the most puzzling and omi-
nous development for whites was that the conspirators were the same
type of relatively highly advantaged men who in the past had seen
slavery as an individual problem and typically resisted as solitary fugitives passing as free men. With this avenue of escape and freedom as

accessible as ever before, why, they asked, did this class of slaves turn, organize, and fight for their freedom in 1800? As John Mayo rode slowly back into Richmond pondering this "strange" and "novel enterprise" of a few very unusual slaves, we can imagine that he was preoccupied with questions such as these.

Six miles northeast of the city, two months earlier, late on the evening of the tenth of July, one of these slaves stood before a wood-pile, axe in hand. He was Ben Woolfolk, a shrewdly intelligent man, hired out to William Young. George Smith, one of the most active recruiters, stepped from the scrubby, pine woods and asked Woolfolk: "would you join a free Mason society?"

> "All free Masons would go to hell."
> "It [is] not a free mason society I have in mind [but] a society to fight the white people for [our] freedom." [9]

Woolfolk hedged, he would give the idea some thought; but Smith persisted, inviting him to a meeting at a neighboring plantation.

Within the next few weeks, Woolfolk, who was to become the State's principal witness, met several conspirators, including Jack Bowler, a proud and physically overpowering man, who ultimately was one of the few insurrectionists to place the rebellion above his own personal ambitions. Bowler, who was also hired out (his owner, a widow, lived in Urbanna, a small, decaying tobacco port on the lower Rappahannock River), was 28 years old, 6 feet 5 inches tall, scarred above one eye, with long hair worn in a queue and twisted at the sides. He was described by one official as "stra[i]ght made and perhaps as Strong a man as any in the State." [10]

The process of enlisting slaves like Woolfolk intensified the confusion at the beginning of the conspiracy, and underscored the search for form and direction. Leadership positions presumably were open to anyone. But only those who were sufficiently resourceful and persuasive to obtain men and arms came to be leaders, and for a while, no one was in charge. No plans were made, few arms were obtained, and organizers and recruitment were uncoordinated. Gabriel, for example, who operated independently of Smith and Bowler, once mentioned to his brother that he first heard about the conspiracy from Bowler, who, another slave testified, was "determined to raise and Enlist Men and Contend for Command with Gabriel." To this end Bowler engaged in a bit of psychological warfare; he frequently visited the blacksmith shop where Gabriel and his brothers worked, and "repeatedly" challenged them with stories of his accomplishments: the acquisition of seven pounds of gunpowder, and the names of two Frenchmen who were allegedly his contacts. The issue of overall command for a time was unresolved because several conspirators, including Bowler, Smith, and Gabriel, were adept at enlisting slaves into the conspiracy by temporarily overcoming their caution and conservatism.[11]

Opportunities for recruiting men were numerous. Slaves late in the century had a rich fraternal and religious life; and recruiters were sufficiently free of any kind of meaningful supervision to travel extensively to meet slaves at barbecues, Sunday afternoon drinking sessions beneath well-known bridges, at meeting-houses, and outdoor "preachings."

Since the conspirators, like the fugitive slaves before them, depended upon the rivers and watermen, they often depended upon the watermen to recruit for them. Stepney, a waterman whose master lived in Goochland, for example, was arrested for recruiting in Carterville, Cumberland County. An official there was so impressed by his effectiveness with other "batteau men," that he organized a patrol, following the discovery of the plot, which surveyed the upper waters of the James River from Powhatan to Buckingham counties. The insurrection also reached in the opposite direction seventy miles down the peninsula into Gloucester County, where it was effectively organized by another waterman and a preacher. A note left by a third conspirator indicates how religious and social gatherings were used by the organizers: "all you in gloster must keep still yet-brother X will come and prech a sermont to you soon, and then you may no more about the bissiness." Jacob, the waterman, was a skipper of a small vessel that operated off Ware Neck. In the weeks following the collapse of the conspiracy he was charged with taking refugees from that tidewater county into the southside.[12]

Additional organizers worked among the slaves at the canal project at the falls of the James River, and at the coal pits at Tuckahoe (a few miles above Westham on the upper James). A black post rider, who rode the route between Richmond and Amherst counties, carried information into the Albemarle piedmont. He contacted slaves at Ross's Iron Works in Goochland and also brought back intelligence from slaves in the neighborhood of Point of Fork. The Fork, about forty-five miles west of Richmond, was the site of the state arsenal. According to Governor Monroe, here at the junction of the Rivanna and James rivers was the "only place of tolerable security [for whites] in the Commonwealth." Slaves in this vicinity instructed the postman to inform Gabriel that he should delay his attack until they had taken the arsenal and were then proceeding down the river to join him.[13]

In addition to Gabriel and Bowler, three other important recruiters were George Smith, Sam Byrd, Jr., and Woolfolk himself. Byrd—like Smith, one of the first organizers—was the son of a free Negro and the slave of a man who allowed him "to hire his own time." Byrd enlisted 37 men at the Hungary Meetinghouse at Deep Run, Henrico County and "50 odd" in the town of Manchester, across the river from Richmond. At the Young's Spring meeting, he talked of several hundred recruits from Louisa, Petersburg, and "adjacent counties," and about additional trips he made to such faraway places as Hanovertown and Charlottesville; the latter is more than one hundred miles due west of Richmond.[14]

Ben Woolfolk coordinated the Henrico and Caroline County contingents. His contact in Caroline was a blacksmith and another highly assimilated recruiter who usually did not work on his home quarter. Thornton, owned by Paul Thilman of Caroline, worked at the Hanover County courthouse. Two weeks before the attack, Thornton, with Woolfolk, left the blacksmith shop, purchased liquor at Ellis's Tavern —"to treat their men that day"—with money from a "subscription" Gabriel conducted, and moved on to recruit at a "preaching" at Little-page's Bridge. Following the sermon, they assembled with the men on the creek, drank grog, and discussed "the War." Afterwards back in his shop, Thornton told Woolfolk that he had "about 20 to 30 men" from four plantations. Gabriel would make him a "Captain of Company," Woolfolk said; but Thornton replied, "he was a General and was to go under the name of Colo. Taylor on this occasion & would make his men obey him." Asked if he needed swords, Thornton stated he would arm his own men. Woolfolk observed that the organizers were "at a loss how to make Cartridges"; and immediately, the blacksmith made one and "gave it to him as a Sample." Thornton, a proud and competent man, was the one recruiter who did not find it necessary to exaggerate his resources in men and materials. But as was so often the case with enlistees, including some of the leading recruiters, he appeared once in the documents and the chronology of events and never again. Woolfolk summarized his Caroline County trip for the trial judges by observing: "he left the shop & knows nothing more of Thornton." [15]

"I COULD KILL A WHITE MAN AS FREE AS EAT"

The accounts of the recruitment procedure reveal what the conspiracy meant for most slaves, and indicate how the first group lost the initiative to Gabriel and his brothers, Martin, a preacher, and Solomon, a blacksmith. Recruitment usually followed a pattern. The organizer contacted one man in a small group of blacks, and in words such as these, asked: "was he willing to fight the white people for his freedoom?" The enlistee often responded by declaring his hatred for whites and his willingness to kill them without compassion, by sharing his views of the insurrection's goals, and by requesting a command position. Sometimes the leader's questions were put in the context of the slave's manhood or toughness. Patrick was asked "if he was a Man?" Woolfolk told Jacob that he "looked so poor and weakly that he could not kill a man." The response was perhaps predictable, Jacob shot back: "do not take me by my looks, I could kill a white man as free as eat." Following a Sunday barbecue, Gabriel revealed his plans to his two brothers, who locked hands and exclaimed "here are our hands & hearts. We will Wade to our Knees in blood sooner than fail in the attempt." But the leaders were seldom so effusive; and some in the face of certain death were quietly eloquent: "my name is Solomon, and [I] am good, what is of me, for fighting." [16]

Challenges were often made before other men. In one trial, a State witness said that when he recruited the defendant, he asked if he was one of George Smith's men:

> He said yes, by God I am—He asked him if he thought he could kill White people stoutly; Yes says he by God I can; and I will fight for my freedom as long as I have breath, and that is as much as any man can do.[17]

This enlistee's little boy, standing nearby while "minding" one of their master's children, gave his father offence, for which he was whipped. When the master's son also cried, the black man turned and said "if you were big enough you would have my shirt off, but I hope you never will be big enough." [18]

Two members of the rank and file have left full accounts of their transformation from fugitives to insurrectionists.[19] Gilbert, a sensitive and intense man, held deep and positive feelings for his master; while King, a waitingman, was a deeply embittered person, whose hatred for whites was unadulterated.

King's life changed dramatically one July market day in Richmond. While lounging with a group of black men before Francis Vanne's Shop, Woolfolk mentioned that he was "encouraged [by King's] language and deportment." The slave replied, he "never intended, or suffered white people to have much their way with him," and the ritual proceeded in this manner:

> Are you a true man?
> Pris[one]r: I am true hearted man.
> Witn[ess]: Can you keep a *proper,* or *important* secret?
> Pris[one]r: Yes
> Witn[ess]: The Negroes are about to rise and fight the White people for their freedom.[20]

"They ought to have taken the rebellion into consideration a long time ago," King said. "Yes, [he] was ready to join them at any moment," and he would "slay the white people like sheep."

After the conspiracy was discovered, King and another slave entered Mary Martin's Grog Shop "as the Guards were going out." "In a surly & abrupt style," he demanded a drink on credit. Mary refused, "I trust nobody." So King paid and turning to his friend who was journeying to visit his wife, he said he wished he could do the same. Mary joined in: "why didn't he visit his wife?" "It was too far," King said, "and the white people ha[ve] turned so comical a man can't go out of his house now but he's taken up to be hanged." He then asked his companion to tell a mutual friend: "We are all alive as yet, looking hard at the bacon, but can't get at it, as we are doing what we can. What we can't do with our Guns, we will do with Bayonets." [21] Placing his finger to his forehead, King concluded, "nobody knows what is here yet." Mary indulged the court further: "she had no bacon in her shop—nor had they any that she saw." Even though his master petitioned for a pardon, King was condemned and executed on October 3.

Few conspirators outside the small leadership clique were as active in promoting the rebellion as William Young's Gilbert. But in his eagerness to get at whites, he encountered a number of petty, frustrating situations. At the Young's Spring meeting, he replied to Martin's vow—"to turn out & fight with his stick"—that: "he was ready with his pistol, but it was in need of Repair." When approached by Gabriel and asked if he had a sword, Gilbert said his master had one hanging up in the house, which he would get and make himself a belt for it. He also depended on the use of his master's horse, but on the day before the rebellion, he expressed "regret . . . that their master was up the Country," he would "take the Bald." There were larger disappointments compounded by the slave's feelings about himself and his owner. During the conversation about the sword, he "asked to be made a Captain," but Gabriel refused, "saying he stuttered too much to give the word of Command." Later Gilbert also said that his "Master and Mistress should be put to death, but by the men under him (as he could not do it himself) because they raised him." [22]

"THE MAIN SPRING AND CHIEF MOVER"

Gilbert first enlisted with George Smith, who seemed unable to distinguish between a plan and its execution. In fact Smith's recruitment in itself indicated that his group was moving too slowly, indecisively, and ceremoniously. So Gilbert joined Gabriel, because, as he later testified, he realized that Gabriel "would carry the business into execution." [23]

This explanation focuses sharply on the style of Gabriel's leadership. More than any other organizer he sensed the narcotic and self-justifying effects of revolutionary rhetoric and organization. Because he was able to make decisions, delegate responsibilities, and pursue routine tasks to their completion in order to avert the strong possibility of disaster, the rebellion came to be his. And it bore his own quietly methodical, businesslike character. But Gabriel cannot be characterized like Woolfolk and Bowler, because his most essential qualities remain hidden and are not revealed in the manuscripts. Although he is referred to in many depositions, he refused to confess when captured. Gabriel was a powerful force pushing the conspiracy toward fruition—a man imbued not so much with messianic fervor as with a grim sense of what had to be done. The whites also recognized his unusual abilities; a county justice, using an especially appropriate mechanical metaphor, noted that Gabriel was "the Main Spring and Chief Mover." [24]

Thus the center of the rebellion shifted to Prosser's blacksmith shop,[25] where Gabriel and his brothers gave form and substance to the notion of revolution. During the early summer months the conspiracy matured under their direction. In the second week of August, when William Young left his plantation for a fortnight, the insurrectionists returned there, ostensibly to bury a Negro child.

"I CAN NO LONGER BEAR WHAT [I HAVE] BORNE"

Saturday afternoon, August 10, the mourners drifted back from the black infant's grave.[26] Gabriel, who often used religious gatherings for his own political purposes, invited the slaves to drink grog with him on the banks of the spring. Understanding that he must build a following among the country people, he ignored secrecy. He asked those assembled who wished to join him to stand, and those who did not to sit. He and Bowler moved among the men, promoting the war and enlisting fighters. Unsatisfied with this cooperative arrangement, Bowler asked rhetorically what Gabriel would do for war material, and before Gabriel replied, Bowler rushed on and asked that those "who have agreed to engage in the Insurrection to give him their Voice for General." "The Votes [were] taken," and "Gabriel [had] by far the greater number." Although he had miscalculated Gabriel's hold on the slaves, Bowler was made second in command, a "Captain of Lighthorse."

Following the election, they debated the critical issue of when to attack. Although the vernacular was religious, the deliberations were practical and realistic. Some, including a few leaders, were apprehensive. While recruiting in the countryside, George Smith came to understand the plantation slave's dual nature: his bitter hatred for whites and his inability to do much about it. So Smith argued that they defer "the business some time longer." But Gabriel replied, "the Summer was About over, & he wished them to enter upon the business before the winter got too cold." At this crucial moment, with the decision in the balance, he suggested that "the Subject should be referred" to his brother Martin, the preacher, who stepped forward and intoned: "there was this expression in the Bible that delays breed danger." But Martin quickly turned from scriptural sanction to more rational, secular considerations and argued that the time for revolution was very near: the country was at peace, the soldiers were discharged, their arms "all put away," and "there were no patrols in the Country." He paused, then crossing what for many was an insurmountable barrier, Martin spoke from within. "I can no longer bear what [I have] borne." The proceedings were open, and the silence was broken by "others who spoke to the company" and said that Woolfolk had "something to say." Woolfolk also used the Bible, but to loosen the spectre of defeat. "He had heard in the days of old, when the Israelites were in Servitude to King Pharaoh, they were taken from him by the power of God—& were carried away by Moses. . . . But I can see nothing of that kind in these days." Martin quickly replied, "their cause was similar to [the] Israelites' "; but that he had read in his Bible "where God Says, if we worship him, we should have peace in all our land," and "five of you shall conquer an hundred & a hundred a thousand of our enemies." At this point Martin held the floor and made the most important decision: "after this they went into consultation upon the time they should execute the plan. [He] spoke & appointed for them to meet in three weeks which was to be a Saturday night (August 30)." With this achieved, Bowler and Gabriel withdrew into "secret conversations," which were interrupted by the appearance of Young's overseer. The conspirators dispersed after agreeing to meet in front of Moore's schoolhouse the following Sunday (while their masters met within the schoolhouse), "where a final Conclusion on the business would take place."

The conspiracy had peaked at the Young's Spring meeting. In the few weeks before the attack a certain indefinable but no less real revolutionary élan was dissipated—if sustained it might have carried the rank and file from words to deeds. During the meeting itself there were clear signs of a potentially disastrous disunity: Woolfolk's comment about the unfulfilled search for a Moses, George Smith's desire to postpone the rebellion, and the recruiters' deceptive responses to questions about the numbers they had actually enlisted.

The recruiters' exaggerated reports conveyed the enlistee's fervent promise, while in company with his friends, and the recruiters' belief that the command he received would be proportionate to the numbers of enlistees he claimed. When asked to produce their lists, moreover, the organizers often couched their response in vague allusions to the "warehouse boys," the "boys across the river" or the "boys in town." Sam Byrd was asked for his record at the Young's Spring meeting, and he said, while he did not have his list "about him," he "supposed he had about five hundred, who were to be assembled by him and given up to Gabriel on the Night [of] the Attack." Some sensed what was going on. Gilbert asked a Richmond free Negro, Matt Scott, who said he had a hundred men, for his list. "Some other time," Scott answered; but Gilbert testified, he "never did see the list." [27]

The recruiters' dangerously misleading estimates of men and material were further distorted by the leaders—but only on those occasions when they addressed groups of slaves in the countryside. In one instance, Gabriel himself (while displaying two bullet molds which he said he had worn out producing several pecks of shot) proclaimed that he had nearly 10,000 men: 1000 in Richmond, about 600 in Caroline County and nearly 500 at the Tuckahoe Coal Pits, "besides others at different places." Significantly, estimates of the number prepared to fight diminished as the point of departure approached. Gabriel's statement was made three weeks before the attack, while addressing the gathering at Young's Spring. A week later, August 20, a slave asked Solomon how many would follow them: the answer was 3,000; and nine days later, Gabriel's wife, Nanny, told a black man "that 1000 Men were to meet her husband near Prosser's Tavern the ensuing Night." [28]

But Gabriel understood what was and was not happening with regard to recruitment in the countryside. He only talked of 10,000 men before gatherings of slaves of all kinds; in the privacy of Prosser's blacksmith shop, he carefully assessed his limited resources and planned accordingly. In its tactical dimensions his rebellion was a coup that would hopefully inspire an insurrection: a small guerrilla force of about two hundred men would enter Richmond at midnight, thoroughly terrorize the city by burning its warehouse district and (initially) killing indiscriminately, capturing stores of arms, and taking the governor as a hostage.

The governor, James Monroe, also understood the real nature of the rebellion. When he addressed the State Legislature in December he referred to it as an "experiment," a "project," undertaken by "bold adventurers," who relied on a "successful . . . first effort," rather than a "very extensive preconcerted combination." [29] Against this background, the nature of the slaves' prolific discussions and recruitment is more understandable. The organizers, the "bold adventurers," sought to build a viable following among the country people who, they hoped, would follow up their initial attack. Thus Gabriel's strategy:

he recognized that unless he struck suddenly, sensationally, and decisively—presenting slaves as well as free men with a *fait accompli*—there would be no mass uprising.[30]

Gabriel's tactics, which were needlessly complicated, were not as astute as his strategy. Even though the city was the key to his plan, it was decided that the conspirators would gather six miles out in the countryside. They would then enter Richmond in three wings (two would be unarmed), from the north and south. One group would fire the wooden buildings in Rockett's, the warehouse district, in order to draw off the townsmen from the residential areas; the others, commanded by Gabriel, would capture the capitol buildings, the store of arms in the penitentiary, and kidnap the governor. When the whites returned from the fires, tired and confused, the insurgents would close with them. If successful, if the "White people agreed to their freedom," Gabriel would raise a white flag in order to notify "their brothers" outside the city, who would presumably rise up and join the fortified insurrectionists.

There were back-up plans based on the slaves' knowledge that the whites were especially vulnerable in their towns. Gabriel said that if they "sustained any considerable loss," they would "bend their course" for either of two small towns, Hanovertown or Yorktown. At this point their plans trailed off into a vague notion of attempting to "form a junction" with some slaves who "they understood from Mr. Gregory's overseer were in rebellion in some quarter of the country."

The question of who was to direct the initial military operations was also a portent of disaster. Slaves knew little of arms and less of tactical leadership. When asked by his brother whether or not Jack Bowler knew "anything about carrying on war," Gabriel replied negatively. Whom would he employ? Solomon continued. A Frenchman from Caroline County, "who was at the Siege of Yorktown," Gabriel said, "was to meet him at the Brook." The Frenchman was to be "Commander & manager the first day, after exercising the Soldiers"; following the attack, "the command was to be resigned to Gabriel."

This Frenchman was allegedly Charles Quersey who, three or four years prior to the conspiracy, had lived at Francis Corbin's in Caroline. William Young's Gilbert credited Quersey with initiating the rebellion: he "frequently advised the negroes to rise & kill the White people, and said he would help them & shew them how to fight." Gilbert had not seen him "since, but is inform'd by several Negroes, that he has

been very active in encouraging the Negroes in this late Business."
Nineteenth-century folk, fighting desperate anti-colonial battles against
overwhelmingly powerful Europeans, often had a similar view: the na-
tionals of a European power hostile to the mother-country would mi-
raculously appear and fight on their side. "They had understood,"
Woolfolk testified, "that the French were at war with this Country—
for the money which was due them & that an army was landed at
South Key which they hoped would assist them." [31]

Sound in strategy but bogged down by confusing tactics, imperiled
by a lack of men and military leadership, the conspiracy moved into its
final days. [32] On the day of the attack, Saturday August 30, at noon, it
began to rain. By mid-evening the thunderstorm had swelled streams
and washed out roads and bridges. Communication, movement, and
morale collapsed. The whites later repeatedly referred to this great
storm as "providential."

Although it is a moot point how many men would have met at
Prosser's the midnight of August 30, no one came either Saturday or
Sunday night when the attack was rescheduled. [33] In the meantime,
security was suddenly broken. For months hundreds of slaves, including women and children, had maintained secrecy while listening
to the discussions and pondering their places in the new scheme of
things. By Saturday morning, however, at least three slaves had informed their masters that this conspiracy was going to become reality.
Monroe dispatched two cavalry troops which swept back and forth
through the area of the rendezvous. But this was unnecessary because
the leaders postponed the attack; one man who came to the Prosser
plantation that stormy night was told by Gabriel to return the next
evening. But another slave informed (her report: three or four hundred, "some from Town & some from the Country" would meet) and
again, the troop commanders' reports were negative. Thus Monroe
noted: "I was on the point of concluding there was no foundation
for the alarm." And even when he came to a partial understanding of
what he was confronting, his deployment of men in the capital indicated the governor's serious misgivings regarding the extent of the
conspiracy's penetration among the plantation Negroes. [34]

In the aftermath, the State proceeded cautiously and confidently
while making arrests, using informers, and conducting the trials. [35]
Within a few days twenty slaves had been captured in Henrico and

Caroline counties. Thereafter arrests continued more slowly. On September 15, Monroe wrote Jefferson that ten slaves had been executed and "at least" twenty would be condemned and "perhaps forty." [36] The former estimate is closer to the total number executed; but the exact number of convictions is unknown because the record of payments to the slaveowners is incomplete. At least twelve slaves were acquitted, one of whom was Sam Byrd's free father, who was accused of recruiting in Hanovertown. Another seven conspirators were pardoned.[37]

"THE BUSINESS ONLY REQUIRED A BEGINNING"

For Gabriel the final scene comprised many of the elements that so often made slavery a tragic and crazy reality for even the most talented and resourceful slaves. In his last moments of real freedom, he was aided by a white and betrayed by a black.

Richardson Taylor, who tried to carry Gabriel to safety, was the master of the schooner *Mary* and an embodiment of the fiercely contradictory values of his post-war society.[38] Taylor was a "family man," an ex-overseer, a ship captain with a crew of slaves, and an anti-slavery Methodist. Although he later feigned innocence by virtue of his ignorance of the matter, Taylor knew about Gabriel. Before he weighed anchor in Richmond and dropped down the James toward Norfolk, several insurrectionists were tried and executed. Late Saturday night, September 17, the *Mary* conveniently ran onto Ward's Reach, four miles below the capital. The following morning Gabriel ran from a patch of woods, crossed the sand bar, and after tossing his bayonet into the water, was taken aboard. Taylor later claimed that he was "unwell" during this episode; when he awoke the ship was underway. Coming on deck he questioned his strange passenger, who said he was a free Negro, Daniel, but unfortunately, he had left his manumission papers ashore. While Taylor let the matter drop, his slave crewmen, Isham and Billy, insisted that the man was Gabriel, and "it was their opinion that he was the person (for whom) the reward was offer[e]d."

The *Mary* was eleven days in passage. Taylor overlooked numerous opportunities to put ashore and either inquire about or dispose of his strange passenger. When he was finally boarded by an official in Norfolk, he said nothing about Gabriel. But Isham, who later testified that he was to be freed if he converted to Methodism, brought the officials back to the ship. They were amazed: "Capt. Taylor is an old inhabitant been an overseer & must have known that neither free blacks nor slaves could travel in this Country without papers." This time Gabriel left in chains; and although he once mentioned he would talk about the rebellion—but only to Monroe—he remained silent while he awaited execution.[39]

In the weeks following the trials, there were a series of small insurrectionary actions throughout the state. In November Paul Thilman, the owner of the Caroline County blacksmith, Thornton, reported that the Negroes "in the neighbourhood" of the Hanover County courthouse had been "very riotous & ungovernable" on a Thursday and Friday. On Saturday they broke into a jail and set free two insurrectionists who were handcuffed and chained to the floor. Once free, the prisoners assaulted the guard, "knocked him down stamped [on] him" and ran off. "A great number of Negroes were present & pretended" to pursue them. Thilman felt that the jail-break was well planned in that "a great number" of slaves had visited the prisoners throughout the week "under the pretence of a preaching." He reported an additional "incident" in Hanover which further indicated that the "concert" between that county's slaves and those in Caroline was still intact. Mr. Paul Woolfolk, "going down his plantation," fell in with two slaves armed with "bayonets." Woolfolk, who was armed with an axe, "threaten[ed] them with an assault" if they did not surrender. The slaves, equal to the occasion, told him "to come on, they were ready for him—that they would go where they pleased." They did, and were last reported crossing Charles Carter's plantation.[40]

But the slaves' unusually open and violent activities were uncoordinated. In the grim days following the discovery of the conspiracy, it became clearly evident that rebellion waited on Gabriel and his few "bold adventurers." In court the following testimony was typical: "all the negroes in Petersburg were to join him [Gabriel] after he had commenced the insurrection"; "as soon as the boys on this side made a *brake,* the boys from Manchester would come over and join them." On the weekend following the storm, about a hundred and fifty slaves actually gathered at Whitlock's Mill outside Norfolk. "They never left this neighborhood until the Tuesday after it was known that the Richmond plan had failed," reported one planter. When a number of "mulattoes, negroes, & some whites, whose connections were with the negroes," were examined, they said that the people at the mill were "to do what those of Richmond were about to do." Nor did the slaves' expectations readily subside. Three months later one Benjamin DuVal wrote Monroe that he had overheard a "parcel" of Richmond Negroes talking about the "Norfolk Cowards." "Cowards & Liberty" was "several times expressed conjoined with other words that I could not distinctly hear." And one Negro said "that there never was or would be a better time than the present," and observed "that the business only required a beginning." [41]

Three weeks after the conspiracy was discovered one of Gabriel's recruiters in Gloucester County hurriedly shoved a note into the neck of a bottle, which he dropped alongside the old road that runs past the court house to Ware's Neck. The letter concerned Jacob, the black skipper who carried refugees from Gloucester into the southside:

September 20 : 1800

dear frind

Tel jacob at john Williams johny is taken up and wil be hanged i is afraide so all you in gloster must keep still yet brother X will come and prech a sermont to you soon, and then you may no more about the bissiness. i must be killed if the white peple catch me and carry me to richmon

i am your tru frind
A.W. [42]

In the bitter aftermath of the rebellion that did not happen, running away was once again the only alternative for slaves who refused to accept slavery. Even though insurrection was in the air, and "only required a beginning," the slaves "looked at the bacon" but "couldn't get at it."

"It is always the individual that really thinks and acts and dreams and revolts," wrote Edward Sapir many years ago. [43] Although the significance of Gabriel's Insurrection lies in its narration, in its tragic, personal dimension, a discussion of its most strategic preconditions completes a view of the revolutionary situation of 1775 and 1800. There are essentially four ways of examining the insurrection's setting and what accounted for its failure. These categories are: the nature of the conspirators' tasks; their understanding of the values of the Revolutionary era; their views of religious revivalism; and the relationship between acculturation levels and patterns of slave behavior in the late eighteenth century.[44]

Depositions and lists supplied by informers offer a fairly complete picture of the conspirators' place and function in society. The insurrectionists were unified by common work experiences. Several were from coal mines, iron foundries, and ropewalks—industries whose growth in scale and number was quickened by the war—or, from such new industries as the Public Canal Works.[45] Privileged domestics, who have not fared too well in studies of American Negro slavery, were as well represented as any other group: Robin and Charles, waiters at the Eagle Tavern and Priddy's Ordinary, janitors and custodians who worked in the Capitol buildings and the penitentiary, as well as the waitingmen, King, and John Mayo's George.[46] Blacksmiths from Goochland, Caroline, and Henrico counties, the only type of highly esteemed craftsmen represented, played a crucial role as recruiters. Several warehousemen were also implicated. Others worked at assignments which required extensive travel; they included several boatmen (from the upper waters of the James between Powhatan and Buckingham counties), and the postman who rode the route between Richmond and Charlottesville. These men were more independent than all the other conspirators, for they only rarely worked in the company of whites. While the insurrectionists' backgrounds cut across several categories—semi-skilled and skilled, routine and artistic—they all thoroughly understood society outside the plantation, in which they traveled so freely.

The conspirators, in fact, were more autonomous than the slaves they would lead. They had a life of their own—masters are conspicuously absent from their lengthy and detailed depositions—and the only whites who participated in any meaningful way in their activities were those whom the slaves could use—Methodists, petty merchants, and tavernkeepers. Several were owned by women; at least three came from estates in probate. Several who were hired out or allowed to hire their own time were also at least a step or two removed from their masters. In this period of economic readjustment and diversification, allowing a slave to hire his own time was an illegal but highly popular and profitable practice. And some were so far removed from their masters that their provenance was difficult to determine. One confused official described William Young's Gilbert in the following manner:

"at the time the Fire took place at Mr. Percells, he was then living with John Young in Caroline County." And Brutus, "alias Julius," who belonged to William Anderson, had been hired out to a prominent Richmond physician, Dr. William Foushee, at which time he ran off and joined the rebellion.[47]

These outwardly rebellious men are by now familiar. They were the same type of slave who had previously possessed the requisite skills to run off and pass as free men. But by the end of the century a significant change had taken place in the revolutionary awareness of men who had previously viewed slavery as an individual problem and resisted it as fugitives. These men and this change, in fact, are the key to the relationship between the social and personal dimensions of the conspiracy. Writing in 1801 about fugitives who became insurrectionists, St. George Tucker, aristocrat and lawyer, analyzed the conspiracy's preconditions for the state legislature. Comparing the slaves' reactions to Dunmore and Gabriel, he discussed their exceptionally rapid material and spiritual development in the "few short years" following the war. He attributed their new outlook to the growth of towns, trades, and a complementary increase in the extent of literacy among slaves. More opportunities for work in commercial areas brought about a "prodigious change" in the skilled slaves' outlook, a change Tucker characterized as the "love of freedom," and that "evolving spirit we fear." While only a few runaways, a "few solitary individuals," joined the British in 1775, the insurrectionists of 1800 organized extensively in order to "assert their claims, while rest[ing] their safety on success alone." The difference between the two rebellions, Tucker argued, was basically ideological: whereas in 1775 slaves "fought [for] freedom merely as a good; now they also claim it as a right." [48]

Thus in the closing years of the century, revolutionary conflict and ideology were resolved for most free men, but not for black men, especially if they were artisans. Between 1775 and 1800, a type of slave who was literate, skilled, mobile, and working in a commercial environment accepted the fact that regardless of his comparatively privileged position, and the whites' efforts to ameliorate slavery, the institution would survive and grow. Skilled slaves had become sufficiently marginal to believe that the values and "rights" of the Revolutionary era were theirs also and that they were sufficiently resourceful and strategically placed to do something about their situation with the aid of other men. Nonetheless, their expanded revolutionary consciousness was still focused by their traditional and relatively advantaged positions. So, to the extent that they were motivated by ideas, these ideas established definite boundaries of their revolutionary action.

The insurrectionists' goals were essentially political. While using the rhetoric of their generation to clearly distinguish between oppressors and victims, white as well as black, they displayed a keen sense of their own time and place. One man testified that he wanted "to fight for his Country," and another said they were to "subdue the whole of the Country where Slavery was permitted but no further." "As far as I understand all the whites were to be massacred, except the Quakers, the Methodists & Frenchmen," Woolfolk testified, and "they were to be spared on account as they conceived of their being friendly to liberty." Prosser's Ben, an 18-year-old who worked beside Gabriel in the blacksmith shop, mentioned that "whites were to [be] murdered & killed indiscriminately excepting French Men, none of whome were to be touched." And another said simply, they "intended to spare all poor white women who had no slaves." The continual discussions of who was to be spared or killed, as well as the occasionally cathartic posturing that characterized the recruitment process, seldom impaired the participant's expression of his clear understanding of the leading principles of the day.[49]

The organizers' discussions regarding Richmond are even more informative of both the origin and political character of their revolutionary style. These rational and calculating men were neither self-indulgent nor self-destructive; for at times, it seemed, they wanted a political settlement, not a reformation. Gabriel once said that all townsmen excepting those who agreed to fight with them would be killed. His brother remarked in passing that they were to possess themselves of the whites' property; and George Smith asked that they preserve the brick storehouses in Rockett's "for their own use." Recall their strategy: the insurgents would fortify the city, take the governor hostage and then—it is assumed—they would negotiate. At this point, Gabriel again set the tone. When the capital was secured, "on the day it should be agreed to," he "would dine and drink with the merchants of the City."[50]

The occupational and ideological values which separated organizers from those they had to recruit were basically a function of their comparatively more thorough acculturation. The slaves' awareness of their profound cultural differences was sharpened by the dramatic quality of religious life at the end of the century.[51] The country people, reluctant and suspicious, came off the quarters and gathered at the large and exciting revival meetings of the Great Awakening. Seeking spiritual assistance, they were confronted by Gabriel and his men, who used the meetings to disguise both their real intentions and the structure of their organization, and to recruit men and discuss tactics. The high point of the revival was the exhortation which, if it had been used by Gabriel, could have been the catalyst for changing religious fervor and concern for the hereafter into revolutionary action in the here-and-now. But this never happened. The leaders and their potential followers were faithful in different ways. The conspiracy was composed of autonomous men confronting religious men. Because of the nature of its leader and the rational, political character of its goals, Gabriel's Rebellion never became a viable part of the great religious revivals.

Because religious and eschatological elements often generate the large-scale rebellions of pre-industrial folk, perhaps it was not merely coincidental that one leader looked beyond the country people's fundamentalism to an even more ancient heritage which leavened their Christianity. For some, like the leader George Smith, Africa was still a very meaningful part of their lives. Smith, who was closer to the soil and the harvest cycles than any other organizer, once proposed that he hire his own time, travel down-country to what he called the "pipeing tree," and enlist the "Outlandish people." For they were "supposed to deal with Witches and Wizards, and thus [would be] useful in Armies to tell when any calamity was about to befall them." [52] Whether or not Smith later talked about bullets turning to water is an intriguing conjecture, but he did announce to the gathering at Young's Spring that when he finished plowing his master's corn field, he would make as many crossbows "as he could," an equally fantastic proposition. Although there was no more said about wizards, crossbows, and Africa, Smith, in his own way, called attention to the one means— charisma—by which the slaves could have transcended their significant cultural and occupational differences. But his proposal (as well as Woolfolk's unfulfilled search for a Moses) calls attention to the relationship between acculturation levels and religious beliefs and practices, on the one hand, and styles of resistance, on the other. Here is the source of Gabriel's failure: at a time when revivalism was a vital force among plantation slaves, those who would lead couched their appeal in political and secular terms. Unlike Nat Turner's magnificent Old Testament visions, which transfigured him and sustained his movement, Gabriel's Rebellion, lacking a sacred dimension, was without a Moses, and thus without a following.[53]

Preliminary research indicates that an understanding of the acculturative experience, as a hitherto neglected dimension of slavery, may also enrich our studies of the other major insurrections about which the slaves have provided ample testimony. The cultural differences among slaves—so evident and divisive in the 1800 rebellion—were also manifested in the religious contexts of the insurrections of Denmark Vesey (Charleston, South Carolina, 1822) and Nat Turner (Southampton County, Virginia, 1831).

Religion and magic sustained Nat Turner's Rebellion.[54] Executed by plantation slaves in an economically backward area, this insurrection was not as politically coherent and extensive as Gabriel's. Turner, who was not a preacher in the conventional sense but a seer and a holy man, also politicized his men by means of dream interpretations and feats of fortune-telling and numerology. In this instance too, a celestial event (an eclipse of the sun) made a tremendous impact on the black country folk; but they were prepared to see it as a favorable sign. Denmark Vesey, the third great insurrectionist, stands midway between Gabriel and Turner. While he normally based his appeal on political grounds, he recognized the connection between religious sanctions and rebellion from below. On a few special occasions he used sermons based on the Bible; and he also delegated to Gullah Jack, a native African and "doctor," the responsibility of forming the rural blacks of the low country's sea islands into "African legions." But, like Gabriel, he failed, because his rebellion was urban-based and restricted to artisans, shopkeepers, and free Negroes. Only Nat Turner, who charged his plan with supernatural signs, and sacred, poetic language that inspired action, was able to transcend the worlds of the plantation and the city. Only Turner led a "sustained" insurrection.

But Gabriel's men were ensnared in an earlier and a different era. Although these artisans, by 1800, had become so much more numerous, strategically placed, and imbued with an ideology supporting collective action, they were still isolated—cut off not only from their own people, but from the new economic realities of the ante-bellum period. There was in this conspiracy, then, a note of cultural despair.

Since the South after the introduction of Eli Whitney's gin was again moving away from manufactures and economic diversification, the occupational strata and milieu productive of this type of slave was rapidly becoming anachronistic. Hence from this threat to their way of life came this group's despair. Isaac declared "if the [insurrection] was not soon he would run off, as he was determined not to serve a white man [for] another year," and Martin said "he could no longer bear what he had borne." To a third, the transformation from slave to free man was forthrightly expressed: "I will kill or be killed." And Solomon, one of the few mulattoes in the conspiracy, joined and died even though he was to be legally free at age thirty-one.[55]

But where were the other slaves? The reality of slavery in post-war Virginia was radically different for leaders and followers. An elite initiated, planned, and dominated Gabriel's Rebellion. In the four months before the insurrection they lived and were sustained by it; they knew one another well. Living with death, they accepted it. Slowly and profoundly freedom, revolution, and death came to be a large part of their lives. Meanwhile, the rank and file simply raised their hands at meetings; a few personalized their commitment by volunteering for specific responsibilities and acquiring weapons. Enlisting in the most inauthentic manner, they did not share the leaders' distinctive revolutionary awareness. Thus their commitment was fragile at best; and in the end, Gabriel and his men stood alone.

Slavery in eighteenth-century Virginia was remarkably flexible and unstructured, in part because the society itself was unsettled, rapidly growing, and insecure. Central to this openness was the planters' overwhelming need for self-sufficiency. Although they were politically and economically subservient to Great Britain, and absolutely dependent on African slaves, patriarchs wished to be "independent on every one but Providence."

In their quest for this goal, slaveowners esteemed highly those Africans who began to change their ways and were then capable, in their masters' eyes, of becoming skilled and of forming the very basis for the planters' vaunted autonomy. Paradoxically, acculturation—the changes by which the African's customs fell away as he acquired English and occupational specialization—ultimately created slaves who were able to challenge the security of the society itself.

Viewing acculturation as another dimension of slave behavior in the colonial period not only clarifies our understanding of adjustments to slavery, but calls attention to the most important ways in which slavery changed as it developed from the colonial to the ante-bellum period. Acculturation and work were the most important variables determining a slave's adjustment. As a new arrival, the African initially reacted to the strange and hostile society on the basis of his communal upbringing. For him, procurement was a brutal but not a brutalizing experience; the "outlandish" African remained a man, and for a time, a highly distinctive slave. In fact, until his prior cultural sanctions proved unworkable, such measurable evidence of acculturation as speaking English did not occur.

Nearly all Africans soon became "new Negroes"—field hands on the up-country quarters. For these men, as well as the field laborers and house servants on the home plantation, resistance was an inward-directed endeavor. Plantation slaves turned their limited rebelliousness back toward the plantation setting itself; their reactions were usually easily contained; they brought a direct, punitive response, and seldom improved the slave's status. But some of this resistance was cooperative, and it was especially effective because the plantation was so vulnerable to acts of sabotage.

A few Africans and many of their American-born children learned proficient English, acquired an intelligent demeanor, advanced in the work hierarchy, and so became relatively assimilated. These men were self-reliant, individualistic, and less cooperative. This is what the colonists desired; slaves who were more like themselves were slaves they could better understand. But these men, in jobs where they learned to function resourcefully in the colonial society outside the plantation, came to understand that they still had little control over their lives. When they resisted, then, it was, for three-quarters of the century, directed away from the plantations; as resourceful fugitives, the skilled slaves went to towns, passed as free men, and found work. They were still unable to escape slavery completely, however; they still contributed their labor to the society, although more on their own terms than previously.

As the assimilateds replaced the Africans in the slave population, traditional arrangements between slaves and free men, in the last quarter of the century, became dangerously outmoded. More slaves were able to resist in ways which challenged their masters' (and the society's) traditional sense of security. These developments, coupled with the changes in the economic and political realities of the revolutionary era, brought about Gabriel's Rebellion. Slavery in the nineteenth century would be based on a heritage more American than African.

Notes

ABBREVIATIONS USED IN THE NOTES

Archives

HEH	Henry E. Huntington Library, San Marino, California
LC	Library of Congress, Washington, D.C.
UVA	Alderman Library, University of Virginia, Charlottesville
CW	Colonial Williamsburg Inc. Research Center (microfilm and manuscript collection)
W&M	William and Mary College Archives
VHS	Virginia Historical Society, Richmond
VSL	Virginia State Library, Richmond
DUL	Duke University Library, Manuscript Department, Durham, North Carolina
SHC	Southern Historical Collection, Chapel Hill, North Carolina

Newspapers and Magazines

MdG	Maryland Gazette
S.C.Gaz.	South Carolina Gazette
Va. Argus	Virginia Argus (Richmond)
VaG	Virginia Gazette (Williamsburg)
VaH & FA	Virginia Herald and Fredericksburg Advertiser
VaH & FFA	Virginia Herald and Fredericksburg and Falmouth Advertiser
VaG & GA	Virginia Gazette and General Advertiser (Richmond)
VaIC	Virginia Independent Chronicle (Richmond)
JSH	Journal of Southern History
VMHB	Virginia Magazine of History and Biography
WMQ	William and Mary Quarterly

Published Primary Sources

Hening	W. W. Hening, Editor. *Statutes at Large: Being a Collection of All the Laws of Virginia from the First Session of the Legislature in the Year 1619.* 13 vols. Richmond and Philadelphia, 1809–23.
JHB	H. R. McIlwaine and J. P. Kennedy, Editors. *Journals of the House of Burgesses of Virginia.* 13 vols. Richmond, 1905–15.
Landon Carter's Diary	Jack P. Greene, Editor. *The Diary of Colonel Landon Carter of Sabine Hall, 1752–1778.* Charlottesville, 1966.
Mount Vernon	M. D. Conway, Editor. *George Washington and Mount Vernon.* Long Island Historical Society *Memoirs,* IV. 4 vols. Brooklyn, 1889.

The Virginia Colonial Records Project

PROCO and VCRP	Public Record Office, Colonial Office Papers part of the Virginia Colonial Records Project (CW microfilm collection)

Introduction

1. William Byrd to the Earl of Orrery, Westover, Virginia, July 5, 1726, *VMHB,* XXXII (Dec. 1924), 27.
2. Robert "King" Carter to Mr. Robert Jones, Corotoman, Virginia, Oct. 10, 1727, Robert "King" Carter Letterbook 1727–28, UVA microfilm.
3. [St. George Tucker], *Letter to a Member of the General Assembly of Virginia on the Subject of the Late Conspiracy of the Slaves, with a Proposal for their Colonization* (Richmond, 1801), VSL microfilm.
4. "Confessions of Ben Alias Ben Woolfolk," Sept. 17, 1800, Executive Papers, Sept.–Dec. 1800, VSL.
5. This introduction is part of a longer paper, "The African Background for American Negro Slavery," presented to a faculty-graduate student seminar in Afro-American history at Stanford University, April 1970. I would like to thank Professor Carl Degler for that opportunity, and Michele Aldrich, Alan Lawson, and Alan Lewis, my colleagues at Smith College, for their helpful criticisms of that essay.
6. Kenneth M. Stampp, *The Peculiar Institution: Slavery in the Ante-Bellum South* (New York, 1956), 35–36.
7. Ulrich B. Phillips, *American Negro Slavery* (New York, 1918), 342–43; see also Lewis C. Gray, *History of Agriculture in the Southern United States to 1860* (2 vols., Washington, D.C., 1933), I, 465–67.
8. Stanley M. Elkins, *Slavery: A Problem in American Institutional and Intellectual Life* (Chicago, 1959), 103–14.
9. George M. Fredrickson and Christopher Lasch, "Resistance to Slavery," *Civil War History,* XIII (Dec. 1967), 315–29.
   Elkins, Fredrickson, and Lasch, and Roy Simon Bryce-Laporte, "The Conceptualization of the American Slave Plantation as a Total Institution" (unpub. Ph.D. thesis, University of California at Los Angeles, 1968) base

their studies on Erving Goffman's definition of a "total institution" in *Asylums: Essays on the Social Situation of Mental Patients and Other Inmates* (New York, 1961), xiii. "A total institution may be defined as a place of residence and work where a large number of like-situated individuals, cut off from the wider society for an appreciable period of time, together lead an enclosed, formally administered round of life."

10. Stampp, *The Peculiar Institution*, 28.

11. Elkins, *Slavery*, 63, 98, see also Part III-2, "Shock and Detachment," for his explanation for "Sambo," the typical product of the infantilizing tendencies of the southern plantation: "Sambo, the typical plantation slave, was docile but irresponsible, loyal but lazy, humble but chronically given to lying and stealing; his behavior was full of infantile silliness and his talk inflated with childish exaggeration. His relationship with his master was one of utter dependence and childlike attachment: it was indeed this childlike quality that was the very key to his being."

This influential thesis has been uncritically accepted by some important interpreters of American slavery and race relations. For example, Charles Silberman, *Crisis in Black and White* (New York, 1964), 74–76, 80; Thomas F. Pettigrew, *A Profile of the Negro American* (Princeton, N.J., 1964), 13–15; and Pierre L. van den Berghe, *Race and Racism: A Comparative Perspective* (New York, 1967), 83ff.

12. For example Stampp, *The Peculiar Institution*, 151, 152ff, 361–62, 363.

13. Jesse Lemisch, "Listening to the 'Inarticulate': William Widger's Dream and the Loyalties of American Revolutionary Seamen in British Prisons," *Journal of Social History*, III (Fall 1969), 2.

14. Marc Bloch, cited in Daniel F. McCall, *Africa in Time-Perspective: A Discussion of Historical Reconstruction from Unwritten Sources* (New York, 1969), 19.

15. Frank Tannenbaum, *Slave and Citizen: The Negro in the Americas* (New York, 1946), 117; see also Tannenbaum, "A Note on the Economic Interpretation of History," *Political Science Quarterly*, LXI (June 1946), 247–48: "In any society where slavery has been institutionalized, the issues between free and slave labor become infinitely variable, and it is often a question of where slavery ends and freedom begins. Stated this way it is better to speak of a slave society rather than slavery, for the effects of the labor system—slave or free—permeate the entire social structure, and influence all of its ways. If we are to speak of slavery, we must do so in its larger setting, as a way of life for both the master and the slave, for both the economy and the culture, for both the family and the community."

16. Tannenbaum, *Slave and Citizen, passim;* Elkins, *Slavery*, 52–80.

17. See too, Harry Hoetink, "Race Relations in Curaçao and Surinam" in Laura Foner and Eugene D. Genovese, eds., *Slavery in the New World: A Reader in Comparative History* (Englewood Cliffs, N.J., 1969), 178–79.

Chapter 1

1. William Byrd to the Earl of Orrery, Westover, Virginia, July 5, 1726, *VMHB* XXXII (Dec. 1924), 27.

2 Winthrop D. Jordan, *White Over Black* (Chapel Hill, 1968), Part I.

3. J. F. D. Smyth, *A Tour in the United States of America* (2 vols., London, 1784), I, 36; François Jean, Marquis de Chastellux, *Travels in North America*

in the Years 1780, 1781 and 1782, trans. and ed. by Howard C. Rice, Jr. (2 vols., Chapel Hill, 1963), II, 395.

4. Arthur P. Middleton, *Tobacco Coast: A Maritime History of Chesapeake Bay in the Colonial Era* (Newport News, 1953).

5. Thomas Lee to the Board of Trade [1750] cited in Carl Bridenbaugh, *Seat of Empire: The Political Role of Eighteenth-Century Williamsburg* (2nd ed. rev., Charlottesville, 1963), 1.

6. Henry Hartwell, James Blair, and Edward Chilton, *The Present State of Virginia, and the College,* ed. by Hunter D. Farish (Charlottesville, 1964 edit. [orig. London, 1698]), 10, 14; Hugh Jones, *The Present State of Virginia* (New York, 1865 edit. [orig. London, 1724]), 35.

7. Jackson Turner Main, "The One Hundred," *WMQ,* 3rd ser., XI (July 1954), 354–56, 358, 362.

8. United States Census Office, *First Census* (Philadelphia, 1791), 50 (transcript); George Maclaren Brydon, *Virginia's Mother Church* (2 vols., Richmond, 1947, Philadelphia, 1952), I, 366ff; *VMHB,* XII (Jan. 1905), 289n. For additional information on the burgeoning growth of the colony's population in the eighteenth century, see the U.S. Bureau of the Census, *A Century of Population Growth, from the First Census to the Twelfth, 1790–1900,* 47, 82, 96f. 100–102, 135–36; Governor Edmund Jenings to the Lords Commissioners of Trade and Plantations, Nov. 27, 1708 PROCO Ser. 5, 1316, 53–54, Virginia Colonial Records Project; see also H. Roy Merrens's relevant criticism of Evarts B. Greene's and Virginia D. Harrington's methodology in their *American Population Before the Federal Census of 1790* (New York, 1932), in *Colonial North Carolina in the Eighteenth Century: A Study in Historical Geography* (Chapel Hill, 1964), Appendix II, 194ff. The population estimates and charts in Robert E. and B. Katherine Brown, *Virginia 1705–1786: Democracy or Aristocracy?* (East Lansing, Mich., 1964), 12–17, and Tables I and II between 72 and 74 are also useful.

9. Hartwell, Blair, and Chilton, *The Present State of Virginia and the College,* 9ff.

10. Hugh Blair Grigsby, *The Virginia Convention of 1776* (Richmond, 1855), 35–36.

11. Andrew Burnaby, *Travels Through the Middle Settlements of North America, 1759–60* (London, 1798; 3rd ed., New York, 1904), 55–56; Robert "King" Carter to Micajah Perry, Sr. and Jr., Rappahannock, May 27, 1721, in Louis B. Wright, ed., *The Letters of Robert Carter, 1720–1727: The Commercial Interests of a Virginia Gentleman* (San Marino, Cal., 1941), 94; Landon Carter to Purdie and Dixon, editors of the *VaG* (Fall 1769) cited in Jack P. Greene, *Landon Carter: An Inquiry into the Personal Values and Social Imperatives of the Eighteenth-Century Gentry* (Charlottesville, 1965), 26.

12. Mallory Papers, UVA.

13. Pocket Plantation Papers, UVA.

14. Peter Fontaine to his brother Moses, March 30, 1757, cited in Ann Maury, *Memoirs of a Huguenot Family* (New York, 1853), 351.

15. "Carter Papers," *VMHB,* VII (July 1899), 65.

16. John Tayloe Account Book, 1776–86; see, for example, his accounts with Landon Carter and Francis Lightfoot Lee, 37v, 126v. Tayloe Family Papers, VHS.

17. Louis Morton, *Robert Carter of Nomini Hall* (Charlottesville, 1941),

205f. Dr. Johann David Schoepf, *Travels in the Confederation,* trans. and ed. by Alfred J. Morrison (Philadelphia, 1911), II, 32–33.

18. Sir Augustus John Foster, *Jeffersonian America: Notes on the United States of America Collected in the Years 1805–6–7 and 11–12,* ed. by Richard Beale Davis (San Marino, Cal., 1954), 140, 142. Duc de La Rochefoucauld-Liancourt, *Travels through the United States of North America, and the Country of the Iroquois, and Upper Canada, in the Years 1795, 1796 and 1797* . . . (2 vols., London, 1799), II, 80.

19. John Page, Rosewell, Gloucester County, Commonplace Book (c. 1794), VHS, 29–32.

20. *VMHB,* XXXVII (Oct. 1929), 294; Thad Tate, *The Negro in Eighteenth-century Williamsburg* (Williamsburg, 1965), 37.

21. Paul L. Haworth, *George Washington: Farmer* (Indianapolis, 1915), 193; Elijah Fletcher to his father, Alexandria, Va., Oct. 1, 1810, Martha von Briesen, ed., *The Letters of Elijah Fletcher* (Charlottesville, 1965), 14.

22. Edmund S. Morgan, *Virginians at Home: Family Life in the Eighteenth Century* (Charlottesville, 1963), 53–54. Morgan's book and Carl Bridenbaugh's brief and unpretentious *Myths and Realities: Societies of the Colonial South* (Baton Rouge, 1952) accurately and most adequately portray the quality of life in eighteenth-century Virginia.

23. Professor Eugene D. Genovese in "The Significance of the Slave Plantation for Southern Economic Development," *JSH,* 29 (Nov. 1962), 422–37, forcefully demonstrates that the ante-bellum plantation was critically lacking in self-sufficiency. In his most recent book, *The World the Slaveowners Made* (New York, 1970), he retreats from this position.

24. *VaG* (Purdie and Dixon), Dec. 1, 1768, B. Moore. The system of notation for newspapers used in this study is the same as that developed by Lester J. Cappon and Stella F. Duff in the *Virginia Gazette Index 1736–80* (Williamsburg, 1950). That is, the newspaper's title, editor (in parentheses), and the date of publication follow in that order. The name of the advertiser (usually referred to as the subscriber), is substituted for a page and column reference, since the quickest way to find a reference while scanning columns of newspaper advertisements is to locate the name of the advertiser.

Editors are important, because after May 1766 there were at least two and sometimes three competing editions of the *Gazette.* A list of these editors follows:

William Parks, 1736–1750
William Hunter, 1751–1761
Joseph Royle, 1761–1765
Alexander Purdie, 1765–1766
Alexander Purdie and John Dixon, 1766–1775
William Rind, 1766–1773
Clementina Rind, 1773–1774
John Pinkney, 1774–1776
John Dixon and William Hunter, Jr., 1775–1778
Alexander Purdie, 1775–1779
John Dixon and Thomas Nicolson, 1779–April 1780
John Clarkson and Augustine Davis, 1779–Dec. 1780

25. Robert "King" Carter, Diary, 1722–27, May 19, 1727, UVA microfilm.

26. Robert "King" Carter to M. Pemberton, Rappahannock, Sept. 15, 1727, Robert Carter Letterbook, UVA microfilm.

27. *Ibid.*, Sept. 16, 1727, Carter Letterbook.

28. Charles Steuart to Messrs. Manville, William Moore, Jr., Isaac De Piza, and Benjamin Messiah, July 5, 1751, Charles Steuart Letterbook, CW microfilm.

29. Governor Jenings to the Board of Trade, Williamsburg, Jan. 11, 1709, PROCO Ser. 5, 1316, f. 133–35, VCRP.

30. Charles Steuart to Messrs. Manville and Co., March 26, 1752, Steuart Letterbook.

31. Thomas E. Campbell, *Colonial Caroline* (Richmond, 1954), 332.

32. Governor Francis Fauquier to the Board of Trade, Williamsburg, Jan. 30, 1763, British Museum, King's 205, p. 264, VCRP; *VaG*, Dec. 12, 1755, Robert Dinwiddie.

33. Hugh Jones and William Byrd II cited in Middleton, *Tobacco Coast,* 135, 136.

34. Philip D. Curtin, *The Atlantic Slave Trade* (Madison, Wis., 1969), 72, 73, 143.

35. Jones, *The Present State of Virginia,* 37–38; Chastellux, *Travels,* II, 439.

36. Jones, *The Present State of Virginia,* 71.

37. William B. Perry, ed., *Historical Collections Relating to the American Colonial Church* (3 vols., Hartford, 1870), I, 264–65.

38. *Ibid.,* 293.

39. *Ibid.,* 281, 299, 301.

40. *Landon Carter's Diary,* II, 1114; Maury, *Memoirs of a Huguenot Family,* 334.

41. *Landon Carter's Diary,* II, 1038.

42. Robert Carter to Richard Dozier, Jan. 27, 1777, Carter Letterbooks, III, 1–92, DUL.

43. *Landon Carter's Diary,* II, 642.

44. *Ibid.,* II, 679.

45. *VaG* (Purdie), March 25, 1775, William Spratley; *VaG* (Dixon and Hunter), May 16, 1777, Josiah Daly; *VaG & GA,* March 14, 1792, Moses Austin and Co.; *VaG* (Purdie and Dixon), Feb. 9, 1769, William Macon, Jr.

46. Richard Henry Lee Account Book, 1776–94, 9, 29, 59–60, HEH.

47. *Ibid.,* 40.

48. *Ibid.,* 4, 11, 106–7.

49. Haworth, *George Washington: Farmer,* 199.

50. *Ibid.*

51. *Ibid.,* 77, 198.

52. *The Journal of John Harrower,* Edward M. Riley, ed. (Williamsburg, 1963), 56; Robert Beverley to Landon Carter, Sept. 24, 1770, Landon Carter Papers, VHS.

53. William Byrd II, *The Secret Diary of William Byrd of Westover, 1709–1712,* Louis B. Wright and Marion Tinling, eds. (Richmond, 1941), Jan. 6–7–8–9, 1711, 283–84.

54. *Landon Carter's Diary,* II, 615, 630, 636.

55. George Pitt to Mr. Robert Prentis, Stratford-on-Avon, England, Feb. 1, 1775, Prentis Family Papers, UVA. Charles Dabney to John Blair, Jr., and Mary Ambler, April 1, 1769, Dabney Papers, CW microfilm; *Landon Carter's Diary,* I, 363; Haworth, *George Washington: Farmer,* 204–5.

56. *VaG* (Dixon and Hunter), Jan. 31, 1777, John Thornton; (Purdie & Dixon), March 7, 1771, Stafford Lightburn, Jr.; *VaG* (Dixon and Hunter), Dec. 26, 1777, Fortunatus Sydnor.

57. Robert "Councillor" Carter to Mr. George Bateman, July 23, 1784, Letterbook, VI, 23. For further examples of the master's use of task allotment, see [Carter] to John South, May 14, 1785; to Jeriah Bonham, W[illia]m Brickey, Rob[er]t Moore, Richard Sutton, April 12, 1779, Letterbook, III, pt. 2, 117, and VI, 150; (Nov. 1776) and June 10 (1784), Daybook, XIII, 221, and XVI, 7–8; [Joseph] Ball to [Joseph] Chinn, Stratford-by-Bow, England, Aug. 5, 1755, Ball Letterbook, CW microfilm; John Hatley Norton to Battaile Muse, Dec. 23, 1781, James Mercer to Muse, July 10, 1777, Muse Papers, DUL; George Washington to William Pearce, Philadelphia, March 15, 1795, in George Washington, *Memoirs of the Long Island Historical Society* (Brooklyn, 1889), IV, *George Washington and Mount Vernon*, 172–73 (hereinafter cited as *Mount Vernon*).

58. Muse to George Nicholas, Berkeley Co., Dec. 18, 1784, Muse Papers; Elijah Fletcher to his father, Alexandria, Va., Oct. 1, 1810, von Briesen, *The Letters of Elijah Fletcher* 140.

59. James Mercer to Muse, July 10, 1777, Muse Papers.

60. Hugh Nelson to Muse, Yorktown, April 12, 1779, Muse Papers.

61. John Hatley Norton to Muse, Hanover Co., Dec. 23, 1781, Muse Papers.

62. *Ibid.*

63. J[ame]s Mercer to Muse, July 10, 1777, Muse Papers.

64. [John Hatley] Norton to Muse, March 5, 1788; Francis Willis, Jr., to Muse, Charlestown, May 25, 1785, Muse Papers.

65. Robert "Councillor" Carter to Charles Haynie, April 21, 1784, Robert "Councillor" Carter Letterbook, V, 201.

66. Robert "Councillor" Carter to Newyear Branson, April 11, 1785, Letterbook, IV, 138; Byrd, *Secret Diary, 1709–12*, 7; James Gordon, Journal, *WMQ*, 1st ser., IX (July 1903), 3; Carter to Branson, April 18, 1785, Letterbook VI, 138.

67. Robert Wormeley Carter to Landon Carter, May 10, 1774, Wellford Papers, UVA.

68. J[ame]s Mercer to Muse, June 13, 1778, June 5, [17]79; John H[atley] Norton to Muse, Winchester, Va., Dec. 17, 1787, Muse Papers.

69. *Landon Carter's Diary*, I, 362, II, 639.

70. James Mercer to Muse, Oct. 5, 1780, Muse Papers; Washington to William Pearce, Philadelphia, Aug. 26, Oct. 27, 1793, July 20 (and a July 21 postscript), 1794, *Mount Vernon*, 5, 8, 9, 92; *Landon Carter's Diary*, I, 302.

Washington and Landon Carter, both rigid, compulsively devoted to order, and plagued by poor managers and balky slaves, used slaves as overseers, they said among the best overseers they had. Washington's Davy cut lambs out of season for his own use, which his master chose to overlook. Carter's Jack Lubbar also took liberties and, like Davy, produced crops while protecting the slaves he was responsible for. Lubbar also drank often and to excess; and on the occasion cited above he left the Fork Quarter strewn with dead cattle and broken fences. Still Carter noted that [he] had "so gratefully discharged his duty as to make me by his care larger crops of Corn, tobacco, and Pease twice over than ever I have had made by anyone." Washington to Pearce, Philadelphia, Dec. 18, 1793, *Mount Vernon*, 13–14, 20; *Landon Carter's Diary*, II, 840.

The only slave overseer who was advertised as a runaway between 1736 and 1800 was rather thoroughly described: "RUN AWAY Tom, some call the slave Tom Salter, middle size, well made for strength, 38 years old; has bad teeth, many small pimples about his beard; can read, play on the fiddle and his common working dress was died brown cotton. He managed several years as an overseer for me, under Capt. Robert Downman, at a plantation of mine on Morattico creek, in Richmond county, where he always lived until lately. He is a dissembling artful fellow, and generally smiles when he speaks. I suspect [he is] lurking . . . near South Wales, where he has a wife named Sebra . . . HENRY LEE," *VaG* (Purdie and Dixon), March 23, 1769.

71. *Landon Carter's Diary,* I, 146; Cornelius Hall to John H. Norton, Oct. 1791, Norton Papers, CW; Charles Dabney to John Blair, Jr., and Mary Ambler, April 1, 1769, Dabney Papers, SHC, CW microfilm.

For additional examples of arrangements between slaves and their supervisors, see H[ugh] Nelson to Muse, Dec. 22, 1778, J[ame]s Mercer to Muse, Dec. 6, 1778, Muse Papers. [Landon Carter] to [John] Broughton, undated and labeled "Rough to Broughton," Wellford Papers, UVA; and one of the most thoroughly documented and revealing accounts of an alliance between whites and blacks involved George Washington's carpenter, Thomas Green, a white man and drunkard, and the slave carpenters and sawyers who worked with him. See the letters from the President to his steward, William Pearce, which were written throughout 1794, in *Mount Vernon,* 5, 8, 9, as well as Pearce to Washington, Feb. 11, 1794, Washington Papers, Ser. 4, LC.

72. Hugh Washington to Muse, n.d. (*ca.* 1788), Muse Papers. George Washington to William Pearce, Philadelphia, May 10, 1795, *Mount Vernon,* 184.

73. Hugh Washington to Muse, May 21, 1788, Muse Papers.

74. Ball to Chinn, Stratford-by-Bow, England, June 27, 1749, Ball Letterbook.

75. James Mercer to Muse, Fredericksburg, Dec. 5, 1778, Muse Papers.

76. Thomas Jefferson Account Book, transcribed by James A. Bear, Jr., UVA, 164.

77. Fairfax to Muse, April 3, 1794, Muse Papers.

78. *Ibid.;* see also Fairfax to Muse, Dec. [?], 1792, Muse Papers.

79. John Blair, Jr., to Charles Dabney, April 1, 1769, Dabney Papers.

Chapter 2

1. See the Introduction.

2. See fn. 35 on acculturation.

3. Eighteenth-century Virginia newspapers that were used were all those available on microfilm in the University of California library. The films were comprised of all of the newspapers printed in the colonial period as well as the major newspaper published in the new state from 1776 to 1801. About seven-eighths of the advertisements were published in various extant editions of the *Virginia Gazette,* the colony's only newspaper before Independence. Only a small number of notices were printed during the first years of publication; for example, there were 20 notices for 30 runaways in the late 1740's. By 1770, about 65 advertisements were published yearly for approximately 70 fugitives.

4. *VaG,* Nov. 21, 1745, Michael Sherman.

5. *VaG* (Purdie and Dixon; and Rind, see both editions), Dec. 24, 1772, Richard Booker.

6. *VaG* (Purdie and Dixon), Oct. 7, 1773, Joseph Hilliard.

7. For a provocative model of man in primitive society complementary to man in maximally politicized civilizations, such as our own, see Stanley Diamond, "Primitive Society in Its Many Dimensions," in Kurth Wolff and Barrington Moore, Jr., eds., *The Critical Spirit, Essays in Honor of Herbert Marcuse* (Boston, 1967), 21–30.

8. *VaG* (Rind), Oct. 8, 1772, Westmoreland jailor; (Dixon and Nicolson), Dec. 18, 1779, Samuel Calland; (Purdie and Dixon), Nov. 5, 1772, James Ball. For additional descriptions of "country marks" and filed teeth see (Purdie and Dixon), Dec. 12, 1771, Peter Pelham; (Purdie), Dec. 5, 1777, Michael Grate; March 1745, Alice Needle; Nov. 14, 1751, Archibald Cary; (Rind), Aug. 8, 1776, T. Poindexter; Aug. 10, 1769, Alexander Spark.

9. The following interpretations of rites of passage were especially useful in writing this section, John S. Mbiti, *African Religions and Philosophy* (New York, 1969); Yehudi A. Cohen, *The Transition from Childhood to Adolescence: Cross-Cultural Studies of Initiation Ceremonies, Legal Systems and Incest Taboos* (Chicago, 1964); David F. Pocock, "The Anthropology of Time Reckoning," in John Middleton, ed., *Myth and Cosmos* (New York, 1967), 301–15; and Paul Bohannan, *The Tiv of Central Nigeria* (London, 1953), 66–67.

10. Mbiti, *African Religions and Philosophy*, 117.

11. *Ibid.*

12. Pocock, "The Anthropology of Time Reckoning," 308–9.

13. In addition to Mbiti and Pocock, see E.E. Evans-Pritchard, "Neur Time-Reckoning," *Africa*, 12 (April 1939), 189–216; Paul Bohannan, "Concepts of Time Among the Tiv of Nigeria," in Middleton, ed., *Myth and Cosmos*, 315–30.

14. *VaG* (Purdie and Dixon), Sept. 12, 1771, George Robertson; see also, Nov. 2, 1739, John Shelton; May 16, 1745, William Hunter; (Purdie and Dixon), Dec. 13, 1770, James Buchanan; (Purdie and Dixon), Oct. 28, 1773, John Burnley's notice for the largest group of runaways advertised in an eighteenth-century Virginia newspaper. "Hanover Town, ranaway, FOURTEEN NEW NEGROES: about 2 months ago."

15. Sir William Gooch to the Board of Trade, Williamsburg, June 29, 1729, Colonial Office Papers, 5/1322, 19, VCRP, CW microfilm; Thomas E. Campbell, *Colonial Caroline* (Richmond, 1954), 72.

16. *S.C. Gaz.*, Feb. 16, 1765, Christopher; Feb. 16, 1734.

17. *S.C. Gaz.*, Jan. 29, 1753, William Edings.

18. *Ibid.*, Feb. 22, 1768, Richard Lambton.

19. *Ibid.*, Oct. 8, 1764, George Tew; Sept. 17, 1754, Supplement, Peter Procher.

20. *Ibid.*, July 21, 1766, George Smith; Oct. 6, 1766, Elias Bell, Feb. 16, 1734, Paine's Plantation.

21. *VaG* (Rind), Oct. 31, 1771, Westmoreland County jailer.

22. *VaG* (Purdie and Dixon), Jan. 28, 1773, John Taylor; (Purdie), Dec. 27, 1776, John Berryman; (Purdie), Nov. 21, 1777, Mary Wills; *S.C. Gaz.*, Feb. [12], 1771, John Brown; Jan. 1, 1771, William Heatley.

23. *VaG* (Purdie and Dixon), Sept. 12, 1771, Robert Owen.

24. *VaG* (Dixon and Hunter), May 16, 1777, Josiah Daly.

25. *VaG* (Purdie and Dixon), July 28, 1775, Samuel Wallace.

26. *VaG* (Rind), Oct. 19, 1769, Supplement, William Garrand.

27. *S.C. Gaz.*, Feb. 25, 1764, M.T. Savage.

28. *Ibid.*, Sept. 10, 1771, John Brown.

29. *VaG* (Dixon and Nicolson), Sept. 18, 1779, Joseph Hightower.

30. *VaG*, July 19, 1754, William Clinch.

31. *Ibid.*

32. *VaG* (Rind), Sept. 22, 1768, John Daniel.

174 NOTES TO PAGES 45–47

33. *VaG* (Rind), Sept. 5, 1771, Edward Hurst; see also (Purdie and Dixon), Jan. 28, 1773, John Taylor.

34. *VaG* (Purdie), Oct. 16, 1778, Hampshire County jailer.

35. Melville J. Herskovits's argument for concrete African "survivals," "Africanisms" (*The Myth of the Negro Past*, Boston, 1941) cannot be applied successfully in North America because, among other problems, there is almost no data on tribal origins. Nor can his methodology, without serious modifications, be applied to the Americas generally if one accepts the conclusions of scholars who have seriously challenged Herskovits's most essential assumption; namely, the West African "cultural (or "focal") area" concept: see M. G. Smith, "The African Heritage in the Caribbean" (and George E. Simpson's reply) in Vera Rubin, ed., *Caribbean Studies: A Symposium* (Seattle, 1960), 34ff; Paul Bohannan, *Africa and Africans* (New York, 1964), 126–28 is particularly devastating in his criticism of the concept. See also G. J. Jones's review of Robin Horton's *Kalabari Sculpture* in *Africa*, 37 (Jan. 1967), 109. "The author's conclusions will shatter many of the fond illusions held by those who postulate a Pan-African cultural unity in the field," Jones writes, "as he shows that Kalabari ideas and practices in this field, differ completely from those of the Yoruba and Bini or for that matter of other Southern Nigerian peoples."

Consequently, it is preferable to talk about a less rigorous but more flexible African "background" (rather than "survivals"), and concentrate on ways of thinking rather than artifacts and other "Africanisms." This is a position Herskovits discussed in one of his last papers, "Ethnophilosophy," in Melford E. Spiro, ed., *Context and Meaning in Cultural Anthropology, in Honor of A. Irving Hallowell* (New York, 1965). At this more general, and manageable, level of analysis the aforementioned paradigm by Stanley Diamond (see fn. 7) is particularly useful, as is Robert A. LeVine, "Africa," in Francis L. K. Hsu, ed., *Psychological Anthropology: Approaches to Culture and Personality* (Homewood, Ill., 1961), 48–92.

36. There were 657 fugitive men advertised between 1736–75; 118 (16 per cent) or about 1 in 6 were Africans. One-half of the native Africans (64) were recently imported "outlandish" slaves who did not learn any English in the first weeks of captivity. During this period about 50 subscribers commented on the slaves' use of English; but only about a dozen included an additional note on the date of importation.

37. *VaG*, Oct. 20, 1752, William Randolph.

38. *VaG* (Rind), Feb. 7, 1771, John Jacob.

39. *VaG*, May 16, 1745, William Hunter.

40. *VaG* (Purdie and Dixon), Nov. 4, 1773, Josiah Daly.

41. Charles Yates to Captain John Duncan, Fredericksburg, April 25, 1775, Yates Letterbook, 1773–83, UVA microfilm collection.

42. *VaG*, Dec. 12, 1755, Daniel Parke Custis.

43. *VaG* (Purdie), Aug. 8, 1777, T. Barbour. Advertisements are an invaluable source for understanding how a planter worked his land and distributed slaves, crops, orchards, and outbuildings. The following notices are especially detailed and informative: *Md.G.*, Aug. 22, 1799, John Francis Mercer; *VaG*, Oct. 3, 1751, Thomas Eldridge; (Purdie), Aug. 22, 1777, Nat. Jones; (Pinkney), June 22, 1775; (Purdie), May 16, 1777, "Supplement," for a description of Augustine Smith's "Shooter's Hill"; (Dixon and Hunter), March 14, 1777, for Adam Fleming's estate near Cabin Point on the lower James River.

44. *VaG* (Purdie), May 16, 1777, William Murray; and Nov. 7, 1777, "Supplement," James Le Grand. For other notices that give an indication of the quarter's isolation and land-slave ratio, see (Purdie), April 18, 1772, "Supplement," Phil. Johnson; Nov. 17, 1775, "Supplement," Anne Burwell; (Dixon and Hunter), Sept. 14, 1776, Robert Walton, Jr.

45. For notices offering to sell plantations worked by fewer than 10 "hands," see (Purdie), Oct. 31, 1777, Robert C. Nicholas; Sept. 5, 1777, John Timberlake; (Dixon and Hunter), Nov. 27, 1778, William Whitlock's executors; (Dixon and Nicolson), March 12, 1779, Otway Byrd.

Occasionally plantation records yielded a detailed letter from a planter to his steward regarding the establishment of a new quarter or home plantation. More than any other type of plantation record, these plans most satisfactorily convey the mood of the up-country quarter. See Hugh Nelson to Battaile Muse, York County, Feb. 10, March 28, and April 12, 1779; and Warner Lewis, Jr., to Muse, Gloucester County, Feb. 25, 1784, Muse Papers, DUL.

For account- and day-books kept by stewards and overseers that are illustrative of life on the quarter, see the Carter's Grove Account Book, 1738–55, Burwell Family Papers, CW microfilm; Nomini [Nomony] Hall Waste Book, 1773–83, CW microfilm, original at UVA; ["Councillor" Carter] Memo Book ("Book of Miscellanies"), 1788–89, LC. This is one of the most informative of its kind; it contains detailed descriptions of Carter's many quarters in Westmoreland and Richmond counties. Carter abandoned these plantations after the Revolutionary War, and leased them to tenants. These descriptions were part of the contracts with the lessees. See also Dudley Digges's reports to Charles W. Dabney, Dabney Papers, SHC, CW microfilm; and James Semple's reports in the Richard Corbin Letterbook, CW microfilm.

46. Custis Papers, VHS.

47. *VMHB*, VII (1899), 64–68.

48. Louis Morton, *Robert Carter of Nomini Hall* (Charlottesville, 1945), Table 9 following 276.

49. Battaile Muse to John Hatley Norton, July 26, 1789, Norton Papers, CW; also Herbert C. Bradshaw, *History of Prince Edward County, Virginia* (Richmond, 1955), 95.

50. "Plantation Accts. with Ch[arles] Payne overseer at Eff[ingham] Forrest," March 18, 1784, Norton Papers, CW.

51. Agreement between Ralph Smith and Hugh George, Jan. 8, 1798, Pocket Plantation Papers, UVA. For additional overseer contracts see, Charles Dabney and Ancel Clarkson, Aug. 21, 1772, Dabney Papers, CW microfilm; Sarah Allaman and Charles Deggs, June 3, 1717, Berkeley-Noland Papers, UVA; and Cornelius Hall and John Hatley Norton, Dec. 16, 1790, Norton Papers, CW. See also Thomas Jefferson's Account Book, Aug. 4, 1773, "Hints for Contracts with Overseers" (transcribed by James A. Bear, Jr.), UVA.

52. John Ferdinand D. Smyth, *A Tour of the United States of America . . .* (2 vols., London, 1784), I, 44; "Councillor" Carter to William Brickey, Jan. 6, 1779, Letterbook III, pt. 2, 86; Carter to Thomas Muse, March 2, 1784, V, 182. See also Carter to [William] Taylor, Dec. 14 [1773], I, 168–69, DUL.

53. La Rochefoucauld-Liancourt, *Travels through the United States of North America* (2 vols., London, 1799), II, 69; Carter to Battaile Muse, March 2, 1784, Letterbook V, 182, DUL; Ball to Joseph Chinn, Stratford-by-Bow, England, Feb. 18, 1774. See also Ball to Chinn, Oct. 22, 1756, Ball Letterbook, CW microfilm; J[ame]s Mercer to Muse, April 3, 1779, Muse Papers, DUL.

54. *VaG* (Purdie and Dixon), Nov. 22, 1770, James Henderson; June 7, 1770

(Purdie and Dixon), Joseph Pleasants; (Rind), July 12, 1770, William Dudley. For a field slave who was described as "well-clothed," see *VaG* (Dixon and Hunter), March 7, 1777. Berryman's Simon ran away with shoes, stockings, two coats, a checked linen shirt, a pair of brown sheeting breeches.

55. For example, Martha Massie's Moll, *VaG*, Nov. 3, 1752. See also the following plantation records: "Councillor" Carter, Nomini Hall Waste Book 1773–83, entries for Nov.–Dec. 1773, CW microfilm collection; Carter to J[ame]s Harrison, March 22, 1785, Letterbook VI, 119–20; Carter to [?], Dec. 18, 1790, IX, 197, DUL; "King" Carter to Thomas Colmore, Feb. 15, 1723/4; and Carter to Robert Jones, Oct. 22, 1729, Carter Letterbook, VHS.

56. *VaG* (Purdie), Sept. 5, 1777, Mordecai Throckmorton; (Dixon and Nicolson), Sept. 25, 1779, John Powell; Dec. 25, 1779, John Potts; *VaH & FA*, June 28, 1792, Job Cart[er]; Ball to Chinn, Feb. 18, 1744, April 23, 1754, Ball Letterbook.

Also Ball to Chinn, Nov. 13, 1746: "I will have no New Quarters built in the forest [one of his quarters] : but you may pull off the Covering; weather boards, studes, & Rafters; and then New Post, Cill, Stud, and Rafter them; and let them be well Cover'd weather boarded, and Lath'd & filled, and the floor rais'd higher within than without, and a Good plank Door, with Iron hinges, & a Good Lock & key; and let there be good Substantial Cills, of which Oak or Chesnut, laid a little way in the Ground."

57. Smyth, *A Tour of the United States,* II, 75.

58. J. H. Norton to Muse, Dec. 23, 1781, Muse Papers; Mary [Browne] to Dr. A. D. Galt, Sept. 13, 1823, Galt Family Papers, CW. See also "Councillor" Carter Daybook (Summer 1793), XVIII, 42: "Negro Sollomon & his Wife sarh I purpose to have as servants here—but not before my Stable is finished"; and "King" Carter to Robert Jones, Oct. 10, 1727, Letterbook, 1727–28, UVA microfilm.

59. See William Tatham, *Historical and Practical Essay on the Culture and Commerce of Tobacco* (London, 1800), which is still the most knowledgeable source. See also Melvin Herndon, "The Sovereign Remedy," *Tobacco in Colonial Virginia* (Williamsburg, 1957); David J. Mays, *Edmund Pendleton, 1721–1803: A Biography* (2 vols., Cambridge, Mass., 1952), I, 9–10, 99ff. Useful primary sources are the Reverend Robert Rose, Account Book and Diary (*ca.* 1727–50) entries for June–July 1748, CW microfilm; Richard Corbin to J. Semple, Jan. 1, 1759, Corbin Letterbook, CW microfilm; *Landon Carter's Diary,* I, 414–15, 426–27, 480, 482; and there is a detailed account on tobacco cultivation in the Wellford Papers (Landon Carter), n.d. [early 1770's], "Rough to [John] Boughton," UVA.

60. "Councillor" Carter to [?], Dec. 18, 1790, Letterbook, IX, 198, DUL.

61. "Councillor" Carter Daybook, Feb. 1777, XIV, 25, DUL.

62. *Ibid.*

63. *Landon Carter's Diary,* I, 355, II, 740.

64. *Ibid.,* I, 397.

65. William Strickland, *Observations on the Agriculture of the United States of America* (London, 1801) cited in Morton, *Carter of Nomini Hall,* 106.

66. *Landon Carter's Diary,* I, 301, 358, 534; also 303, 369.

67. Haworth, *George Washington: Farmer,* 198; see also George Washington to William Pearce, Philadelphia, Feb. 22, 1794, *Mount Vernon,* 166.

68. *Landon Carter's Diary,* I, 386; see also 445.

69. "King" Carter to [?], Corotoman, March 3, 1720/21; Carter to Mr.

Edward Tucker, May 11, 1727, Carter Letterbooks, 1720–21, 1727–28, UVA microfilm. Louis B. Wright, ed., *Letters of Robert Carter, 1720–1727: The Commercial Interests of a Virginia Gentleman* (San Marino, Cal., 1940), 85–87. Robert Carter Nicholas to John H. Norton, Oct. 14, 1771, Norton Papers, CW.

70. J[ame]s Mercer to Muse, June 13, 1778, Muse Papers, DUL; Washington to Pearce, Philadelphia, March 8, 22, 1795, *Mount Vernon*, 175, 179, see also 94, 194. Washington required frequent "sick reports" from his steward Pearce. See Pearce to Washington, Mount Vernon, Feb. 1, 8, 1794, Washington Papers, Ser. 4, LC; *Landon Carter's Diary* I, 371, 373.

71. "King" Carter to Mr. Robert Jones, Corotoman, Oct. 10, 1727, Letterbook 1727–28, UVA microfilm.

72. John Tayloe to Landon Carter, Mount Airy, "Easter Sunday," March 21, 1771, Wellford Papers, UVA.

73. "Councillor" Carter Daybook, June 15, 1784, XVI, 11–12 DUL; see Acting Governor Edmund Jenings's Proclamation (March 1709) warning overseers and planters who were too lenient in allowing slaves to "go abroad and remaining absent longer time than the Law allows." March 12, 1709, Colonial Office Papers, ser. 5/1316, 166, 167, VCRP, CW.

74. *Landon Carter's Diary*, I, 291, 371, 389.

75. *VaG* (Rind), April 11, 1766, Thomas Watkins.

76. For the first remedial legislation on runaways, see *Hening*, II, 299–300 (1672).

77. *VaG* (Rind), Feb. 4, 1768, John Smith; (Rind), Feb. 27, 1772, Thomas Lawson; (Rind), May 23, 1771, Morris Ramsay; (Purdie and Dixon), Aug. 10, 1769, Edward Cary.

78. *Landon Carter's Diary*, II, 754. *VaG* (Rind), May 23, 1771, Joseph Calland; (Purdie and Dixon), April 18, 1771, George Narthsworthy; (Purdie), Jan. 17, 1777, John Greenhow.

79. *Va. Argus*, Sept. 5, 1800; also *VaIC*, Aug. 16, 1786, Francis Alison; *VaH & FA*, Aug. 16, 1792; *VMHB*, VII (Jan. 1900), 444; and James Hugo Johnston, *Race Relations and Miscegenation in the South, 1776–1860* (Amherst, Mass., 1970), 24, 26, 317ff.

80. *VaG* (Rind), Jan. 25, 1770. The small and sporadic eighteenth-century conspiracies before Gabriel's insurrection (1800), analyzed by Herbert Aptheker, *American Negro Slave Revolts* (New York, 1943), Ch. VIII, can be compared to the rebellious styles discussed in this chapter.

81. For example, J. P. Kennedy and Henry R. McIlwaine, eds., *Journals of the House of Burgesses, 1619–1776* (13 vols., Richmond, 1905–15), 1726–40, 254, 262, 263. Three suicides were reported in all issues of the *VaG*, July 10, 1752; March 17 and Sept. 17, 1775.

82. *VaG*, Aug. 14, 1752, William Lightfoot.

83. *JHB*, 1752–55, 258.

84. *Landon Carter's Diary*, I, 359. Washington to Pearce, Philadelphia, Nov. 23, 1794, *Mount Vernon*, 35–36, 129–30, 189–90.

85. Ball to Chinn, Stratford-by-Bow, Eng., Feb. 18, 1744, Ball Letterbook; J[ame]s Mercer to Muse, April 3, 1779, Muse Papers. Hugh Jones, *The Present State of Virginia* (New York, [1724] 1865), 132.

86. *VaG* (Rind), March 17, 1768, B——E——; March 29, 1770. On Feb. 3, 1772, Landon Carter noted that he was dissatisfied with the House of Burgesses; they had not passed a law prohibiting "those night shops," nor had

they listened to his "repeated letters in Public against allowing these night shops." Professor Greene's note to the above (*Landon Carter's Diary*, II, 649n) reads: "a search of copies of the *Gazette* failed to reveal any of these letters." But the tone of the letters cited above, and fact that Carter, a staunch patriot or anti-court man, would not publish in Purdie and Dixon's edition of the *VaG*, suggests that the letters are his.

On several occasions, slaves gave to their masters money and jewelry they found along the roads and river banks; the masters, in turn, advertised the lost article in the *Gazette*. One of Landon Carter's "servants" found a money bag with £204 near Littlepage's Bridge, see *VaG* (Dixon and Nicolson), Feb. 19, 1779; also (Dixon and Hunter), Sept. 21, 1776, Gabriel Jones; April 13, 1776, James Cocke; June 8, 1776, Thomas Fenner; (Pinkney), Nov. 2, 1775, James Bray Johnson. There are several more.

87. Richmond County Court Minute Book, Slave and Criminal Trials, 1710–54, VSL. I am indebted to Mr. William J. Van Schreeven, formerly the State Archivist, for calling this source to my attention.

88. Frank Tannenbaum, *Slave and Citizen: The Negro in the Americas* (New York, 1946), 115.

89. Adrienne Koch and William Peden, eds., *The Life and Selected Writings of Thomas Jefferson* (New York, 1944), 278.

90. The paternalistic aspect of American Negro slavery, an essential feature of Stanley Elkins's interpretation (*Slavery*, 103–4), is an especially controversial issue; for it involves the now familiar problem of whether or not accommodationist behavior was a prominent feature of the slave's adjustment. Ulrich B. Phillips wrote most fully on this subject—at times as a scholar, at other times as an apologist. See his *American Negro Slavery* (Gloucester, Mass., 1959) *passim*, but esp. 512, 513; and *Life and Labor in the Old South* (Boston, 1963), ch. XI, "Life in Thraldom," in which he makes the following statement which he unfortunately does not follow up: "The simplicity of the social structure on the plantations facilitated Negro adjustment, the master taking the place of the accustomed chief." Professor Genovese, like Elkins, also emphasizes Southern paternalism as a key factor in slavery; see his introduction to a new paperback edition of the 1918 *American Negro Slavery* (Baton Rouge, 1967); "The Legacy of Slavery and the Roots of Black Nationalism," *Studies on the Left*, VI (Nov.–Dec. 1966), 6f, 9, 11, 14; and most recently, *The World the Slaveholders Made* (New York, 1969).

91. For biographical information on William Byrd II, see John Spencer Bassett's useful introduction to *The Writings of "Colonel William Byrd of Westover in Virginia Esqr"* (New York, 1901); Louis B. Wright, *The First Gentlemen of Virginia* (Charlottesville, 1940), Ch. XI; and Wright's introduction to the most recent edition of Byrd's writings, *The Prose Works of William Byrd of Westover* (Cambridge, Mass., 1966), as well as the introductions to Byrd's two Virginia diaries: L. B. Wright and Marion Tinling, eds., *The Secret Diary of William Byrd of Westover, 1709–1712* (Richmond, 1941); and M. Tinling and Maude H. Woodfin, eds., *Another Secret Diary of William Byrd of Westover, 1739–1741* (Richmond, 1942).

92. For example, Wright and Tinling, eds., *The Secret Diary, 1709–1712*, 15, 412, 419; and Tinling and Woodfin, eds., *Another Secret Diary, 1739–1741*, 1, 6, 7, 129, 171.

93. *The Secret Diary, 1709–1712*, 205.

94. *Ibid.*, 307.

95. *Ibid.*, 22, 42, 79, 224.

96. *Ibid.*, 192.

97. *Ibid.*, 7.

98. *Ibid.*, 45, 46, 112, 113. The entry p. 46 reads "George B-th brought home my boy Eugene . . . [he] was whipped for running away and had the bit put on him." Byrd's style of paternalism was not simply restricted to his black "people." See, *ibid.*, 13, 75. "I proceeded to Falling Creek where I found Mr. Grills [an overseer] drunk. . . . I scolded at Mr. Grills till he cried and then was peevish." And "I denied my man Grills to go to a horse race because there was nothing but sewaring and drinking there."

99. William Byrd, Commonplace Book (ca. 1722–32), 50, 78, 79, VHS.

100. Jack P. Greene, *Landon Carter: An Inquiry into the Personal Values and Social Imperatives of the Eighteenth-Century Virginia Gentry* (Charlottesville, 1967), 10.

101. Greene, *Landon Carter*, 76–83. For another side of Robert Wormeley—that is, more from the young man's point of view and less from his father's—see his daybooks and plantation records, which he kept for his father while acting in the capacity of a steward during the early 1770's. This material is in the Wellford Papers, UVA, and in the Carter Papers, William and Mary College Library. See also Louis Morton, ed., "The Daybook of Robert Wormeley Carter of Sabine Hall, 1766," *VMHB*, LXVIII (July 1960), 301–16. In Morton's article (313–14), Carter writes on Aug. 25, 1766: "Determined [to take up residence] at Hiccory Thicket [for] myself & Family, as the [only method] to avoid the frequent quarrels between Father & me; discoursing about the matter [with] Mr Parker I recd from him some hints, that Father looks upon it [gambling] in so heinous a light as to threaten to make an alteration in his will to the prejudice of me & my Children; upon this I discoursed with the old Gent on the affair; I understood from him that he would take away the maids that tended my Children, & that he would not aid me but distress me; this prevailing reason obliged me to lay aside my design & with it bid adieu to all Satisfaction, being compelled to live with him who told me I was his daily curse; and who [attributed] to me his Negroes running away, &c." Then after this intriguing observation, young Carter noted, "But he is still my Father & I must bear with every thing from him; in order [to lead a?] quiet life."

102. *Landon Carter's Diary*, I, 310.

103. *Ibid.*, I, 369; see also, 378.

104. *Ibid.*

105. *Ibid.*, 397.

106. [Landon Carter] to [John] Boughton, n.d. This document is labeled "Rough to Boughton," Wellford Papers, UVA.

107. One of the finest biographies of a colonial aristocrat is Louis Morton's *Robert Carter of Nomini Hall*. Although I used the Carter material at Duke, the Library of Congress, and Virginia Historical Society for different purposes than did Professor Morton, our conclusions about Carter as a slave master are similar.

108. Hunter Dickinson Farish, ed., *The Journal and Letters of Philip Vickers Fithian 1773–1774: A Plantation Tutor of the Old Dominion* (Williamsburg, new edit., 1965), 37.

109. Carter to John Pound, March 16, 1779, Letterbook, III, part 2, 110. See also Morton, *Carter*, 107–8, 109; Carter to Newyear Branson, Aug. 22,

1788, Letterbook, VIII, 170; to Elder William Hazard, Jan. 3, 1783, Letterbook, V, 89; and to William Dawson, Feb. 6, 1788, Letterbook, VIII, 78. See also Carter to General B. Barnes, Jan. 19, 1777, Letterbook, III, part 2, 4: "Your Favor of New Years day got to hand last Saturday advising of Negro Tom a runaway—I thank you for your care and Attention towards him." It is interesting to compare Carter's reception of this runaway with Byrd's reaction to Eugene. (Note: this runaway, Tom, was one of at least two fugitives that left Northern Neck quarters and, when later committed to jail, claimed that Carter was their master.) See Peter Durling [?] to Carter, Jan. 17, 1800, Carter Papers, VHS.

For another indication of Carter's sensitivity to the inevitable problems which occurred between overseers and crop hands, see his handling of a fiasco at the Billingsgate quarter in the summer of 1781, Letterbook, VI, 31; IV, 75, 87, 93, 105.

Carter's convictions about slavery are also well illustrated in his recommendations for overseers. See Letterbook VI, 23: "The Subscriber doth herein certify that Mr Youell Rust, Overseer, Made for him five Crops. . . . That said Negroes appeared to have an affection for both him and her"; and Letterbook, VII, 311–12: "Mr James Harrison . . . during his tenure was humane to the Negroes under his authority." Also see Carter to Samuel Carter, March 10, [1781], Letterbook, IV, 48: "Negro George, Carpenter has a daughter, Betty, about 7 years old, Motherless, now at Colespoint plantation, George wishes to have Betty to live at Aires, with his wife who lives there—If Betty is not useful where she now lives—I desire to indulge George in the Request mentioned above and you will accordingly permit him to take his daughter"; Carter to Mr. John Latham, Dec. 22, 1792, Letterbook, X, 37: "Negro Samson Robinson, a free man, applies to me wishing to hire said Rose (Samson's wife and his two Children of tender years) & to take her children—I am very much inclined to come into Samson's proposal touching his wife & Children." And again his tone of address, the manner in which he speaks of Africans, that is, as people, is as important for our purposes as his actions. And finally, see Carter to George Newman, Dec. 29, 1789, Letterbook, IX, 72: "Negro Argy of Cancer Plantation requested of me that I would consent to his removal from said Plantation, and to be hired to Mr. Richd Neale of Loudoun who has a Negro woman, his Wife—I do agree that Argy be hired to Mr. R. Neale for the Year 1790."

110. Carter to Newyear Branson, Feb. 2, 1790, Letterbook, IX, 93, DUL.

111. For Carter's speech, see his Daybook, 1773–76, 175–79; and Morton, *Carter*, 55–56.

112. [unsigned] to Carter, Frederick County, [Aug. 5], 1796, Carter Papers, LC.

113. *VaG* (Rind), Sept. 26, 1771; (Purdie), Oct. 25, 1776; (Purdie) Nov. 21, 1777, William Pollard; (Purdie), Feb. 16, 1776; (Purdie and Dixon), Dec. 10, 1772; *VaH & FFA*, Oct. 30, 1795, Alexander Voss; *VaG* (Rind), Jan. 31, 1771, Richard Randolph; (Purdie and Dixon), April 14, 1774, Thomas Lawson for John Tayloe; May 7, 1767, Robert Hart.

Cf. Winthrop D. Jordan, "American Chiaroscuro: The Status and Definition of Mulattoes in the British Colonies," *WMQ*, 3rd ser., XIX (April 1962), 183–200.

114. Charles Yates to Messrs. Collin, Wilson & Ponsonby of St. Kitts, Fredericksburg, March 15, 1780, Yates Letterbook, 1773–83, UVA microfilm.

115. *Mount Vernon,* 172–73.

116. *Ibid.,* 21, 216, 244.

117. Ball to Aron, Stratford-by-Bow, Eng., Aug. 31, 1754, Ball Letterbook.

118. Ball to Joseph Chinn, Aug. 31, 1754, Ball Letterbook. These letters were in one cover.

119. *ValC,* July 11, 1787, James Heron; *VaG* (Purdie and Dixon), March 23, 1769, Henry Lee. See also a runaway notice for "George," of "sulky looks and temper, except when he chooses to force a deceitful smile." He "is a *very* complete domestic servant," his owner concluded, "when [he] pleases." And Matt's owner warned that his slave, "being very clever as a waitingman," would probably "endeavour to hire himself to some Gentleman" (Dixon and Nicolson), May 22, 1779, Hamilton Ballantine; April 2, 1779, Alexander G. Strachan. For additional notices for runaway waitingmen, see *VaG & GA,* March 11, 1795, M. Anderson; *VaH & FA,* Aug. 11, 1796, Adam Hunter; April 26, 1792, George French; *VaG,* March 21, 1745, Alice Needle; (Purdie and Dixon), Aug. 17, 1769, Thomas Barnes.

120. *VaG* (Purdie and Dixon), April 14, 1774, Thomas Lawson for Tayloe.

121. *Ibid.,* March 19, 1772, James Mercer.

122. James Mercer to John Francis Mercer, March 3, 1787; see also [to same] Jan. 26, Mercer Papers, VHS.

123. *ValC,* March 4, 1780, Austin Brockenbrough.

124. *Landon Carter's Diary,* II, 778.

125. *Ibid.,* I, 290, 378, II, 665.

126. *Ibid.,* II, 778, also I, 378.

127. *VaG* (Rind), March 3, 1768, Landon Carter; see also *Landon Carter Diary* I, 363, 373; II, 778, 784, 793, 798.

128. *Landon Carter's Diary,* II, 782, 784, 793, 797–98. The runaway notice, in a mutilated condition, is labeled: Clerk of Lunenburgh Parish upper Church "is requested to publish this outlawry at his Church this day—19 Oct 1777," Carter Papers, folder 3, W & M.

129. *Ibid.,* II, 760.

130. *Ibid.*

131. *Ibid.*

132. Morton, *Carter,* 225. The family tutor, Philip Vickers Fithian, made insightful comments on Carter's sons. See *Fithian Journal,* 26, 49–50, 64, 70, 75, 86, 187, 190.

133. J[ame]s Mercer to Muse, May 18, 1780, Muse Papers, DUL.

134. *VaG,* Dec. 17, 1736, Nathaniel-Bacon Burwell; *VaH & FA,* Sept. 25, 1795, Daniel Triplett; *VaG & GA,* July 10, 1797, John Hopkins.

135. *VaG & GA,* Feb. 7, 1800, John Mayo; March 11, 1795, M. Anderson; *VaG* (Rind), Jan. 31, 1771, Richard Randolph.

Chapter 3

1. *VaG* (Rind), Feb. 2, 1769, Josiah Sumner; Aug. 17, 1769, John Graham; Dec. 1, 1768, Bernard Moore; April 14, 1768, also Moore; May 26, 1768, Mann Page; Jan. 28, 1768, Richard Graves; Sept. 3, 1767, Thomas Moore; May 19, 1768, Thomas Boswell.

2. *ValC,* Oct. 31, 1787, Archibald Cary.

3. *VaG* (Rind), Nov. 16, 1768, William Kennon.

4. *Ibid.* (Purdie), July 25, 1777, Francis Jaram; Nov. 4, 1763, Samuel Smith:

May 9, 1777, Dalton & Carlyle. *MdG,* May 24, 1759, A. McRae. John Ritchie to Battaile Muse, n.p. January 28, [17]68, Muse Papers, DUL.

5. "Councillor" Carter to Mr. Richard Oharrow; to John Ballandine, Letter-book, III, pt. 1, 138–39; V, 120; Tayloe Account Book, 1776–86, Tayloe Family Papers, VHS.

See also "Councillor" Carter to William Mathis, July 24, 1775; Carter to William Mitchell, May 15, 1776, Letterbook, III, 16–17, III, pt. 1, 27–28; "Councillor" Carter Daybook, 1773–76, June 29, 1774, for an agreement with Hugh Burnie, cooper, "a sober man," to "work and instruct" his slaves in cooperage; Sept. 10, 1776, an agreement with the widow of a river boat pilot, who "understood the Woolin & Linen Branches completely [to] instruct his Negroes at Aires."

6. Estate of Robert Poole, Princess Anne County, Deed Book 6, 1740–47, p. 79 VSL; *VaG* (Purdie), May 9, 1777, Dalton and Carlyle; Dec. 12, 1777, Alexander Saunders for the estate of William Bond; Jan. 1, 1767; Sept. 12, 1755; Oct. 10, 1745, John Brown; July 19, 1754, William Lightfoot; June 11, 1772, Matthew Tuell; (Dixon and Nicolson), May 15, 1779; and Thad Tate, *The Negro in Eighteenth-Century Wiliamsburg* (Charlottesville, 1965), 68–69; *VaH & FA,* Sept. 18, 1794, Michael Wallace.

7. *Hening,* VIII, 364–66; *VaG* (Hunter and Dixon), Feb. 21, 1777, James Tait; Mar. 7, 1777, Mary M. Pearson; (Purdie), March 7, 1777, Mary M. Pearson; Jan. 3, 1777, John Strode; *VaIC,* Jan. 24, 1787 Hunter Estate; *VaG* (Purdie and Dixon), April 11, 1771, James Hunter.

8. Norfolk County Order Book, 1796–1801, Norfolk Parish Register, part 1.

9. *VaG* (Purdie), Jan. 5, 1775, Isaac Zane; Feb. 14, 1777, David Ross; (Dixon and Hunter), Feb. 7, 1777, "The Manufacturing Society"; (Purdie), Oct. 31, 1777, David Ross; Nov. 28, 1777, B. Johnston, Thomas Waring. See also *VaIC,* Jan. 7, 1789, James Harris (Canal Works on the James River); Jan. 23, 1788, Harris; *VaG* (Purdie), Nov. 28, 1777; Jan. 7, 1775, John Ballendine (Potomac Canal and Navigation project); *VaH & FA,* Nov. 28, 1793, Daniel Triplett (Falmouth Nail Manufactory); Jan. 12, 1792, Thomas West and Co. (Nail Manufactory).

10. *VaH & FA,* Dec. 19, 1793, Thornton Fitzhugh.

11. *VaG* (Rind), Dec. 24, 1767.

12. *VaIC,* Jan. 23, 1788, James Harris.

13. *Ibid.,* Jan. 7, 1789, Harris.

14. John Ritchie to Battaile Muse, n.p. Jan. 28, [17]86, Muse Papers, DUL. "Councillor" Carter to Stephen Johnson Mason, March 21, 1785, VI, 116; to Joseph Dozier, May 13, 1777, III, pt. 1, 133.

15. Carter to George Howe, Sept. 10, 1784, "Councillor" Carter Letterbook, VI, 32. *VaG* (Rind), April 19, 1770, William Garthright, Jr.; (Purdie and Dixon), Sept. 15, 1774, John West.

16. *VaG.* (Rind), Feb. 6, 1772, Thomas Jones.

17. Lee Account Book, 1776–94, 59–60, Brock Collection, HEH. For additional examples of artisans and jobbers who traveled extensively among quarters, see Edward Ambler to Charles Dabney, Dec. 7, 1767, April 1, 1769 (about the carpenter "Sharper"), Dabney Papers, SHC, CW microfilm.

18. Erik Erikson, *Ghandi's Truth: the Origins of Militant Nonviolence* (New York, 1969), 195.

19. *VaIC,* March 4, 1789, Nathaniel Pope; *VaG* (Rind), March 24, 1768, Henry Brodnax; *VaH & FA,* May 8, 1795, Lawrence Brooke; *VaG & GA,* March 28, 1798, Thomas Owen; Jan. 16, 1761, Christopher Wright.

20. *VaIC,* July 11, 1787, James Heron; *VaG* (Dixon and Nicolson), Feb. 12, 1779, Thomas Lundie; *VaG & GA,* March 30, 1791, Sampson Mathews.
21. *Landon Carter's Diary,* II, 754. *VaG,* (Purdie and Dixon), May 19, 1774, Postscript, John Hartwell Cocke; (Dixon and Hunter), May 16; (Purdie), May 23, 1777, Bennett Browne.
22. *VaG* (Dixon and Hunter), April 4, 1777, Robert Beverley; (Purdie and Dixon), Feb. 20, 1772, Grymes's Estate; (Rind), April 19, 1770, William Garthright, Jr. See also J. F. D. Smyth, *A Tour in the United States of America* (2 vols., London, 1784, reprinted New York, 1969), I, 59:

> You cannot understand all of them [the slaves] as great numbers, being Africans are incapable of acquiring our language and at best but very imperfectly, if at all. Many of the others [the American-born] also speak a mixed dialect between the Guinea and English.

23. *VaG* (Purdie and Dixon), Feb. 9, 1769, William Macon, Jr.
    See also (Rind), April 23, 1772, John Fox; (Purdie and Dixon), April 5, 1770, Joshua Jones; March 5, 1772, James Walker.
24. For runaways who played the fiddle, see *VaG* (Rind), July 18, 1771, Judith Harbert; (Purdie and Dixon), May 7, 1767, Richard King; (Purdie), May 3, 1776, Thomas Penistone; Feb. 3, 1775, Townshed Dade's "Harry," who was "very fond of playing on the fiddle, though but a poor hand."
    For runaways who played the violin and "banger," see *VaG* (Dixon and Nicolson), June 12, 1779, [?] Isaac; *VaH & FA,* March 27, 1794, Betty Lewis; *VaG,* Oct. 27, 1752, James Cocke; and (Dixon and Nicolson), Jan. 8, 1780, John Giles's "Charles," who had "remarkably short teeth which he keeps very dirty . . . is very fond of playing on the banger." Note: one of the precious few illustrations of slave life (c. 1800) is a painting, "The Old Plantation," by an unknown artist, which includes a man playing a banjo ("banger") in the Abby Aldrich Rockefeller Collection, CW; it is also reproduced in Morgan's *Virginians at Home,* 60 ff.
25. *VaG,* April 4, 1766, Sarah Gist.
26. *VaH & FA,* Jan. 15, 1795, Jacob Christman; *VaG* (Purdie and Dixon), Sept. 15, 1774, Peterfield Trent; (Dixon and Nicolson), July 31, 1779, John Banister.
27. *VaG* (Purdie and Dixon), Nov. 3, 1775, John Aylett; (Purdie), May 29, 1778, John Gordon.
28. *VaG* (Purdie and Dixon), April 18, 1766, John Greenhow; Dec. 13, 1770, William Black.
29. *VaH & FA,* Sept. 18, 1794, Michael Wallace; *VaG* (Purdie and Dixon), April 1, 1774, Thomas Lawson for John Tayloe; *VaIC,* May 7, 1788, L. A. Pauly; *VaG,* May 14, 1767, J. Jones.
30. For additional notices for runaway blacksmiths, shoemakers, and woodworkers, see *VaG* (Purdie), Jan. 19, 1776, John Evans; Nov. 8, 1776, Richard Burnley; (Dixon and Hunter), March 14, 1777, Daniel Trueheart; Dec. 5, 1777, William Black; Oct. 17, 1777, John Jouet's Adam, who was described as a young mulatto, "a fine Shoemaker, dresses tolerably well and has been used to wait in the House for several Years"; June 27, 1777, Anthony Thornton, Jr.'s Abraham, a strong and well made shoemaker and a "fine Plantation Hand"; (Purdie), June 13, 1777, John Murchie.
    See: *Sailors, VaIC,* Jan. 2, 1788, Thomas Ker; *VaG* (Purdie), June 12, 1778; William Hepburn's Ishmael, "bred to the sea by Mr. Cornelius Calvert of Norfolk"; (Rind), Oct. 19, 1769, Supplement: Henry Minson's 16-year-old

boy, "remarkably smart and sensible" and "had two voyages to sea"; (Purdie and Dixon), Aug. 24, 1769, Robert Donald's "Spaniard," Brazil, a skipper of one of Donald's flats and "a very good seaman." *Carters, VaG,* (Purdie), March 8, 1776, Scrivener; (Dixon and Nicolson), July 24, 1779, John Saunders; (Hunter), Oct. 10, 1756, Francis Willis, Sr. *Coachmen,* (Purdie), April 18, 1745, Benjamin Grymes; Sept. 12, 1745, John Mercer; (Purdie and Dixon), Feb. 24, 1774, William Griffin's "noted old Fellow," once a coachman for Speaker John Robinson. *Cooks,* April 25, 1751, Bolling; *VaH & FA,* Sept. 13, 1782, Cyrus. *Gardeners, VaG,* Sept. 19, 1751, James Spi[c]ks' "Dick," who was also a "Ferry-Man"; (Dixon and Hunter), Sept. 15, 1777, John West; (Rind), May 12, 1768, Peter Wagener's Jack Yarmouth, formerly Governor William Gooch's gardener; *VaG & GA,* July 15, 1795, John Tyler. *Ploughman, VaG,* Oct. 10, 1756, Francis Willis, Sr. *Overseer,* (Purdie and Dixon), March 23, 1769, Henry Lee. *Wagoners, VaG & Ga,* April 3, 1793, Samuel Higgenbotham; *VaIC,* March 4, 1789, Nathaniel Pope's Davy, "drove a waggon many years at the Deep Run coal pits for Samuel Du Val"; *VaG* (Dixon and Nicolson), July 24, 1779, James Saunders. *"Tobacco-maker," VaG,* Oct. 27, 1752, James Cocke (this runaway also played the violin). *Wheelwrights,* (Dixon and Hunter), Jan. 6, 1776, Ruffin's Lewis, an excellent wheelwright and wagon maker; (Purdie and Dixon), Aug. 10, 1769, B. Green. *Millers,* Oct. 18, 1770, May 28, 1767, April 7, 1774, Jan. 14, 1775, Benjamin Harrison's "Nick," an habitual runaway. *Stocking weaver, VaG,* (Purdie and Dixon), Nov. 30, 1775, Isaac Zane. *Whiskey distiller, VaG & GA,* March 16, 1796, Edward Mosely, Sr.'s Will, tall, forty years old, "almost white," round-shouldered and a "good Shoemaker," also "under[stood] distilling whiskey," "rather too fond of spirits." *Hostlers and jockeys, VaH & FA,* June 12, 1795, William T. Alexander's "Parlor." His "profession as a groom for the last ten years," wrote Alexander, "has attached him very much to horses." *VaG* (Pinkney), Jan. 6, 1776, John Scott. *Harness maker, VaG* (Purdie and Dixon), April 22, 1775, Daniel Dodson. *Slave workers in "factories;" Dismal Swamp Land Co., VaG* (Rind), June 23, 1768, John Washington; (Purdie and Dixon), Dec. 5, 1771, J. Washington. *Salt works laborers, VaG* (Dixon and Hunter), Nov. 13, 1778, William Clopton; Dec. 19, 1777, Ben Timberlake, Jr.'s Ned, a stutterer, "remarkably dirty having been employed some Time in making Salt." *Ropemakers, VaG & GA,* March 30, 1791, Sampson Mathews; July 10, 1798, William Nicholson. *Lead mines laborers, VaG & GA,* March 14, 1792, Moses Austin & Co. *"Striker" at the Fredericksburg gunnery, VaIC,* Aug. 29, 1789, Charles Porter. *Laborers at Westham, the Public Armory, VaG* (Purdie), Aug. 1, 1777, Richard Adams, Nathaniel Wilkinson, and Turner Southall. *Bricklayers,* (Purdie and Dixon), April 5, 1770, William Byrd; (Dixon and Hunter), Sept. 15, 1777, John West; (Purdie and Dixon), July 7, 1774, Chapman Manson. *Laborers at Estave's vineyard,* Oct. 22, 1772; Nov. 18, 1773; (Pinkney), March 24, 1774. For *hired-out slaves* that ran off, see *VaG* (Rind), April 25, 1772, William Gatewood's Joe, hired to "Doctor Clements last year who employed him some times to work upon his plantation"; (Purdie and Dixon), July 30, 1772, Enoch George's Daniel, a waterman, "hired this present Year to Mr. Robert Gilmour . . . and went in a Vessel of his when he made his Elopement . . . went off with one Charles . . . broke into a Catpoint warehouse"; Oct. 13, 1774, Josiah Parker's slave, hired "eight weeks ago to Mr. Rice Pierce, a waterman; Jan. 14, 1775, Benjamin Harrison's Nick. *Laborers at ironworks, VaG,* (Pinkney), Nov. 30, 1775, Isaac Zane; (Dixon and Hunter), Jan. 31, 1777, Hunter;

May 2, 1777, William Lawson; (Purdie), Feb. 14, 1777, John Thornton; (Dixon and Hunter), Jan. 23, 1778, Lawson; (Rind), July 28, 1768 and Feb. 9, 1769, Thomas Lawson at Tayloe's Neabsco Ironworks in Prince William County. More slaves ran off from iron foundries than from any other non-agricultural industry.

31. *VaG* (Purdie and Dixon), April 1, 1774, Thomas Lawson for John Tayloe. For additional examples of runaways skilled in more than one craft or non-field task, see *VaG* (Purdie and Dixon), April 16, 1767, William Trebell's Bob, a sawyer, shoemaker, currier, and carpenter; May 28, 1768, Charles Floyd's Charles, a sawyer, shoemaker, and preacher; March 3, 1768, John Fox's Ben, "by trade a farmer & Gardner, and is very handy at many other businesses"; April 1, 1774, John Tayloe's Billy, a founder, miller, and stone mason, also his ex-valet; and (Purdie), May 9, 1777, William Green's Sam, a carpenter, cooper, fiddler, and "pretends to a deal of religion"; May 5, 1738, James Ball's mulatto Will, a carpenter, sawyer, shoemaker, and cooper; he left with a "lopping Ax, and a Fiddle." Also see *VaH & FA*, July 12, 1792, Griffin Garland. John Tayloe, Jr.'s overseer, in this instance, advertised for a "strong" and "active" slave who was described as "a compleat Wheelwright and house carpenter, and a tolerable good joiner and carpenter." He was also "pert, smooth tongued, sensible, and very artful." The slave was also "fond of dressing in fine cloaths and russle."

32. *MdG,* May 24, 1759, A. McRae; *VaIC,* May 7, 1788, L. A. Pauly; *VaG & GA,* July 15, 1795, John Tyler.

33. *VaG* (Purdie and Dixon), Nov. 5, 1772, Thomas Gaskins.

34. *VaG* (Rind), Sept. 22, 1768, Thomson Mason.

35. *Ibid.*

36. *VaIC,* March 3, 1790, Francis Bright; *VaG* (Purdie), Nov. 14, 1777, Beverley Randolph; July 5, 1776, Postscript, Mungo Harvey; March 12, 1752, Edmund Walker; (Purdie and Dixon), Nov. 12, 1772, George Bird.

37. *VaG,* July 25, Aug. 16, 1751, Thomas Dansie; (Purdie and Dixon), May 5, 1774, John Austin Finnie; (Dixon and Hunter), Dec. 19, 1777, Benjamin Timberlake, Jr.; *VaG & GA,* March 30, 1791 and April 12, 1797, "Extra," Sampson Mathews; Dec. 29, 1790, Alexander Quarrier; *VaIC,* Jan. 28, 1789, Tom Cox, pressman; *VaG,* April 25, 1766, R. Armistead.

38. *VaG* (Purdie), April 18, 1777, Supplement, Lodowick Jones; *VaG & GA,* March 11, 1795, M. Anderson.

39. *VaG* (Dixon and Hunter), Nov. 13, 1778, William Clopton; (Dixon and Nicolson), March 12, 1779, Mr. David Jones "at the hospital in York garrison"; (Purdie and Dixon), Sept. 15, 1768, William Heath; Jan. 2, 1772, John Stratton; (Dixon and Hunter), May 18, 1776, Robert Hart; *VaIC,* Jan. 21, 1789, Arthur Branch.

40. *VaG,* April 25, 1766, R. Armistead.
Note: Given the description of Pompey's affliction, that is, a speech defect attributable to "fright," it is doubtful that Virginians made a distinction between "stuttering" and "stammering." Such a distinction, however, is made today. According to the derivation, stuttering stands for labored, difficult, hesitant speech with resultant defective conversation. Stammering refers to defects of articulation and should never be confused with stuttering. Stammering depends on performance, stuttering depends on emotional disturbances. See Dominick Barbara, *Stuttering, a Psychodynamic Approach to Its Understanding and Treatment* (New York, 1954), 4.

41. *VaIC,* Feb. 25, 1789, Thomas Anderson; *VaG* (Purdie and Dixon), April

16, 1767, John Brown; *VaH & FA,* Sept. 11, 1794, Catesby Jones; *VaG* (Pinkney), Aug. 3, 1775, Clement Parker; (Purdie), Sept. 13, 1776, John Bannister; *VaH & FA,* July 12, 1792, George· Turberville.

42. See the following advertisements as examples of the slaveowners' sensitivity to intemperate slaves: *VaG & GA,* Sept. 28, 1796, "A VALUABLE young negro man, who is a good hand·at the house joiners trade, and a very faithful well instructed house servant, he will not drink any kind of spirituous liquor. For terms, apply to WILLIAM HOWERTON." See also *VaH & FA,* Jan. 5, 1792, Wm. W. Hening: "To be hired for the ensuing years, SEVERAL valuable NEGROES, of different ages, sizes and sexes: There is among them, a good *Waggoner,* who can be particularly recommended for his honesty and sobriety."

43. *VaG* (Purdie and Dixon), Sept. 17, 1772, W. Johnson; (Rind), March 31, 1774, James Fairlie; (Purdie and Dixon), Sept. 14, 1769, Thomas Jefferson.

For additional examples of runaway slaves who were "turbulent" while drunk, see *VaG* (Purdie and Dixon), May 4, 1769, William Gregory; (Purdie), June 12, 1778, James Belches; (Dixon and Hunter), Oct. 3, 1777, William Jackson; (Rind), Sept. 27, 1770, Mann Page; *VaH & FA,* April 11, 1793, Francis Jerdone.

See also Jacob Wray's curious notice: *VaG,* Nov. 4, 1775: Argyle "loves Drink, and is very bold in his Cups, but dastardly when sober."

Only three subscribers, incidentally, chose to mention that their runaways used *tobacco:* Peter always had a great "Quid of Tobacco in his mouth," and Dick, "who commonly carried a book with him," was "a great snuff taker." Robert Ruffin's Caesar and Kate, husband and wife, were habitual users of the staple for their "Teeth [were] somewhat worn with Pipes." *VaG,* May 9, 1745, Henry Armistead; (Dixon and Nicolson), July 31, 1779, Peter Royster; (Purdie and Dixon), Sept. 24, 1772, Robert Ruffin; and July 28, 1768, Thomas Lawson.

44. *VaG* (Purdie), March 15, 1776, Turberville; July 25, 1777, Thomas Poindexter. On the Chiswell murder case, see Carl Bridenbaugh, *Seat of Empire,* 69–70; and Lucille Griffith, *The Virginia House of Burgesses, 1750–1774* (Northport, Ala., 1963), 182, 190n.

45. In writing this brief section on the speech defects of runaway slaves, the following texts were especially useful: Barbara, *Stuttering: A Psychodynamic Approach to Its Understanding and Treatment;* Travis, *Handbook of Speech Pathology;* and Charles F. Diehl, *A Compendium of Research and Theory on Stuttering* (Springfield, Ill., 1958). Diehl sees the basic divisive issue in theory and treatment as between those who see stuttering as a physiological deviation and those who see it as a psychological deviation—the latter certainly seem to have carried the field. This book is an excellent and thorough summary of about 190 articles (over 2,000 have been written in English) on stuttering. See also Eugene F. Hahn, *Stuttering, Significant Theories and Therapies* (Stanford, 1943).

One prevalent explanation for stuttering, that it often occurs in those who must learn a second language under stressful, critical conditions, will not do in this instance; for all but one of the slaves manifesting this particular speech defect were Virginia-born.

46. See John W. Kinch, "A Formalized Theory of the Self-Concept," *American Journal of Sociology,* XLVIII (Jan. 1963), 481–86. For another approach, see Erik Erikson, "The Concept of Identity in Race Relations: Notes and Queries," *Daedalus,* The Negro American-2 (Winter 1966), 145–71. Erikson's views are

especially appropriate at this point in my argument; see his reference to a letter from William James, p. 147.

47. On the "marginal man" concept, see Robert Ezra Park, *Race and Culture* (Gencoe, Ill., 1950), 356, 370, 386–92; and my comments in the conclusion of this chapter.

48. James Baldwin, "Letter from a Region in My Mind," *The New Yorker*, Nov. 17, 1962, 68.

49. *VaG* (see both editions; Pinkney, and Rind), Jan. 20, 1774, John Draper for Robert Carter; (Dixon and Nicolson), Dec. 18, 1779, William Dandridge; (Purdie and Dixon), Jan. 28, 1775, Executors of the Royle estate. *Va. Argus*, Sept. 12, 1800, John Williamson; (Purdie), July 28, 1775, Samuel Wallace.

50. The incidence of motives offered by owners for a woman's decision to run away:

—going to town	printed in 30 notices	
—will visit relatives	" " 42 "	
—left with another man	" " 14 "	
—will attempt to board a vessel	" " 7 "	

Note: One hundred and forty-two women were advertised as runaways from 1737 to 1801 in the newspapers used in this study. Thirty-eight were advertised as runaway slaves committed to jail during this same period. Twenty-five of the former, about one-sixth, ran off in the company of men. Three were accompanied by children and six were pregnant. Four of the women taken up were pregnant and two were accompanied by their children.

For examples of women who ran off with their husbands and children, see *VaG* (Purdie), July 10, 1778, Mary Burwell; (Purdie and Dixon), April 8, 1775, William Allegre; (Purdie), Dec. 13, 1776, Peter Perkins; (Dixon and Hunter), Aug. 29, 1777, Richard Lucas; Jan. 23, 1778, notice for "a negro wench and three children . . . now in Lewis Town in Pennsylvania, who say they belong to one Meredith, near Hampton, in Virginia." See also *VaH & FA*, April 20, 1795, William Jessee.

For examples of female runaways who were pregnant, see *VaG* (Purdie and Dixon), James Johnson's "Grace," "somewhat fat, middling large and appears to be young with child"; July 9, 1772, William Black's slave "pretty far gone with Child" ran off with "an Indented Scotch Servant," a 25-year-old seaman—"it is supposed the Servant Man carried her away."

For additional examples of women who ran off with white men, see *VaG* (Purdie and Dixon), Nov. 21, 1771, John Blair; May 6, 1774, John A. Strange; (Rind), July 13, 1769, Cuthbert Bullitt.

51. *VaG* (Purdie and Dixon), April 8, 1775, William Allegre; (Purdie), Nov. 21, 1777, Charles Beazley; Nov. 3, 1752, Martha Massie; *VaG & GA*, July 24, 1793, Benjamin Tallman; *VaG* (Purdie and Dixon), July 28, 1768, William Holt, executor for the estate of John Thompson; (Dixon and Hunter), Oct. 17, 1777, Thomas Fenner.

52. *VaG* (Dixon and Nicolson), Feb. 26, 1780, Susannah Williamson; (Purdie and Dixon), June 30, 1768, Jane Vobe; (Purdie), Aug. 8, 1777, J. W. Bradley; *VaH & FA*, April 20, 1795, William Jessee.

53. *VaG* (Purdie and Dixon), Sept. 10, 1772, William Watts; (Dixon and Hunter), March 7, 1777, Thomas Barnes; see also *VaIC*, Dec. 27, 1786, Elizabeth Jones.

54. The following lists the types and incidences of problems of health among females who ran away.

ailment, injury, or scar	frequency
contracted smallpox	2
"poor" teeth	7
whip marks	3
burns	1
brands	1
lumps, wounds	2
limp	2

For examples, see *VaG* (Purdie), Dec. 5, 1777, William Smith; (Dixon and Hunter), Sept. 4, 1777, John Cary; Feb. 12, 1779, Henry Vaughan.

55. A measurement of the reliability of the information in the runaway notices, especially that material which deals with the slaves' motives and destination is, of course, crucial for this chapter. The only way to check the accuracy of the subscriber's estimates of his runaway's actions while at large is to correlate the notice with a later advertisement for the same slave committed to jail. This leaves much to be desired: the material is not readily available, for most runaways committed were usually immediately claimed and thus not advertised by jailers; and, in fact, the number advertised both as runaways and later as taken up is only 16 of more than 1,500. There are other difficulties. Many slaves in this competent group were probably not recaptured at a very early date—if ever. There are notices for runaways out for eight and ten years. Since many left to visit their relatives on other quarters, it is possible that many returned voluntarily (see *Landon Carter's Diary*).

Thus 380 advertisements for runaways committed to jail, the only large sample available, were used to test the reliability of the subscribers' estimates. The hypothesis is that slaves usually ran off along the rivers in a southeasterly direction and into the oldest areas of settlement; specifically they ran to the peninsula formed by the York and James rivers. Using one sample of runaways to test a hypothesis regarding another is not the soundest or most desirable technique. Nonetheless there is a high correlation between the subscribers' estimates of their runaways' destinations and the jailers' publication of where the runaways were intercepted.

Correlations between runaway advertisements and notices for the same slave taken up:

Owner and (slave)	Master's estimation of runaway's destination	Home County	Taken up at	Dates of notices in VaG
Henry Brodnax (Harry)	"Indianfield," York Co.	Dinwiddie	James City Co.	(R) 3/24/69, 5/26/69; (P&D) 5/11/69
Edward Hall (Daniel)	Northern Neck	Augusta	New Kent Co.	5/2, 5/23/66
Henry Thomas (Tom)	Smithfield, Isle of Wight	Southampton	Norfolkborough	(P&D) 9/1, 9/15/68
John Fox (Adam)	to "Carolina" 2nd ad: South	"Greenwich" Gloucester Co.	Orange Co. North Carolina	(R) 2/22/70, (P&D)

	Carolina 3rd ad: North Carolina			4/19/70, 7/12/70
Brett Randolph (Charles)	will "pass as free" will "perhaps board a vessel"	Cumberland	Alexandria, Fredericksburg (broke jail in both ports)	(P&D) 3/28, 9/26/71 (R) 8/15/71 (P&D) 6/20, 8/1/71
Robert Munford (Cuffy)	"neighbour-hood" of York or Norfolk	Mecklenburg	Elizabeth City Co.	(P&D) 5/16/72 (R) 3/12/72
Estate of William Lightfoot, Esq. (Harry)	Sussex or "Brandy Quarter," Brunswick (wife there)	"Sandy Point" Charles City	Pittsylvania	(P&D) 10/17/71, 3/12/72, 4/22/73
Thomas Gaskins (David)	"endeavour for some foreign Part; or make for Carolina"	Northumberland	Nansemond	(P&D) 11/5, 11/19/72
Hardin Perkins (Tom)	Williamsburg	Buckingham	Charles City	(P&D) 3/5, 5/28/72
Griffin Stith (David [Sam?])	York Co.	Brunswick	Charles City	(P&D) 5/13/73 8/17/74; (R) 9/1/74
William Penn (Burton)	"Ragged Is-lands" Isle of Wight, or Norfolk, or "neighbour-hood of Capt. *Williamson* on *Backwater*"	Amherst	James City	(P&D)11/25, 9/30/73
John Austin Finnie (Amy)	Portsmouth	"Cabin Point" Surry Co.	Charles City	(R) 9/1/74
John Edloe (Harry Perfume or Sharper)	Philadelphia	Charles City	Gloucester	(P&D) 1/6, 2/17/74; (P) 3/10/75
John H. Norton (Cornelius)	Carolina	Yorktown	Gloucestertown, Fredericksburg	(P&D) 6/30, 7/28/74
Robert Munford (Cuthie)	York Co.	Mecklenburg	Hampton	(D&H) 10/16/78 (D&N) 3/5/79
James Huie, Jr. (Molly)	Fredericksburg or Port Royal	Dumfries	Fredericksburg (with a Negro man who called himself Aaron Timothy)	*VaH & FA,* 7/10, 8/28/94

56. *VaG* (Rind), Sept. 22, 1774, John Harrison, Jr.; (Purdie and Dixon), Nov. 10, 1774 Postscript, Nathan Yancy.

57. *Ibid.*, Feb. 3, 1774, Peter Pelham; (Purdie and Dixon), May 4, 1769, William Gregory.

58. Campbell, *Colonial Caroline*, 342.

59. *VaH & FA*, April 17, 1794; the exploits of Tayloe's Duke and Bob can be followed in *VaH & FA*, July 12, 1792, March 28, 1793, and April 17, 1794.

60. *VaG* (Rind), Jan. 31, 1771, Richard Randolph; (Purdie and Dixon), April 1, 1774, Thomas Lawson; (Purdie), June 16, 1775, Gabriel Jones.

61. *Ibid.* (Purdie), Aug. 21, 1778, John Edmondson; (Purdie and Dixon), Feb. 3, 1774, James Southall.

62. *VaH & FA*, Aug. 7, 1794, John Daingerfield; June 2, 1795, Garratt Minor; *VaG* (Purdie), July 25, 1777, Robey Coke; (Purdie and Dixon), Sept. 17, 1772, W. Johnson.

63. *VaG* (Rind), Aug. 4, 1768, Richard Edwards; Nov. 8, 1770, Cuthbert Bullitt; (Dixon and Hunter), Oct. 31, 1777, James French; (Purdie and Dixon), April 21 and May 5, 1768, John Holiday (also Holladay); (Dixon and Hunter), Dec. 5, 1777, William Black; *VaH & FA*, Nov. 14, 1793, Charles Taylor.

64. Governor Nicholson cited in Hugh Talmadge Lefler and Albert Ray Newsome, *North Carolina: The History of a Southern State* (Chapel Hill, 1954), 116.

65. *VaG* (Rind), July 28, Aug. 4, 1768; Feb. 9, 1769, Thomas Lawson.

66. *Ibid.* (Purdie and Dixon), April 16, 1767, William Trebell.

67. Lefler and Newsome, *North Carolina*, 399. See also Edward Phifer, "Slavery in Microcosm: Burke County, North Carolina," *Journal of Southern History*, XXVIII (May 1962), 137–65—the most successful article of its kind available; and Harry Roy Merrens, *Colonial North Carolina in the Eighteenth Century: A Study in Historical Geography* (Chapel Hill, 1964), see especially 75ff., and Table 1, 76–77, on the dispersal of the slave population and of slaveholding families.

68. The following slaves were allegedly running to North Carolina: *VaG*, Nov. 21, 1751, Griffin Stith's Tom; Oct. 10, 1755, Francis Willis, Sr.'s Ben, a ploughman and carter; Nov. 4, 1763, Richard Eggleston's Jacob, a crippled shoemaker; (Purdie and Dixon), May 21, 1767, Charles Bruce's Harry Spence, age 50. Harry had run previously to North Carolina, "where he staid a considerable time." His owner at that time was Governor Alexander Spotswood; (Rind), July 23, 1767, Benjamin Harrison's Johney, or John Brookes, a waitingman; March 3, 1768, John Fox's Ben, a farmer and gardener, and "very handy at other businesses"; (Purdie and Dixon), Dec. 21, 1769, Richard Chilton's Lancaster, who played the fiddle, could read and write "a little," and was also "a very smart fellow"; Sept. 21, 1769, John Genter's George, a tailor from Yorktown; Nov. 9, 1769, two mulattoes, who belonged to Carter Braxton, one a waitingman; Nov. 23, 1769, John Snelson's Charles, a carpenter, who took a mare with him; Aug. 16, Nov. 8, 1770, Lawrence Taliaferro's Milford, a waterman; Nov. 22, 1770, Peter Jones's African and field hand; Oct. 18, 1770, Benjamin Harrison's Nick, a millwright; (Rind), Jan. 31, 1771, Richard Randolph's two house servants who had been to North Carolina "once before"; (Purdie and Dixon), Sept. 17, 1771, Richard W. Chandler's James, a carpenter and blacksmith.

69. *VaG*, March 11, 1737, Charles Carter.

70. *VaH & FA*, Jan. 15, 1795, Jacob Christianson.

71. *VaG* (Purdie), April 7, 1775, John Aylett.

72. *VaG*, Sept. 12, 1745, John Mercer.

73. *Ibid.*

74. *VaH & FA,* July 12, 1792, George Turberville, Sr.; *VaG* (Rind), May 31, 1770, John Hardaway.

75. *VaG* (Purdie and Dixon), Feb. 7, 1771, Anthony Martin.

76. *VaG* (Purdie and Dixon), March 22, 1770, Henry James. For another example of a female runaway disguised in men's clothing, see (Rind), Aug. 8, 1771, Edmund Bacon.

77. *VaG* (Purdie and Dixon), Sept. 6, 1770, John Verell's Davy ran off with Anne Ashwell, "a woman of infamous character in this neighbourhood . . . she has advised him to run away, as I am informed she did before, when he stayed out near two months."

For examples of runaways with white women, see *ibid.,* Oct. 17, 1751, Colonel Fitzhugh's Charles in company with one Mary Marshall, "an Irish Woman"; *VaH & FA,* Sept. 11, 1794, and Sept. 18, 1795, Catesby Jones's Jacob, in the "house business from his infancy"; he ran off with an Irish woman "who left her husband [Patrick Larkin] a few weeks ago." This woman had borne Jacob's son who was at this time fourteen years of age! See also *VaG* (Rind), March 17, 1774, Joseph Calland's mulatto, Sancho, a carpenter and cooper, who ran off with Elizabeth Beaver of "fresh complexion . . . but thick."

For descriptions of slaves who ran off with white men, see *VaG* (Dixon and Hunter), July 10, 1778, John Hasalgrove's Sam, who ran off with a white man, a prisoner from the *Phoenix,* a frigate of war; this man was a "parole of honour." (Rind), April 19, 1770, George Murrill's Harry; (Purdie and Dixon), Sept. 23, 1775, Andrew Lewis's Plim.

For descriptions of white men who aided, hired out, or otherwise encouraged ("entertained" was the term they used) runaways, see *VaG* (Purdie and Dixon), July 27, 1769, William Black; Jan. 14, 1775, Benjamin Harrison's habitual runaway, Nick, a millwright, "he is so artful that he will escape from any One who is not extremely careful." Nick "ran away some Time ago and hired himself as a Freeman at a Saw Mill either in *Isle of Wight* or *Nansemond,* and it is supposed he may take the Same Route"; *VaH & FA,* Sept. 18, 1794, Michael Wallace's Gerrard; "a blacksmith by trade, and perhaps inferior to none . . . I have reason to believe . . . [he] went off in company with some ill disposed white person, and will endeavour to pass as a free man, to some of the northern states, either under the protection of such a person, or by changing his name"; and *VaG* (Purdie and Dixon), May 16, 1771, Thomas Tunstall.

78. *VaG* (Purdie), June 21, 1776, William Graves; Dec. 22, 1738, Thomas Godwin, Jr.; April 10, 1752, Charles Beale. For additional notices for slaves who were "seduced" or "carried" away, see (Purdie and Dixon), July 2, 1772, John Wormeley; Aug. 8, 1771, John Bailey; (Rind), May 12, 1768; and Feb. 7, 1751, Henry Wythe's "battle ham'd" Charles.

Another type of notice dealt with those who hired slaves and then never returned them to their lawful owners. See *VaG,* April 15, 1737, Joseph Wright; (Purdie and Dixon), June 11, 1772, Matthew Tuell; July 15, 1775, Bennett Browne; (Purdie), Jan. 24, 1777, Thomas Fiveash.

For an account of an exchange between an outraged owner and the alleged thief of his slave property, see *VaG* (Dixon and Hunter), May 23, 1777, Richard Phillips. The slave in question, "Abraham alias Will," was carried out to the Watauga River from Louisa County. The accused thief, Joseph Cook, replied in *VaG* (Dixon and Hunter), Aug. 15, 1777.

For notices of trials and condemnations of "negro stealers," see *VaG* (Rind), April 21, March 31, 1774, for the trial of the Bragg brothers of Richmond, who were accused of taking up a negro woman, Winnie; Landon Carter, a magistrate at their trial, commented on the same in his Diary (*WMQ*, 1st Ser., XVI, 41–42). See also Hugh Rankin, *Criminal Trial Proceedings in the General Court of Colonial Virginia* (Williamsburg, 1965), 169–71.

79. *VaG* (Purdie and Dixon), Dec. 2, 1773, Samuel Meredith, Sr.

80. *Ibid.* (Rind), Nov. 29, 1770, David Scott. See also: (Purdie and Dixon), Dec. 29, 1774, James Lyle's African Harry. "I am told he was seen lately employed on board an Oyster Boat on James River, near the Hundred"; (Purdie), March 15, 1776, George Turberville's blacksmith, Will.

81. *VaG* (Purdie and Dixon), April 16, 1772, Edward Ker. There are two other detailed accounts of men who stole slave property. See May 14, 1772; and (Rind), Oct. 22, 1772, Mary Purnall's Simon. Simon was carried to Norfolk by one McFaling, who also had a Maryland runaway with him, *VaG* (Purdie and Dixon), Nov. 19, 1772, James Atkinson and Barnabas Lorrain. See also Jan. 23, May 2, June 11, 1772, for John Stratton's Jack, from the Eastern Shore, who was taken off by a pilot, one Peter Geossegon or "Gossigon"; the latter saved his neck following his trial by "agreeing" to serve aboard a British man-of-war.

82. *VaG* (Pinkney), Jan. 12, 1775, Richard Hipkins.

83. *VaG*, May 9, 1766; *VaG & GA*, Jan. 27, 1796, Lewis.

84. *VaG*, Oct. 6, 1752, Benjamin Harrison; (Purdie), Aug. 21, 1778, Peyton Skipwith; Sept. 5, 1755, John Norton; see also (Purdie), May 26, 1775, Edmund Wilkins.

Note: Runaways very seldom took with them a means of conveyance, such as a boat or a horse. For descriptions of *runaways on horseback*, see *VaG*, March 26, 1772, John Neallie; *VaH & FA*, June 2, 1795, Garratt Minor; June 12, 1795, William T. Alexander; *VaG* (Purdie and Dixon), May 30, 1766, Col. Tabb. For *runaways in boats*, see (Purdie and Dixon), Feb. 4, 1775, William Slater; Dec. 17, 1736, Nathaniel-Bacon Burwell; July 21, 1738, Nathaniel Harrison; (Purdie and Dixon), June 18, 1772, Allen Jones.

Numbers of Runaways by Month
(totals, taken from advertisements, 1736–1801, inclusive)

January	29	July	51
February	41	August	47
March	39	September	31
April	79	October	35
May	51	November	28
June	60	December	44

This tabulation is incomplete; since subscribers made a practice of not advertising for runaways until some two to four months after the fact, they often did not mention the date, or even the month or season of the slave's flight. Nevertheless, winter months, because of the severity of the weather, were unpopular. The first January runaway was not reported until 1768, thirty-two years after the first *Gazette* went to press. Yet nearly as many slaves ran off in December as August. Notice the jump in numbers of runaways from March to April. Since most of the runaways were in non-field positions, their work schedule would not necessarily depend on the harvest seasons; thus prolonged stretches of little or no crop work, or pending "holidays," which were important to the crop laborer, would not necessarily influence the artisan's decision to run off.

85. *VaG & GA*, March 16, 1796, William Dandridge.

VaG (Rind; Purdie and Dixon), Feb. 11, 1768, Lewis Burwell. This is one of the few notices to be placed in more than one newspaper. For Jack Ash's 1805 venture, see *The Richmond Enquirer* (Ritchie), March 1, 1805. Jack, then fifty, lived in Amherst County; he was suspected of heading for Manchester. He "has thought proper," his master reported, at this time, "to abuse this indulgence [to visit his wife] by not returning to his master."

86. *VaG* (Purdie and Dixon), Sept. 15, 1768, William Heath; May 19, 1774, Postscript, John Hartwell Cocke; on Cocke, see John B. Boddie, *Colonial Surry* (Baltimore, 1959), 161, 170.

87. *VaH & FA,* April 23, 1795, John Minor.

88. *VaG,* Aug. 24, 1751, William Lightfoot; (Purdie and Dixon), Aug. 16, Nov. 8, 1770, William Watt; (Rind), July 26, 1770, Mitchel, York County jailer; and see Watt's third notice, March 7, 1771.

89. *VaG* (Purdie), July 10, 1778, Edward C. Travis; (Rind), May 26 and March 24, 1768, Henry Brodnax; (Purdie), March 8, 1776, Joseph Scrivener. For additional descriptions of runaways in Williamsburg, see (Purdie and Dixon), Sept. 15, 1774, Lewis Burwell's Isaac Bee, from Mecklenburg County and "well known in Williamsburg"; May 13, 1775, Samuel Apperson's Michael, who ran away from a plantation in New Kent County in late April; he was seen in early May "in Williamsburg, offering to hire himself"; Aug. 5, 1775, John Walker's Billy, from Albemarle County, was a shoemaker suspected of hiding in the city; and Nov. 1, 1770, M. Mayes's Sam, from Amelia County, was "harboured" at one Matthew Ashby's; the latter was a mulatto who lived in Williamsburg. This slave, his master wrote, "pretends to lay claim to freedom."

90. *VaG* (Rind), Aug. 8, 1771, Edmund Bacon; (Purdie and Dixon), Feb. 5, 1767, William Carter; (Purdie), Aug. 21, 1778, Patrick Robertson.

91. *VaG* (Purdie and Dixon), Dec. 13, 1770, William Black. After Sarah was recaptured she ran off again; see May 6, 1776: "she is lurking near *Maycox, Merchant's Hope,* or up near *Petersburg*"; (Purdie), May 2, 1777, Supplement, William Spratley; *VaIC,* April 9, 1788, Peter Aylett; Jan. 23, 1788, Richard Stewart; *VaG* (Rind), Dec. 24, 1767, Benjamin Harrison; *Va. Argus,* Aug. 5, 1800, John Hunnicut.

92. *VaG & GA,* July 10, 1798, James Miller; *VaG* (Purdie and Dixon), March 7, 1771; *MdG,* March 7, 1771, Stafford Lightburn, Jr.; *VaG* (Purdie and Dixon), Aug. 18, 1774, James Ball.

93. *VaG* (Purdie and Dixon), Jan. 14, 1775, Anthony Lamb; (Purdie), Nov. 17, 1775, Supplement, John Lamb.

94. *VaG* (Purdie and Dixon), Sept. 17, 1772, John Edmondson; (Rind), Aug. 8, 1771, Richard Banks; (Purdie and Dixon), Sept. 1, 1774, Supplement, King and Queen County jailer.

95. *VaG* (Purdie and Dixon), Dec. 29, 1774, James Lyle; (Rind), March 17, 1768, Robert Hening, Jr.

96. *VaG* (Purdie and Dixon), Sept. 30, 1773, John Austin Finnie; (Purdie), Sept. 19, 1777, Nelson Anderson, Jr.

97. *VaG* (Dixon and Hunter), Jan. 23, 1778, Thomas Lawson.

98. For assessments of the Elkins-Tannenbaum thesis see David Brion Davis, *Slavery: A Problem in Western Culture* (New York, 1966); Eugene D. Genovese, "Rebelliousness and Docility in the Negro Slave: A Critique of the Elkins Thesis," *Civil War History,* 13 (Dec. 1967), 293–314; and Laura Foner and Genovese, eds., *Slavery in the New World: A Reader in Comparative History* (Englewood Cliffs, N.J., 1969).

99. Robert Blauner, *Alienation and Freedom: The Factory Worker* (Chicago, 1965), viii.

100. Frantz Fanon, *Black Skin, White Masks,* trans. by Charles L. Markmann (New York, 1967); Albert Memmi, *The Colonizer and the Colonized,* trans. by Howard Greenfield (New York, 1965).

101. Virginia artisans were marginal men, but not in the classic sense of the concept developed by Robert Ezra Parke and others, that is, alienated from both cultures. Rather, they were productive men in white society, and there is no evidence that they were not so among plantation slaves. Such "captains" as Landon Carter's Nassau and Austin Brockenbrough's Romeo, in fact, evidently received important privileges for helping their masters, while they also protected slaves on the plantation—including those who wished to run away. These men were not suspended ineffectually between two cultures; instead they were mediators, political go-betweens—what the anthropologist Malcolm McGee has called the "150 per cent acculturated man." "The 150% Man: A Product of Blackfoot Acculturation," *American Anthropologist,* 70 (1968), 1096–1103; also useful is Yehudi A. Cohen, ed., *Social Structure and Personality: A Casebook* (New York, 1961), 452–53, esp. Cohen's summary of George Spindler's "Menomini Acculturation."

Chapter 4

1. Henry Adams, *The United States in 1800* (Ithaca, N.Y., 1961), 98. (This is a separate edition of the first six chapters of Adams' *History of the United States During the First Administration of Thomas Jefferson.*)

2. Lewis C. Gray, *History of Agriculture in the Southern United States to 1860,* (2 vols., New York, 1941), II, 611ff.; Louis Morton, *Robert Carter of Nomini Hall* (Charlottesville, 1941), 118–85; David J. Mays, *Edmund Pendleton, 1721–1803: A Biography* (2 vols., Cambridge, Mass., 1952), I, chap. ix, "The Decline of the Plantation System"; see also the "Amicus" articles which were printed in the *VaIC* throughout June 1787; for example, see the June 20 article. Charles R. Lingley, *The Transition in Virginia from Colony to Commonwealth* (New York, 1910), 14ff.; N. F. Cabell (with notes by Earl G. Swemm), "Some Fragments of an Intended Report on the Post Revolutionary History of Agriculture in Virginia," *WMQ,* 1st ser. (Jan. 1918), 145–68.

3. See Nathaniel Littleton Savage to John Norton, Virginia, July 22, 1766, Norton-Savage-Dixon Papers, Brock Collection, HEH: "The only recipe that can be prescribed, at this juncture is Frugality & Industry which is a potion scarcely to be swallowed by Virginians, brought up from their Cradles, in Idleness, Luxury, & Extravagance, depending on their myriads of Slaves, that Bane (if not Curse) of this Country; how happy are you to have had it in your power to rid yourself of that load of trouble, which is Inseparable from a Virginia Estate . . . had it been in my power . . . [I] should have almost doubled my Fortune & rendered my Life easy & free from those perplexing cares, which I have at the thoughts of leaving my Children in a country where they make Shipping Negroes their chief employ." And see Charles Yates to Samuel Martin, Fredericksburg, Sept. [?], 1775, Yates Letterbook: "Nobody denys but America may be much distressed . . . necisity the mother of invention removes them in every known such manner [?] that a stoppage of Imports for 5 Years (I now speak perticularly for Virginia) would make British goods as little necessary as they are to any of the best regulated European Nations. . . .

Buildings for Workmen now going forward & Materials laying in as fast as possible that there be no delay—having such plenty of Iron & the compleatest Forge on the Contenent within two Miles I expect a Slitting Mill will be erected out of hand & Nails be made to supply all demands within our Capes— the increase of Wools will be very great as no Sheep have been killed & all possable attention paid to increasing the Stock. The Crops of Cotton have been extended to at least five times the quantity ever before grown in Virginia & scarce a plantation or Farm but has made Flax & Hemp more than they can use. Spinning & weaving of course & plain goods are such simple operations that they are performed without difficulty, and having [?] for Tobacco or Wheat, will be undertaken in every Family. You will say an Accomadation will bring all things into their usual Channell—but it must happen soon, for if the people get once used to provid[ing] for themselves without being obliged to look out for necessarys at a distance they will continued to follow it to such a degree as will lesson the imports considerably."

4. The following scholars have made succinct and accurate statements concerning the colony's economy in transition after 1760. In addition to Freeman, Gray, Morton, and Mays (see above, n. 3), see Middleton, *Tobacco Coast, A Maritime History of the Chesapeake Bay in the Colonial Era*, 157 ff.; Lingley, *The Transition in Virginia from Colony to Commonwealth* (New York, 1910), 14; Robert S. Hilldrup, "A Campaign to Promote the Prosperity of Colonial Virginia," *VMHB*, LXVII (Oct. 1959), 410–28. See also Robert Carter Daybook, XVII, 1 ff., "April 1787—The Patriotic Society in order to guard agst any mistake or misrepresentation of their Views, have published this as containing the principles of their Institution" (the Society's pamphlet is pasted into the Daybook following Carter's introductory note); J[ame]s Mercer to Muse, July 1, 1779, Muse Papers. For illustrations of the planters' awareness of the acute economic problems in the tidewater, see J[ame]s Mercer to Battaile Muse, July 1, 1779, H[ugh] Nelson to Muse, Fauquier County, Feb. 10, 1779, Muse Papers; Robert Carter Nicholas to John H. Norton, Williamsburg, Aug. 4, 1772, Norton Papers; Charles Yates to George McCall, Fredericksburg, July 10, 1773, Yates Letterbook, 1773–1783.

See also Clement Eaton, *The Growth of Southern Civilization, 1790–1860* (New York, 1963), chap. i; and George T. Starnes's little known but very useful book, *Sixty Years of Branch Banking in Virginia* (New York, 1931); also *ValC*, May 2, 1787.

5. Carter Braxton to Robert Prentis, Williamsburg, May 17, 1784, Prentis Family Papers, UVA.

6. John H. Norton to Muse, Winchester, Frederick County, Nov. 25, 1784, Muse Papers. "Colo Thurston informs me that Mr. Robt Morris Philadelphia has wrote to Mr. Edwd. Snickers of this County disiring to know if there are any fine Lands for Sale in this part of the World as he wants to become a purchaser to a Considerable Amt."

7. See Paul Leland Haworth, *George Washington: Farmer* (Indianapolis, 1915), chap. vii, "Agricultural Operations and Experiments before the Revolution"; also Gray, *Southern Agriculture*, II, chap. xxvi.

8. This material on the distribution of the new state's slave population was taken from Harold Eugene Cox, "Federalism and Anti-Federalism in Virginia, 1787: A Study of Political and Economic Motivations" (unpublished Ph.D. thesis, University of Virginia, 1958). See especially, Cox's excellent maps and pp. 30, 39f.

9. Ulrich B. Phillips, *American Negro Slavery* (New York, 1918), chap. x, "The Westward Movement"; Joseph C. Robert, *The Tobacco Kingdom: Plantation, Market, and Factory in Virginia and North Carolina, 1800–1860* (Durham, 1938), 77f.

10. U.S. Census, *Second Census,* 1800 (Philadelphia, 1801), 2. Transcript of the original at San Francisco State College Library. See Norton to Muse, Winchester, Jan. 6, 1786, Muse Papers: "I consider that as many Northward Farmers are settled in the Neighbourhood of this Land & numbers coming in daily to purchase, the value of this Tract will be increasing every Year." (Note: Norton was discussing Mrs. Burwell's holdings in the Valley—n. 11—see *VaG* (Purdie), Nov. 17, 1775, Supplement, for a description of this tract.)

11. Frederic Bancroft, *Slave-Trading in the Old South* (Baltimore, 1931), 7.

12. *Hening,* XI, 39f. There were approximately 2,000 free Negroes in Virginia before the 1782 statute; there were 12,866 in 1790, 20,124 in 1800, and 30,570 in 1810. See Phillips, *American Negro Slavery,* 124.

13. *VaG & GA,* July 22, 1795.

14. *VaH & FA,* Sept. 18, 1794, George Shepherd. Sept. 25, 1795, Daniel Triplett. For additional examples of multilingual sailors, see *VaG* (Purdie and Dixon), Dec. 7, 1769, Maxmillian Calvert's Brazil, who ran away from Norfolk. He spoke English, "some" French, and Spanish; Nov. 19, 1772, Stafford Lightburn.

15. *VaG* (Purdie and Dixon), April 18, 1771, Sarah Floyd. Also, (Rind), Oct. 27, 1768, Charles Floyd. *VaH & FA,* June 18, 1793, Aug. 18, 1795, Thomas MaGee [sic]; *VaG* (Purdie and Dixon), July 18, 1771, John Fox. Also, (Rind), April 23, 1772, John Fox; (Rind), Feb. 22, 1770, John Fox, April 19, 1770, John Fox; and July 12, 1770, John Fox.

16. See Wesley M. Gewehr, *The Great Awakening in Virginia, 1740–1790* (Durham, 1930), 187f., 235ff.

17. For the legal aspects of the Somerset Case see Helen T. Catterall, ed., *Judicial Cases Concerning Slavery and the Negro* (5 vols., Washington, 1924–26), I, 4–5, 14–15; Eric Williams, *Capitalism and Slavery,* 44f.; *VMHB,* XVI (1909–10), 144–45, 145n.

18. *VaG* (Purdie and Dixon), June 30, 1774, Gabriel Jones.

19. *Ibid.,* Sept. 30, 1773, John Austin Finnie.

20. *WMQ,* 1st ser., XVI (1907–08), 44f. Note: For a sketch of Dunmore's career, see *WMQ,* 1st ser., XVI (1907–08), 35f; Louise B. Dunbar, "The Royal Governors in the Middle and Southern Colonies on the Eve of the Revolution: A Study in Imperial Personnel," in *The Era of the American Revolution,* ed. by Richard B. Morris (New York, 1939, 1965), 240–46.

The most recent, thorough, and scholarly treatment of Dunmore's "Ethiopian Regiment" is Professor Benjamin Quarles' *The Negro in the American Revolution* (Chapel Hill, 1961), 19–32.

21. There is little agreement among scholars regarding how many slaves responded to Dunmore. Professor Quarles estimates that 800 slaves eventually joined his fleet; this figure is also accepted by Professor Thad Tate. See Quarles, *The Negro in the American Revolution,* 31, and Tate, *The Negro in Eighteenth-Century Williamsburg,* 218. Perhaps their estimate is too conservative; the slaveowners certainly believed that at least twice that number joined the governor. In addition to the examples in the text, see Robert Carter to Messrs. Thomas & Rowland Hunt, Nomini Hall, Westmoreland County, April 18, 1777, Letterbook, 1776–77, reproduced in the CW abstract file, original in the Cheuvenet Collection; and *VaG* (Dixon and Hunter), Oct. 4, 1776.

22. *VaG* (Purdie), Jan. 26, 1776.

23. *Ibid.*

24. Dunmore to the Secretary of State, Virginia, June 26, 1776 cited, in George W. Williams, *History of the Negro Race in America from 1619–1800* (New York, 1885), 342.

25. Edmund Pendleton to Richard Lee, Virginia, Nov. 27, 1775, in *American Archives*, ed. by Peter Force (Washington, 1837–53), 4th ser., IV, 202.

   Washington to Joseph Reed, Dec. 15, 1775, cited in Williams, *History of the Negro Race,* 341.

26. Mercer to Muse, Aug. 9, 1782, Muse Papers.

27. *VaG* (Purdie), April 5, 1776, Landon Carter; Nov. 17, 1775, Supplement, Robert Brent.

28. *VaG* (Purdie), March 29, 1776; (Dixon and Hunter), April 13, 1776. For reports of "boatloads of slaves" fleeing to Dunmore's fleet, see *VaG* (Pinkney), Nov. 30, 1775; (Dixon and Hunter), Dec. 2, 1775. Many of these notices merely tantalize; but the Proclamation obviously had stirred considerable numbers of slaves. See, for example, *VaG* (Purdie), June 5, 1778, James Willison's runaway notice for Sam, who went off "with other negroes of the set."

29. *VaG* (Dixon and Clarkson), Oct. 21, 1780, Thomas Nelson, Jr.; (Dixon and Hunter), July 10, 1778, Richard Wynne; (Purdie), June 5, 1778, Jacob Wray. For other black enlistees advertised as runaways see: Oct. 31, 1777, Edward C. Travis; Sept. 12, 1777, Charles Jones; June 13, 1777, John Wilson; Aug. 21, 1778, Peyton Skipwith; *Hening,* XI, 308, 309

30. Henry R. McIlwaine, ed., *Official Letters of the Governors of Virginia* (Richmond, 1929), III, 8, 257, 266.

31. For an indication of the bitter reaction to Dunmore's foraging, see Robert Carter to George Wythe, Westmoreland County, Letterbook, III, part 1, 3–4; also *VaG* (Purdie), May 31, 1776; (Purdie), March 29, 1776.

32. *VaG* (Purdie), March 15, 1776.

33. *VaG,* Nov. 17, 1775.

34. *VaG* (Dixon and Hunter), Nov. 25, 1775.

35. *Ibid.*, as part of the wartime propaganda formulated to oppose Dunmore's proclamation, Virginians claimed that he would send slaves to the West Indies "to defray expenses" and also for "his own private emolument." See *VaG* (Dixon and Hunter), Aug. 31, Oct. 4, 1776.

   Evidently some slaves were sent from the islands to aid Dunmore. See a curious notice signed by "a Warehouseman" at Layton's (Essex County). This advertisement told of an African with country marks who said "he was sent here in a ship with many others from *Barbados*, by his master there to fight for lord Dunmore." *VaG* (Purdie), July 26, 1776, Supplement, Jas. Bowdrie.

36. *VaG* (Purdie), Nov. 17, 1775.

37. This section on Richmond in the 1790's is based on Samuel Mordecai, *Richmond in By-Gone Days* (Richmond, 1860), and W. Asbury Christian, *Richmond, Her Past and Present* (Richmond, 1912).

38. Christian, *Richmond,* 41.

Chapter 5

1. A version of this chapter was presented to the Wayne State University Convocation (May 1969), "The Black Man in America: 350 Years, 1619–1969," and has been published in Peter I. Rose, ed., *Americans from Africa* (2

vols., New York, 1970), II, 53–74; and in August Meier, Elliott Rudwick, John H. Bracey, Jr., eds., *American Slavery: The Question of Resistance* (Belmont, Calif., 1971), 160–78.

2. Unless otherwise indicated, sources for this are the Executive Papers (Sept.–Dec. 1800) in the Virginia State Library (Richmond). These two boxes contain 8 x 11 file folders marked "Negro Insurrection 1800," and the approximately 105 items include the following types of documents: letters from officials and ranking state politicians and military men to Governor James Monroe; "certificates from the Examining Magistrates (the Justices of Henrico and Caroline Counties)," who recorded the depositions of the conspirators; resolutions concerning the conspiracy from the Richmond, Williamsburg, and Petersburg Common Halls; "Informations" taken from slave informers and transcribed by clerks of the court; court transcripts and depositions submitted as evidence, including the testimony of the most important informers, Paul Grayham's Ben Woolfolk, Thomas H. Prosser's Solomon and Ben, and William Young's Gilbert; and many bits and pieces of undated and unendorsed documents, including some important lists of suspects used by officials while making arrests.

About two-thirds of this material is reprinted in Henry W. Flournoy, ed., *Calendar of Virginia State Papers and Other Manuscripts Preserved in the Capital at Richmond* (11 vols., Richmond, 1875–93), IX. Some depositions are also reprinted in the *Richmond Recorder*, April 13, 1803 ("Documents respecting the Insurrection of the Slaves"), State Library microfilm. All of the major correspondence and trial transcripts are in Governor Monroe's copybook, Executive Communications, Sept.–Dec. 1800, State Library.

The Evidence. The slaves were imprisoned separately, and although about four of the accused were pardoned, only a small number were spared because they confessed. The following endorsements of depositions indicate that the evidence was handled in a careful and critical manner: "the Witness was at Mr. Young's on the night spoken of by Prosser's Ben (whose testimony is Confirmed by him in every Part)." "He confirms Verbatem Prossers Ben's Testimony." When the clerks or justices knowingly imposed themselves between what was said and what they heard, they usually made a note of it: "This statement is made with the aid of some notes, but principally from recollection; minute circumstance is detailed in it, they feel assured that no material circumstance is omitted." (From the trial of William Young's Gilbert.)

3. *Va. Argus,* Oct. 3, 1800.

4. *VaG & GA,* Feb. 7, 1800.

5. *Va. Argus,* Oct. 3, 1800.

6. *Hening,* XI, 24–25, 390–94. See also, Robert E. and B. Katherine Brown, *Virginia 1705–1786; Aristocracy or Democracy?* (East Lansing, Michigan, 1964), 285f; and Robert McColley, *Slavery and Jeffersonian Virginia* (Urbana, Ill., 1964), chs. 7–8.

7. The following plantation accounts and newspaper advertisements offering slaves for sale indicate that some Virginians in the last quarter of the century were reluctant to separate slave children from their mothers. *VaH & FA,* Oct. 11, 1792 (subscriber, James Lewis); Oct. 24, 1793 (John Minor, Jr.); July 25, 1793 (Burges Ball); Nov. 14, 1793 (Charles Taylor), and Oct. 30, 1794 (Robert Patton and John Mercer). See also the will of Young Short (Sept. 4, 1795); the Hawkes and McGehee Family Papers; Thomas Jefferson to T.M. Randolph, Sr., Oct. 22, 1790, Edgehill-Randolph Papers, UVA.

8. Monroe to Governor John Drayton of South Carolina, Richmond, Oct. 21, 1800, Executive Letterbooks, VSL microfilm.

9. Ben Woolfolk's testimony at the trial of Smith's George; see also "Confessions of Ben Alias Ben Woolfolk Sept 17th 1800 Nos. 4." This, the most important document in the collection, hereafter will be cited as "Woolfolk's Confessions." (It is reprinted in Flournoy, ed., *Calendar*, 150–52.)

10. Bowler's description is taken from a small and tattered slip of paper which reads: "Jack Bowler alias Jack Ditcher, the property Wm Bowlers wife (?) of Urrbina [Urbanna] is a Black man. . . . [H]e has a Scare over one of his Eyes But which I do not Recollect His hair Grows Wiry down his forehead He by trade a Ditcher Rick Bowler Septr 17. 1800."

11. "Evidence adduced against Solomon the property of Thomas Henry Prosser on his trial on the 11th September 1800"; and the testimony of Prosser's Ben at the trial of Jack Bowler.

12. See fn. 42.

13. Confession of William Young's Gilbert.

14. Woolfolk at the trial of George from Jacob Smith's estate; Mrs. Price's John and B. Woolfolk at Byrd's trial; Woolfolk's Confessions.

15. Testimony of Prosser's Ben at Gabriel's trial; Woolfolk at the trial of Paul Thilman's Dick; Woolfolk at the trial of George from Jacob Smith's estate; Sam alias Sam Graham's Information; Woolfolk at Thornton's trial: see the Caroline County Order Book, Oct. 30, 1800, p. 221. Thornton, a blacksmith, was rated at $500 when condemned; to that date, four others had been convicted and rated between $300 and $334, VSL microfilm.

16. Testimony of Prosser's Ben at the trial of John Holman's Doby; John Williams's Daniel at the trial of Mary Jones's John; "Trial of Charles, Testimony of Patrick & Ben against him & Patrick"; trial of Judith Owen's Michael; Testimony of Benjamin Mosby's Wiltshire and Prosser's Ben at the trial of Anne Parson's Nat.

17. "Woolfolk's Confessions."

18. *Ibid.*

19. The documents relating to Gilbert and King are: "Information from Mr Foster respecting the intended Insurrection 1800 September 23d," and the material within this file is endorsed: "The above information given by Gilbert 23d. Sepr 1800 to Jno. Foster"; "[The trial of] Sam Bird, James & others no date. . . . Communications made by Gilbert"; "The Application, by Philip N. Nicholas, esqr. to the court of Oyer & terminer, which tried & condemned a negroe man Slave named *King*. . . ." See also the testimony of the following slaves and free men, Ben Woolfolk, Mrs. Mary Martin, "Colonel Goodall's Man," Mr. (Philip N.) Nicholas, and Larkin Stanard.

20. Woolfolk's and Mary Martin's testimonies at King's trial.

21. *Ibid.*

22. The testimony of William Young's Gilbert at the trial of William Galt's Armstead.

23. Woolfolk at the trial of William Young's Gilbert; Prosser's Ben at Gabriel's trial. Only one slave openly demonstrated a strong attachment to Gabriel: John Williamson's Laddis told the gathering at Young's Spring that "he would join Gabriel & stand by him till the last."

24. "Certificate of the examining Magistrates respecting the intended insurrection . . . 8th Sept 1800 To the Governor of Virginia at Richmond," Executive Papers.

25. In 1783 Prosser's father, John Ambler, and George Nicholas recorded the following deed; Thomas H. Prosser's plantation was carved from this tract, which was the setting for the conspiracy of 1800: "all the lands begining at the Mouth of West Ham Creek on James River. Thence on the Old lines of the land of the late Wm Byrd Esq. dec'd. to the lands [of the] Late Ben: Clarks [Smith's group often used the widow Clarke's plantation for their meetings], thence up the Back lines of the lands of R.C. Nichols Estate, & so on the Lands of Colo. Tho. Randolph & thence down James Randolph & thence down James River to the beginning. Warrant for 6000 acres, certified by my hand & seal, 22 May 1783. Signed Tho. Prosser I.H.C." The Ambler Mss. Library of Congress, reprinted in *Virginia Colonial Abstracts, James City County, 1634–1904,* Ser. II, Vol. 4, Lindsay Duvall, compiler (1957).

In 1800 Thomas H. Prosser, one of the wealthier men in Henrico County, paid personal and property taxes on 3 white and 48 black tithables, 17 horses and mules ($23.16) and 1,945 acres ($17.06). Evidently he moved and sold most of his holdings shortly after the conspiracy was broken, because in 1801 he only paid taxes on 200 acres. Henrico County Personal and Land Tax Books, 1800, VSL.

26. For the Young Spring meeting see, "Woolfolk's Confessions," Prosser's Ben at Jack Bowler's trial; and a letter "from a gentleman in this city [Richmond], to his friend in New-York" (dated September 20, 1800) in *Va. Argus,* Oct. 14, 1800.

27. "Communications made by [William Young's] Gilbert" (no date); Woolfolk at the trial of Thomas Goode's Michael; Prosser's Ben at the trial of Mrs. Price's John; Woolfolk at Sam Byrd's trial; and Billey and Ben at the trial of Mr. Gregory's Martin.

28. Prosser's Ben at the trials of Gabriel, Solomon, Pharaoh, and John Holman's Doby; William Burton's Daniel at the trial of Mary Jones's John. "Information" on Ned, the property of Judith Owen; see also, the trial of Philip Sheppard's Pharaoh.

29. Monroe to Governor John Drayton (South Carolina), Richmond, Oct. 21, 1800, Executive Letterbooks, VSL microfilm; Monroe to the Speaker of the General Assembly, Richmond, Dec. 5, 1800 in Stanislaus M. Hamilton, ed., *The Writings of James Monroe* (7 vols., New York, 1898–1903), III, 239ff.

30. The testimony of Woolfolk and Prosser's Ben at Gabriel's trial.

31. Prosser's Ben at Gabriel's trial; Woolfolk's testimony at Gabriel's trial; Woolfolk at Sam Byrd, Jr.'s trial; and "Woolfolk's Confessions." Because of the "cold war" with France and the candidacy of Thomas Jefferson for the Presidency, the French and the French Revolution were topics of everyday conversation in Virginia in 1800. There were references to the French throughout the trials (no small embarrassment for Monroe and other Jeffersonian Republicans).

32. The organizers were more successful in obtaining weapons than men. There is hard evidence for 500 bullets, 12 dozen swords, six "guns," several kegs of gun powder and Jack Bowler's 50 spears, which he made by cutting wheat scythes in two and attaching them to long poles. So Gabriel was forced to provide weapons for his men on the very night of the attack. Plans to this end involved meeting various janitors and caretakers at taverns and public buildings and obtaining keys to the arms rooms.

33. Herbert Aptheker states that 1,000 slaves met Saturday night. See *American Negro Slave Revolts* (New York, 1943), 221–22, 222n; see also John Killens, "The Confessions of Willie Styron," in John Henrik Clarke, ed., *William*

Styron's Nat Turner, Ten Black Writers Respond (Boston, 1968), 39. Overlooking for the moment Gabriel's decision made early in the evening to postpone the attack, and the commanders' negative reports to Monroe, it is difficult to see how 1,000 slaves would have assembled and then returned home without detection.

34. Monroe to the General Assembly, Dec. 5, 1800, *Writings of Monroe*, III, 235–36. "The close of the day (Aug. 30) was marked by one of the most extraordinary falls of rain ever known in our country. . . . Nothing occurred in the night, of the kind suspected." It is noteworthy, however, that the one movement in support of Gabriel came from the city not the countryside. Monroe continued, "In the morning the officer commanding the Horse reported he had seen but one circumstance unusual in the neighbourhood, which was, that all the negroes he passed on the road, in the intervals of the storm, were going from town, whereas it was their custom to visit it every Saturday night. This circumstance was not otherwise important than as it was said the first rendezvous of the negroes was to be in the country."

See also, William Mosby to Monroe, Henrico County, Sept. (?), and Nov. 10, 1800; Monroe to Colonel David Lambert, Richmond, Sept. 2, 1800; Monroe to the Mayor of Richmond, Dec. 27, 1800, *Writings of Monroe*, III, 203, 246–47.

35. *Va. Argus*, Oct. 14, 1800. A gentleman who witnessed the trials wrote to his "friend in New-York":

> The Judges conduct themselves with a degree of humanity highly honorable. The least doubt, the smallest suspicion, or contradiction on the part of the witnesses (who are kept in separate apartments) will often acquit Negroes who are really criminal.

This is a fairly accurate picture of the proceedings. The court on at least one occasion silenced a slave informer who implicated some black men from Petersburg, who had not been formally charged. The slaves' legal counsel, James Rind, seems to have conducted himself in an unexceptional way. He and other officials secured at least six pardons.

36. Monroe to Jefferson, Richmond, Sept. 15, 1800, *Writings of Monroe*, III, 208. The Governor's activities regarding informers, pardons, arrests, and the trials may be conveniently followed in the Executive Letterbooks; see especially, Monroe to Colonel David Lambert, Sept. 2, 1800; to Colonel Matthew Cheatham, Sept. 6; "General Orders," Richmond, Sept. 10 and 15, VSL microfilm.

37. Professor Aptheker has made a careful study of the appropriate vouchers and warrants dealing with the executions. See *American Negro Slave Revolts*, 222–23, 223n. "Altogether merely in executed slaves the Gabriel plot cost the State of Virginia $14,242.31, plus one hundred pounds paid to a Mr. Michael Ocletree. Other expenses, as for slaves banished, rewards, costs of guards and militia, would bring the plot's expense to about $25,000 (Auditor's Papers, Box 187, VSL), no small item," he concludes, "when it is remembered that the total planned budget of the State for the fiscal year 1801–1802 was $377,703."

Nearly all slaves were valued at £100 or $333.33; but Gabriel and Prosser's Tom were rated at $833.33 and William Young's Gilbert and William at $700. Auditor's Journal 155 (see entries dated 1 Sept. through 11 Dec. 1800).

38. Monroe to the President and Members of the Council of State, Richmond, Sept. 27, 1800. See also Thomas Newton (Recorder for the City of Norfolk) to Monroe, Norfolk, Sept. 24, 1800; John Moss to Monroe, Sept. 28, 1800; Richard E. Lee to Monroe, Sept. 28, 1800; Newton to Obadiah Gunn and Robert Wilson, Norfolk, Sept. 23, 1800. On Monroe's expectations that Gabriel

would "confess" only to him, see Monroe to the Council Sept. 27, 28; to Captain Thomas Nicholas, Sept. 28, and to Thomas Newton, Oct. 5.

Newton's letter to Monroe (Sept. 24) read in part: "I confess I think Mr Taylor knew much better than he acts, what to do in such a case, having Long had the management of negroes. . . . His conduct appears extradinary to me. . . . Taylor told the men that he had emancipated his negro Isham, but on [exa]mination Isham told me that he had never given him any papers but promised him to do it, when he was a methodist, but as he was not turn'd again he was afraid he should not be given his freedom—both Billy & Isham say they saw the Negroes hung before they left Richmond. . . . Mr. Taylor must have known that circumstance & undoubtedly have heard of Gabriels before he left. . . . I hope for the sake of his family, he may be able to clear himself of the opinion entertaind of him here. Gabriels says he will give your Excy. a full information he will confess to no one else. . . . Billey one of Taylors men has a wife at a Mr Harris's on Shockoe hill she may probably know whether Gabriel had concerted any measure, to get on board this vessel with the hands. Gabriel will set off this day under a guard, in a vessel . . . should your Excy think proper a guard may be sent down the River & take him from Osborns by land but they will proceed by water as fast as possible & I believe there will be no danger of a rescue."

39. Executive Letterbook, Sept. 28–Oct. 7; Minutes of the Governor's Council, Sept. 28, Oct. 3, 7, 16, VSL microfilm. Gabriel's last few weeks as a prisoner in the capital can be followed in these sources. When he was returned from Norfolk he was brought directly to Monroe's residence, 4 P.M. Sept. 28, and "a great crowd of blacks as well as whites gathered around him." (Monroe to the Council, Sept. 28.) After his trial his execution was twice stayed in the hope that he would confess. But on October 5 Monroe wrote to Newton, the Mayor of Norfolk (who had suggested that Gabriel would confess, but only to the Governor): "On his arrival here he declined making it. From what he said to me, he seemed to have made up his mind to die, and to be resolved to say but little on the subject of this conspiracy."

40. "Mr [Paul] Thilman's information respecting the Slaves in Hanover" file cover is dated "Nov 1800."

41. (Lexington) Kentucky *Gazette,* Nov. 3, 1800; Benjamin DuVal to Monroe, Richmond, Dec. 26, 1800.

42. Jacob's letter was sent in a cover endorsed: "Thomas Booth to Captain Alexander McRae, Gloucester County, Oct. 5, 1800."

43. Edward Sapir cited in Elman R. Service, *Primitive Social Organization* (New York, 1964), 10.

44. The following general statements on "internal war" have been especially useful. Harry Eckstein, "On the Etiology of Internal War," *History and Theory,* IV (1965), 133–63, particularly 148–52 for a discussion of structural and behavioral hypotheses (action theory and the "orientation process"); Chambers Johnson, *Revolutionary Change* (Boston, 1966), IV, 6off.; William Nisbet, *The Sociological Tradition* (New York, 1966), VI, "The Sacred (charisma)"; and James C. Davies, "Toward a Theory of Revolution," *American Sociological Review,* XXVII (1962), 5–19, especially 17ff for his attempts to reconcile the views of Marx and de Tocqueville on the antecedents of revolution.

45. "Communications made by [William Young's] Gilbert," Monroe to the Assembly Dec. 5, 1800. Hamilton, ed., *Writings of Monroe,* III, 239.

46. Bob Cooley or Cowley was a famous Richmond black man and keeper of

the capitol's keys. He was implicated in at least one confession, prompting Monroe to write: "Although Robert Cowley has been intrusted with the keys . . . for some time past, and has acted in such a manner as to inspire the Executive with high confidence in his fidelity," if there was "the slightest doubt" about him he should be "removed" from his job. In the 5″ by 8″ obituary file, VHS, is this notice: "Departed this life on Tuesday the 8th Inst[ant] (Feb. 8, 1820), Robert Cowley, a man of colour, aged one-hundred-and-twenty-five years. For many years he had been doorkeeper to the Capitol."

47. Gilbert, cited in a document labeled "Information from Mr Foster respecting the intended Insurrection 1800 Sepr 23d."

48. [St. George Tucker], *Letter to a Member of the General Assembly of Virginia on the Subject of the Late Conspiracy of the Slaves, with a Proposal for their Colonization* (Richmond, 1801). VSL microfilm.

Imbued with the mood and themes of the Enlightenment and revolutionary idealism, Tucker's prescient analysis is worth citing at length; for it deals with nearly all of the major preconditions for insurrection.

"There is a progress in human affairs which may indeed be retarded, but which nothing can arrest. . . . Of such sort is the advancement of knowledge among the negroes of this country. . . . Every year adds to the number of those who can read and write; and he who has made any proficiency in letters, becomes a little centre of instruction to others. This increase of knowledge is the principal agent in the spirit we have to fear. The love of freedom, sir, is an inborn sentiment . . . long may it be kept under by the arbitrary institutions of society, but, at the first favorable moment, it springs forth, and flourishes with a vigour that defies all check.

"In our infant country, where population and wealth increase with unexampled rapidity. . . . The growth and multiplication of our towns tend a thousand ways to enlight and inform them. The very nature of our government, which leads us to recur perpetually to the discussion of natural rights, favors speculation and enquiry.

"But many of those, who see and acknowledge this change in the temper and views of the Negroes, ascribe it principally to the mild treatment they have of late years experienced. . . .

"We have hitherto placed much reliance on the difficulty of their acting in concert. Late experience has shewn us . . . they have maintained a correspondence, which, whether we consider its extent, or duration, is truly astonishing. . . . Fanaticism is spreading fast among the Negroes of this country, and may form in time the connecting link between the black religionists and the white. Do you not, already, sir, discover something like a sympathy between them? It certainly would not be a novelty, in the history of the world, if Religion were made to sanctify plots and conspiracies."

49. "Woolfolk's Confessions"; Prosser's Ben at Woolfolk's trial.

50. Solomon's "Communications" (Sept. 13); "Information from Mr. Foster"; Prosser's Ben at the trial of John Mosby Yincor's [?] Will; Woolfolk at Gabriel's trial; Prosser's Ben at Gabriel's trial.

51. Robert McColley, *Slavery and Jeffersonian Virginia* (Urbana, Ill., 1964), ch. vii. Wesley M. Gewehr, *The Great Awakening in Virginia, 1740–90* (Durham, 1930), ch. vii.

52. Woolfolk at the trial of George Smith.

53. On the relationship between charismatic leaders, chiliasm, and the rebellious activities of pre-industrial folk, see E. J. Hobsbawm, *Primitive Rebels* (New

York, 1959); George M. Fredrickson and Christopher Lasch, "Resistance to Slavery," *Civil War History,* XIII (Dec. 1967), 317–18; 317n–18n.

54. From data collected for an extended study on the role of cultural change and slave insurrections tentatively entitled: "Religion, Acculturation, and American Negro Slave Rebellions."

55. Prosser's Ben at the trial of James Allen's Isaac; Ben at the trial of William Burton's Isaac; "Information" of William Young's Gilbert given to John Foster (Sept. 23).

Bibliography

Manuscript Sources

Henry E. Huntington Library (San Marino, California)
    Bolling Family Papers
    Fairfax Papers
    Richard Henry Lee Memorandum Book, 1776–1794
    Edmund J. Randolph, "The History of Virginia" (transcript)
    Randolph-Tucker Correspondence and Documents
    Robert Rose Diary, 1746–1751

Duke University, Manuscript Division (Durham, North Carolina)
    William Bolling Papers
    Robert "Councillor" Carter Papers
    Dismal Swamp and Land Company Papers
    Henry Fitzhugh Papers
    Battaile Muse Papers

The Alderman Library, University of Virginia (Charlottesville)
    Berkeley-Noland Papers
    Robert "King" Carter Letterbooks (microfilm)
    Carter Letterbook, 1732–1781
    Edgehill-Randolph Papers
    Hawkins and McGehee Family Papers
    Thomas Jefferson Account Book (transcribed by James A. Bear)
    Lee Family Papers
    Nathan Mallory Papers
    Pocket Plantation Papers
    Wellford Family Papers
    Charles Yates Letterbook, 1773–1783 (microfilm)

Colonial Williamsburg Inc., Research Center
    (If microfilm, location of the original manuscript is indicated in paren-
    theses)
    Elizabeth Barbour Ambler Papers (UVA)
    Joseph Ball Letterbook, 1743–1780 (LC)
    Burwell Papers (privately owned, CW restricted file)
    Robert "Councillor" Carter, Miscellaneous MSS
    Corbin Family Papers
    Charles W. Dabney Papers (SHC)
    Galt Family Papers
    Lieutenant Governor William Gooch Letters, 1727–1751
        (typescripts and microfilm of originals which are privately owned)
    E. W. Hubard Papers (SHC)
    Norton Family Papers
    Turner Southall Receipt Book, 1776–1780
    Charles Steuart Letterbooks, 1751–1753; 1754–1763
        (Pennsylvania Historical Society)

Virginia Historical Society (Richmond)
    William Byrd II Commonplace Book, ca. 1722–1732
    Robert "Councillor" Carter Account Books, 1773–1774, 1785–1792
    Custis Family Papers
    Mercer Family Papers
    Tayloe Family Papers

Virginia State Library
    Executive Papers, August–December, 1800
    Executive Letterbook, September–October, 1800
    Governor's Council Minutes, September–October, 1800
    Richmond County Court Minute Book, Slave and Criminal Trials, 1710–
    1754

William and Mary College Archives
    Carter Family Papers

Newspapers

Kentucky (Lexington) Gazette
Maryland Gazette
South Carolina Gazette (Charleston)
Virginia Argus (Richmond)
Virginia Gazette (Williamsburg)
Virginia Gazette and General Advertiser (Richmond)
Virginia Herald and Fredericksburg Advertiser
Virginia Herald and Fredericksburg and Falmouth Advertiser
Virginia Independent Chronicle (Richmond)

Printed Sources

Anburey, Thomas. *Travels Through the Interior Parts of America; in a Series
    of Letters.* By an Officer. New edition, 2 vols. London: 1791.

Beverley, Robert. *The History and Present State of Virginia* [1705], edited by Louis B. Wright. Chapel Hill, 1947.

Burnaby, Andrew. *Travels through the Middle Settlements in North-America in the years 1759 and 1760.* 2nd ed. Ithaca, N. Y., 1960.

Byrd, William. *The Secret Diary of William Byrd of Westover, 1709–1712,* edited by Louis B. Wright and Marion Tinling. Richmond, 1941.

———. *Another Secret Diary of William Byrd of Westover, 1739–1741,* edited by Maude H. Woodfin, transcribed by Marion Tinling. Richmond, 1942.

———. *The Prose Works of William Byrd of Westover,* edited by Louis B. Wright. Cambridge, Mass., 1966.

———. *The Writings of Colonel William Byrd of Westover in Virginia Esqr,* edited by John Spencer Bassett. New York, 1901.

Calendar of Virginia State Papers and Other Manuscripts, 1652–1869, Preserved at the Capitol in Richmond. William Palmer, Sherwin McRae and H. W. Flournoy, eds. 11 vols. Richmond, 1875–93. Vol. IX edited by H. W. Flournoy.

Carter, Landon. *The Diary of Colonel Landon Carter of Sabine Hall, 1752–1778.* Jack P. Greene, ed. Charlottesville, 1966.

———. *The Landon Carter Papers in the University of Virginia Library: A Calendar and Biographical Sketch.* Walter Ray Wineman, ed. Charlottesville, 1962.

Carter, Robert "King." *Letters of Robert Carter, 1720–1727: The Commercial Interests of a Virginia Gentleman.* Louis B. Wright, ed. San Marino, Cal., 1940.

Catterall, Helen T. *Judicial Cases Concerning American Slavery and the Negro.* 5 vols. Washington, 1924–26.

Chastellux, Marquis de [François Jean],*Travels in North America in the Years 1780, 1781 and 1782,* revd. transl., Howard C. Rice, Jr., 2 vols. Chapel Hill, 1963.

Creecy, Harvie John. *Princess Anne County Loose Papers, 1700–1789.* (Volume I of the *Virginia Antiquary.*) Richmond, 1954.

Evans, Emory G. (ed.). "A Question of Complexion: Documents Concerning the Negro and the Franchise in Eighteenth-Century Virginia," *Virginia Magazine of History and Biography,* LXXI (October 1963), 411–15.

Fithian, Philip Vickers. *The Journal and Letters of Philip Vickers Fithian, 1773–1774: A Plantation Tutor of the Old Dominion,* Hunter Dickinson Farish, ed. New edition. Williamsburg, 1965.

Fletcher, Elijah. *The Letters of Elijah Fletcher,* Martha von Briesen, ed. Charlottesville, 1965.

Foster, Sir Augustus John. *Jeffersonian America, Notes on the United States of America, Collected in the Years 1805–6–7 and 11–12,* Richard Beale Davis, ed. San Marino, Cal., 1954.

Hening, William W. (ed.). *The Statutes at Large: Being a Collection of All the Laws of Virginia from the First Session of the Legislature in the Year 1619.* 13 vols. Richmond and Philadelphia, 1809–23.

———, and Munford, William (eds.). *A Collection of all Such Acts of the General Assembly of Virginia of a Public and Permanent Nature as Have Passed since the Session of 1801.* 2 vols. Richmond, 1808.

Jefferson, Thomas. *The Life and Selected Writings of Thomas Jefferson.* Adrienne Koch and William Peden, eds. New York, 1944.

————. *Notes on Virginia.* William Peden, ed. Chapel Hill, 1955.

Jones, Hugh. *The Present State of Virginia* [1724]. Richard L. Morton, ed. Chapel Hill, 1956.

Journals of the House of Burgesses, 1619–1776. J. P. Kennedy and H. R. McIlwaine, eds. 13 vols. Richmond, 1905–15.

Legislative Journals of the Council of Colonial Virginia. H. R. McIlwaine, ed. 3 vols. Richmond, 1918, 1919.

Monroe, James. *The Writings of James Monroe.* Stanislaus M. Hamilton, ed. 7 vols. Vol. III, 1796–1803. New York, 1900.

Norton, John. *John Norton and Sons Merchants of London and Virginia (Being the Papers from Their Counting House for the Years 1750 to 1795).* Frances Norton Mason, ed. Richmond, 1937.

Schoepf, Johann David. *Travels in the Confederation (1783–1784).* Alfred J. Morrison, ed. Philadelphia, 1911.

Smyth, John Ferdinand D. *A Tour in the United States of America.* 2 vols. London, 1784.

Statutes at Large of Virginia, from October Session 1792, to December Session 1806, Inclusive. Samuel Shepherd, ed. 3 vols. Richmond, 1835.

Tatham, William. *An Historical and Practical Essay on the Culture and Commerce of Tobacco.* London, 1800.

Toulmin, Harry. *The Western Country in 1793: Reports on Kentucky and Virginia,* Marion Tinling and Godfrey Davies, eds. San Marino, Cal., 1948.

United States Census Office. *First Census.* Philadelphia, 1791 (transcript).

————. *Second Census,* Philadelphia, 1801 (transcript).

Washington, George. *The Diaries of George Washington, 1748–1799.* John C. Fitzpatrick, ed. 4 vols. Boston, 1925.

————. *Memoirs of the Long Island Historical Society.* Vol. IV: *George Washington and Mount Vernon.* M. D. Conway, ed. Brooklyn, 1889.

Selected Secondary Materials

Adams, Henry. *The United States in 1800.* A separate edition of the first six chapters of *The History of the United States of America during the First Administration of Thomas Jefferson.* Ithaca, N.Y., 1961.

Adams, James Truslow. *Provincial Society, 1690–1763.* New York, 1927.

Agee, Helene Barret. *Facets of Goochland County's History.* Richmond, 1962.

Ambler, Charles Henry. *Sectionalism in Virginia from 1776 to 1861.* Chicago, 1910.

Ammon, Harry. "Formation of the Jeffersonian Party in Virginia, 1789–1796," *Journal of Southern History,* LXXI (April 1963), 153–67.

Aptheker, Herbert. *American Negro Slave Revolts.* New York, 1963.

Bailyn, Bernard. "Political and Social Structure in Colonial Virginia," *Seventeenth-Century America,* James M. Smith, ed. Chapel Hill, 1959. Pp. 90–115.

Ballagh, James Curtis. *A History of Slavery in Virginia.* Baltimore, 1902.

Bancroft, Frederick. *Slave-Trading in the Old South.* Baltimore, 1931.

Barbara, Dominick. *Stuttering, a Psychodynamic Approach to Its Understanding and Treatment.* New York, 1954.

Barrow, Robert Mangum. "Williamsburg and Norfolk: Municipal Government and Justice in Colonial Virginia." Unpublished Master's thesis, College of William and Mary, 1960.

Bassett, John Spencer. *Slavery and Servitude in the Colony of North Carolina.* Baltimore, 1896.

Berkeley, Francis Lewis, Jr. "The Berkeleys of Barn Elms, Planters of Colonial Virginia and a Calendar of the Berkeley Papers, 1653–1767." Unpublished Master's thesis, University of Virginia, 1940.

Blanton, Wyndham B. *Medicine in Virginia in the Eighteenth Century.* Richmond, 1931.

Boddie, John B. *Colonial Surry.* Baltimore, 1959.

Bohannan, Paul. "Concepts of Time Among the Tiv of Nigeria," *Myth and Cosmos: Readings in Mythology and Symbolism,* John Middleton, ed. New York, 1967.

Boorstin, Daniel J. *The Americans: The Colonial Experience.* New York, 1958.

Bradshaw, Herbert Clarence. *History of Prince Edward County, Virginia.* Richmond, 1955.

Bridenbaugh, Carl. *Myths and Realities: Societies of the Colonial South.* New York (1952), 1963.

———. *Seat of Empire: The Political Role of Eighteenth-Century Williamsburg.* Charlottesville (1950), 1963.

Brown, Robert E. and B. Katherine. *Virginia 1705–1786: Democracy or Aristocracy?* East Lansing, Mich., 1964.

Brydon, George MacLaren. *Virginia's Mother Church, and the Political Conditions under which It Grew.* 2 vols. Richmond and Philadelphia, 1947, 1952.

Cabell, N. F. "Some Fragments of an Intended Report on the Post Revolutionary History of Agriculture in Virginia" with notes by Earl G. Swem, *William and Mary Quarterly,* XXVI (January 1918), 145–68.

Campbell, Thomas E. *Colonial Caroline: A History of Caroline County, Virginia.* Richmond, 1954.

Cohen, Yehudi A. (ed.). *Social Structure and Personality: A Casebook.* New York. 1961.

———. *The Transition from Childhood to Adolescence.* Chicago, 1964.

Cox, Harold Eugene. "Federalism and Anti-Federalism in Virginia—1787: A Study of Political and Economic Motivations." Unpublished Ph.D. dissertation, University of Virginia, 1958.

Craven, Avery O. *Soil Exhaustion as a Factor in the Agricultural History of Virginia and Maryland, 1606–1860.* Urbana, 1926.

Darter, Oscar H. *Colonial Fredericksburg and Neighborhood in Perspective.* New York, 1957.

Davidson, Basil. *The African Slave Trade: Precolonial History, 1450–1850.* Boston, 1961.

Davies, James C. "Toward a Theory of Revolution," *American Sociological Review,* 27 (1962), 5–19.

Davis, David Brion. *The Problem of Slavery in Western Culture.* Ithaca, N.Y., 1966.

———. "Slavery," *The Comparative Approach to American History.* C. Vann Woodward, ed. New York, 1968. Pp. 121–34.

Degler, Carl. *Out of the Past: The Forces That Shaped Modern America.* New York, 1959.

———. "Slavery and the Genesis of American Race Prejudice," *Comparative Studies in Society and History,* II (October 1959), 49–66.

Diehl, Charles F. *A Compendium of Research and Theory on Stuttering.* Springfield, Ill., 1958.

Donnan, Elizabeth. "Eighteenth-Century English Merchants, Micajah Perry,"

Journal of Economic and Busines History, IV (1931–32), 70–98.

Eaton, Clement. "Slave-Hiring in the Upper South: A Step Toward Freedom," *Mississippi Valley Historical Review,* XLVI (March 1960), 663–78.

Eckenrode, Hamilton J. *The Revolution in Virginia.* Boston and New York, 1916.

Eckstein, Harry. "On the Etiology of Internal Wars," *History and Theory,* IV, 2(1965), 133–63.

Elkins, Stanley M. *Slavery: A Problem in American Institutional and Intellectual Life.* New York, 1963.

Erikson, Erik H. "The Concept of Identity in Race Relations: Notes and Queries," *Daedalus,* "The Negro-American-2" (Winter 1966), 145–71.

Evans, Emory G. "The Nelsons: A Biographical Study of a Virginia Family in the Eighteenth Century." Unpublished Ph.D. dissertation, University of Virginia, 1957.

Evans-Pritchard, E. E. "Neur Time-Reckoning," *Africa,* vol. 12, no. 2 (April 1939), 189–216.

Fage, J. D. *An Introduction to the History of West Africa.* Cambridge, England, 1962.

Forde, Daryll (ed.). *African Worlds: Studies in the Cosmological Ideas and Social Values of African Peoples.* London and New York, 1960.

Fredrickson, George M., and Lasch, Christopher. "Resistance to Slavery," *Civil War History,* XIII (December 1967), 315–29.

Freeman, Douglas Southall. *George Washington.* 6 vols. New York, 1948–54.

Genovese, Eugene D. "The Legacy of Slavery and the Roots of Black Nationalism." An Address to the Socialist Scholars Conference, 1966, with comments by Herbert Aptheker, C. Vann Woodward, and Frank Kofsky. *Studies on the Left,* VI (November–December 1966), 3–65.

————. *The Political Economy of Slavery: Studies in the Economy and Society of the Slave South.* New York, 1965.

Gewehr, Wesley M. *The Great Awakening in Virginia.* Gloucester, Mass., 1965.

Goffman, Erving. *Asylums: Essays on the Social Situation of Mental Patients and Other Inmates.* New York, 1961.

————. "Characteristics of Total Institutions," *Identity and Anxiety, Survival of the Person in Mass Society,* Maurice Stein and others, eds. New York, 1960. Pp. 449–79.

————. *Interaction Ritual: Essays on Face-to-Face Behavior.* New York, 1967.

Goodwin, Mary F. "Christianizing and Educating the Negro in Colonial Virginia," *Historical Magazine of the Protestant Episcopal Church,* I (Sept. 1932), 143–52.

Gray, Lewis Cecil. *History of Agriculture in the Southern United States to 1860.* 2 vols. New York, 1941.

Greene, Evarts B., and Harrington, Virginia D. *American Population Before the Federal Census of 1790.* New York, 1932.

Greene, Jack P. "Foundations of Political Power in the Virginia House of Burgesses, 1720–1776," *William and Mary Quarterly,* 3rd ser., XVI (Oct. 1959), 485–506.

————. *Landon Carter: An Inquiry into the Personal Values and Social Imperatives of the Eighteenth-Century Virginia Gentry.* Charlottesville, 1967.

Greene, Lorenzo J. "The New England Negro as Seen in Advertisements for Runaway Slaves," *Journal of Negro History,* XXIX (1944), 125–46.

Griffith, Lucille B. *The Virginia House of Burgesses: 1750–1774.* Northport, Ala., 1963.

Handlin, Oscar and Mary F. "Origins of the Southern Labor System," *William and Mary Quarterly,* 3rd ser., VII (April 1950), 199–222.

Harris, Malcolm H. *A History of Louisa County, Virginia.* Richmond, 1936.

Haworth, Paul Leland. *George Washington: Farmer.* Indianapolis, 1915.

——. *George Washington: Country Gentleman.* Indianapolis, 1925.

Haynie, Miriam. *The Stronghold: A Story of Historic Northern Neck of Virginia and Its People.* Richmond, 1959.

Haywood, Robert C. "Mercantilism and Colonial Slave Labor, 1700–1763," *Journal of Southern History,* XXIII (1957), 454–64.

Herskovits, Melville J. "The Ahistorical Approach to Afroamerican Studies: a Critique," *Journal of American Anthropology,* LXII (1960), 559–68.

——. "The Culture Areas of Africa," *Africa,* III (1930), 59–77.

——. *The Myth of the Negro Past.* Boston, 1962.

Hilldrup, Robert S. "A Campaign to Promote the Prosperity of Colonial Virginia: Charles Carter and the Society for the Promotion of Useful Knowledge," *Virginia Magazine of History and Biography,* LXVII (Oct. 1959), 410–28.

Honigmann, John J. *Culture and Personality.* New York, 1954.

——. *Understanding Culture.* New York, 1963.

Hume, Noel Ivor. *Here Lies Virginia: An Archaeologist's View of Colonial Life and History.* New York, 1963.

Hunt, Robert (ed.). *Personalities and Culture: Readings in Psychological Anthropology.* Garden City, N.Y., 1967.

Jahn, Janheinz. *Mantu: An Outline of the New African Culture.* New York, 1961.

Johnston, James Hugh. "The Participation of White Men in Virginia Negro Insurrections," *Journal of Negro History,* XVI (April 1931), 158–67.

Jordan, Winthrop D. "American Chiaroscuro: The Status and Definition of Mulattoes in the British Colonies," *William and Mary Quarterly,* 3rd ser., XIX (April 1962), 183–200.

——. "Modern Tensions and the Origins of American Slavery," *Journal of Southern History,* XXVIII (Feb. 1962), 18–30.

——. *White Over Black.* Chapel Hill, 1968.

Kemp, Louise Singleton. "Battaile Muse," *Magazine of the Jefferson County Historical Society,* XI (Dec. 1945), 21–23.

Kilson, Marion D. "Towards Freedom: An Analysis of Slave Revolts in the United States," *Phylon,* XXV (1954), 175–89.

Kinch, John W. "A Formalized Theory of the Self-Concept," *American Journal of Sociology,* LXVIII (Jan. 1963), 481–86.

Lefler, Hugh Talmadge, and Newsome, Albert Ray. *North Carolina: The History of a Southern State.* Chapel Hill, 1963.

Lemisch, Jesse. "Listening to the 'Inarticulate': William Widger's Dream and the Loyalties of American Revolutionary Seamen in British Prisons," *Journal of Social History* 3(Fall 1969), 1–29.

Lingley, Charles Ramsdell. *The Transition in Virginia from Colony to Commonwealth.* New York, 1910.

Little, John P. *History of Richmond.* Richmond, 1933.

McCall, Daniel F. *Africa in Time-Perspective: A Discussion of Historical Reconstruction from Unwritten Sources.* New York, 1969.

McColley, Robert. *Slavery and Jeffersonian Virginia.* Urbana, 1964.

McGee, Malcolm. "The 150% Man, A Product of Blackfoot Acculturation," *American Anthropologist,* 70 (1968), 1096–1103.

McKitrick, Eric L. "The Age of Deference," *The New York Review of Books*, VI (Feb. 17, 1966), 28–29.

Main, Jackson Turner. "The One Hundred," *William and Mary Quarterly*, 3rd ser., XI (July 1954), 354–84.

Mays, David J. *Edmund Pendleton 1721–1803: A Biography*. 2 vols. Cambridge, Mass., 1952.

Mbiti, John S. *African Religions and Philosophy*. New York, 1969.

Merrens, Harry Roy. *Colonial North Carolina in the Eighteenth Century: A Study in Historical Geography*. Chapel Hill, 1964.

Middleton, Arthur Price. *Tobacco Coast: A Maritime History of Chesapeake Bay in the Colonial Era*. Edited for the Mariner's Museum by George Carrington Mason. Newport News, 1953.

Mintz, Sidney W. Review of Stanley Elkins' *Slavery*, *American Anthropologist*, LXI (June 1961), 579–87.

Moore, Gay Montague. *Seaport in Virginia: George Washington's Alexandria*. Richmond, 1949.

Mordecai, Samuel. *Richmond in By-Gone Days*. Richmond, 1860.

Morgan, Edmund S. *Virginians at Home: Family Life in the Eighteenth Century*. Charlottesville, 1963.

Morton, Louis. *Robert Carter of Nomini Hall; a Virginia Tobacco Planter of the Eighteenth Century*. Charlottesville, 1964.

Park, Robert Ezra. *Race and Culture*. Glencoe, Ill., 1950.

Phifer, Edward W. "Slavery in Microcosm: Burke County, North Carolina," *Journal of Southern History*, XXVIII (May 1962), 137–65.

Phillips, Ulrich B. *American Negro Slavery*. Gloucester, Mass., 1918, 1959.

———. *Life and Labor in the Old South*. New York, 1929, 1963.

Pinchbeck, Raymond B. *The Virginia Negro Artisan and Tradesman*. Richmond, 1926.

Pocock, David F. "The Anthropology of Time-Reckoning," *Myth and Cosmos: Readings in Mythology and Symbolism*. John Middleton, ed. New York, 1967. 301–15.

Pole, John R. "Historians and the Problem of Early American Democracy," *American Historical Review*, LXVII (April 1962), 626–46.

Quarles, Benjamin. *The Negro in the American Revolution*. Chapel Hill, 1961.

Rankin, Hugh. *Criminal Trial Proceedings in the General Court of Colonial Virginia*. Williamsburg, 1965.

Read, Allen W. "The Speech of Negroes in Colonial America," *Journal of Negro History*, XXIV (July 1939), 247–58.

Riley, Edward M. "The Town Acts of Colonial Virginia," *Journal of Southern History*, XVI (Aug. 1950), 306–23.

Robert, Joseph Clarke. *The Tobacco Kingdom: Plantation, Market, and Factory in Virginia and North Carolina, 1800–1860*. Durham, 1938.

Rosenblatt, Samuel Michael. "The House of John Norton & Sons: A Study of the Consignment Method of Marketing Tobacco from Virginia to England." Unpublished Ph.D. dissertation, Rutgers University, 1960.

Rubin, Vera (ed.). *Caribbean Studies: A Symposium*. Seattle, 1960.

Soltow, James H. *The Economic Role of Williamsburg*. Charlottesville, 1965.

Stampp, Kenneth M. *The Peculiar Institution: Slavery in the Ante-Bellum South*. New York, 1956.

Stanton, William. *The Leopard's Spots: Scientific Attitudes Toward Race in America, 1815–1859*. Chicago, 1960.

Starnes, George T. *Sixty Years of Branch Banking in Virginia.* New York, 1931.

Sydnor, Charles S. *American Revolutionaries in the Making: Political Practices in Washington's Virginia.* New York, 1965.

Tannenbaum, Frank. *Slave and Citizen: The Negro in the Americas.* New York, 1946.

———. "A Note on the Economic Interpretation of History," *Political Science Quarterly,* 61 (June 1946), 247–48.

Tate, Thad W. *The Negro in Eighteenth-Century Williamsburg.* Williamsburg, 1965.

Thompson, Edgar T. "Economic Institutions: The Plantation" and "The Race Making Frontier: Five Historical Situations, Virginia," *Race, Individual and Collective Behavior.* Edgar T. Thompson and Everett C. Hughes, eds. New York, 1965. Pp. 225–36, 256–64.

Travis, Lee Edward. *Handbook of Speech Pathology.* New York, 1957.

van den Berghe, Pierre L. "Paternalistic versus Competitive Race Relations: An Ideal-Type Approach," *Racial and Ethnic Relations: Selected Readings.* Bernard E. Segal, ed. New York, 1966. Pp. 53–69.

———. Race and Racism: A Comparative Perspective. New York, 1967.

Ver Steeg, Clarence L. "Historians and the Southern Colonies," *The Reinterpretation of Early American History: Essays in Honor of John Edwin Pomfret.* Ray Allen Billington, ed. San Marino, Cal., 1966. Pp. 18–100.

Wallace, Anthony F. C. *Culture and Personality.* New York, 1961.

Wertenbaker, Thomas J. *Norfolk: Historic Southern Port.* Durham, 1931.

———. *The Old South: The Founding of American Civilization.* New York, 1942.

———. *The Shaping of Colonial Virginia.* New York, 1958.

Williams, David Alan. "Political Alignments in Colonial Virginia, 1698–1750." Unpublished Ph.D. dissertation, Northwestern University, 1959.

Williams, Eric. *Capitalism and Slavery.* Chapel Hill, 1944.

Williams, George W. *History of the Negro Race in America from 1610–1880.* New York, 1885.

WPA Virginia, comp. *The Negro in Virginia.* Writers' Program of the Work Projects Administration. New York, 1940.

———. *Dinwiddie County, "The Countrey of the Apamatica."* Writers' Program of the Work Projects Administration, Richmond, 1942.

Yinger, J. Milton. "Research Implications of a Field View of Personality," *American Journal of Sociology,* LXVIII (March 1963), 580–92.

Index